Before the
Civil Rights
Revolution

Recent Titles in
Contributions in Legal Studies
Series Editor: Paul L. Murphy

BEFORE THE CIVIL RIGHTS REVOLUTION

The Old Court and Individual Rights

John Braeman

CONTRIBUTIONS IN LEGAL STUDIES, NUMBER 41
Greenwood Press

NEW YORK • WESTPORT, CONNECTICUT • LONDON

Library of Congress Cataloging-in-Publication Data

Braeman, John.
    Before the Civil Rights revolution : the old Court and individual
rights / John Braeman.
        p.   cm. — (Contributions in legal studies, ISSN 0147–1074 ;
no. 41)
    Bibliography: p.
    Includes index.
    ISBN 0–313–26205–5 (lib. bdg. : alk. paper)
    1. Civil rights—United States—History.   2. United States.
Supreme Court.—History.   I. Title.   II. Series.
KF4749.B647 1988
342.73′085—dc 19
[347.30285]   87–32291

British Library Cataloguing in Publication Data is available.

Library of Congress Catalog Card Number: 87–32291
ISBN: 0–313–26205–5
ISSN: 0147–1074

First published in 1988

Greenwood Press, Inc.
88 Post Road West, Westport, Connecticut 06881

Printed in the United States of America

The paper used in this book complies with the
Permanent Paper Standard issued by the National
Information Standards Organization (Z39.48-1984).

10 9 8 7 6 5 4 3 2 1

Contents

Preface

The subject matter of this study is known and unknown. Supreme Court decisions—if not their motivations—are a matter of public record, available on the shelves of any law library. But the record of the Supreme Court vis-à-vis civil rights/civil liberties issues before the 1937 switch-in-time that saved nine has received scant attention. Looking at the case books for constitutional law courses, one would gain the impression that, except for a few isolated so-called landmark decisions, the justices did not deal with such questions in a significant way until at least the Roosevelt Court—or even the 1960s. While this lack of historical perspective may be excusable in texts whose purpose is to instruct would-be new practitioners in the latest developments in the law, constitutional historians have largely been guilty of similar neglect. The predominant note in the work that has been done—such as, for example, on the Court's interpretation of the Reconstruction-era amendments for the protection of the Negro—has been to contrast the Old Court's solicitude for property with its benighted attitude toward human rights and personal freedoms.

The present account is an offshoot of a larger study underway of the post-1937 civil rights revolution. My attention was drawn to the prior developments, partly because of my surprise at the degree to which the Modern Court has quoted earlier precedents in support of what have been regarded as new departures, partly because of my realization that one could not assess the scope of the resulting changes without a base line for comparison. My first chapter examines how the existence of the federal system complicated the definition of what individual rights were guaranteed by the United States Constitution while simultaneously exacerbating the problem of their protection against violation. The second chapter explores the substantive content that the Old Court gave to constitutionally protected rights outside the criminal procedure area. Chapter three deals with the Old Court's response to what has been, and remains, the most intractable issue in the American polity: race discrimination. Chapter four surveys the Old Court's decision-making in the criminal procedure area, focusing upon the twin questions of the meaning of the criminal law guarantees of the Bill of Rights and the limits imposed by the Constitution upon state autonomy in the administration of criminal justice. The final chapter assays an over-all appraisal that aims to elucidate the values defining the parameters of the Old Court's treatment of civil liberties/civil rights issues.

My conclusions may be briefly stated. The first is that the widely held assumption that the post-1937 justices were writing upon a largely blank slate in this area is mythology. The second—and more significant—is that the Old Court's record on civil rights/civil liberties issues was far from simply one of judicial negativism. On the contrary, much of what the Modern Court has done when viewed in long-term perspective appears incremental expansions upon precedents laid down by the Old Court. Before the first of Franklin D. Roosevelt's appointees took his seat on the bench, the Court had made the crucial breakthrough of applying the First Amendment to the states via the Fourteenth. The Old Court's interpretation of the criminal procedure guarantees of the Bill of Rights remains to this day the governing definition of many of those provisions. And the first step had been taken toward imposing those limitations upon the states. Last—but crucially important—the Old Court developed the enforcement mechanisms upon which the Modern Court has relied for the guardianship of individual rights.

There is no question that from the standpoint of contemporary liberal thinking the Old Court had its blindspots. Examples include its treatment of women, blacks, and aliens. But the changes that have occurred in their legal status reflect primarily changes that have taken place in the attitudes and values of the larger society. Even where the Modern Court has broken with the one-time accepted interpretation, the discarded precedents were not without their influence. As an institution, the Supreme Court maintains its legitimacy by preserving the appearance of continuity to avoid making too visible its policy-making role. Much of the hesitancy, wavering, stops and starts that marked the post-1937 Court's decision-making in the civil liberties/civil rights area—at least until the mid-1960s—reflected divisions among the justices over how fast and how far they could, or should, depart from inherited constitutional doctrine. Nor was the Warren Court immune to the pressure to avoid too sharp breaks with the past. The most important example was its refusal to abandon the state-action requirement for the Fourteenth Amendment. And many of its most innovative decisions strove as much as possible—at times to the point of strain—to appeal to the earlier precedents dealt with in this study.

I wish to thank Professor Philip B. Kurland of the University of Chicago

Law School for his judicious reading of the text. Commiseration is due my wife, who put up (more or less) with the moods—ranging from abstraction to grumpiness with not much between—induced by my writing. I bear sole responsibility for any errors of fact or eccentricities of interpretation.

Before the
Civil Rights
Revolution

1 Individual Rights in a Federal System

The Supreme Court of the United States holds a unique position among the world's judicial bodies. In form the justices simply decide controversies between opposing litigants. From the start, however, the Court was deeply involved in broader policy making. One way of doing this was via statutory interpretation. Disputes over the scope and/or meaning of a statutory provision grow out of the clash of interests between different parties. The Court's answer will thus favor one or the other view of what the policy should be. But the Court's major impact has come from its power to declare a law, an official action, or a lower court judgment in violation of the Constitution. One group of constitutional issues that comes before the tribunal consists of questions about the distribution of power among different government organs (e.g., whether a given power belongs to Congress or to the president, to the national government or to the states). A second group revolves around the limitations upon governmental power (i.e., whether a particular power has been exercised properly or even exists). Deciding such questions makes the Court, Felix Frankfurter has written, "for all practical purposes, the adjuster of governmental powers in our complicated federal system."[1]

A long, inconclusive, and largely futile debate has gone on over whether the framers of the Constitution had intended the Supreme Court to review the constitutionality of governmental actions or whether that power had been "usurped."[2] What can be said without dispute is that the text of the Constitution offers scant guidance to understanding what the role of the Court has become. The so-called supremacy clause in Article VI stipulated that "This Constitution, and the Laws of the United States which shall be made in Pursuance thereof . . . shall be the supreme Law of the Land; and the Judges in every State shall be bound thereby, any Thing in the Constitution or Laws of any State to the Contrary notwithstanding." There is no question that the purpose was to affirm the superiority of the Constitution to state laws and constitutions and acts of Congress not "made in Pursuance thereof." But the Constitution did not say what governmental organ should interpret and enforce that higher law. Article III simply provided that the "judicial Power of the United States . . . shall extend to all Cases, in Law and Equity, arising under this Constitution, the Laws of the United States, and Treaties made, or which shall be made, under their Authority."

In what became the classic rationale for the power of the Supreme Court to declare acts of Congress unconstitutional, Chief Justice John Marshall in *Marbury v. Madison* relied partly upon this text. He pointed out that the supremacy clause legitimized only acts of Congress "made in *pursuance* of the constitution." And noting that the judicial power of the United States extended to all cases arising under the Constitution, he asked: "Could it be the intention of those who gave this power, to say that, in using it, the constitution should not be looked into?" But the major thrust of his argument rested upon what he saw as the inescapable logic of a written constitution. "To what purpose are powers limited, and to what purpose is that limitation committed to writing, if these limits may, at any time, be passed by those intended to be restrained?" Accordingly, "essentially attached to a written constitution" was "that an act of the legislature, repugnant to the constitution, is void." The question still remained, why should the primary responsibility for deciding if a law conflicted with the Constitution belong to the judiciary? Marshall's answer was: "It is emphatically the province and the duty of the judicial department to say what the law is. Those who apply the rule to particular cases, must of necessity expound and interpret that rule."[3]

Commentators have differed over whether Marshall was asserting a judicial monopoly of constitutional interpretation.[4] The decision as such was not incompatible with the alternative so-called tripartite theory of constitutional interpretation "that each of the three departments has equally the right to decide for itself what is its duty under the constitution."[5] At issue in *Marbury* was the scope of the judicial power—a question appropriate under the tripartite theory for the Court to decide. More important, Marshall appeared to suggest that judicial determination of constitutional questions was limited to cases affecting "individual rights," and did not extend to the exercise by the other branches of their "political powers."[6] In his famous 1819 decision in *McCulloch v. Maryland* upholding the constitutionality of the Second Bank of the United States, he affirmed that Congress had the primary responsibility under the "necessary and proper" clause[7] for adapting the "great outlines" of the Constitution to the changing needs of society. "Let the end be legitimate," he declared, "let it be within the scope of the constitution, and all means which are appropriate, which are plainly adapted to that end, which are not prohibited, but consist with the letter and spirit of the constitution, are constitutional."[8]

On the other hand, there is no question that Marshall assumed in *Mar-*

bury—at the minimum—that the Court had final say on which questions were political and which were judicially reviewable. There was similarly in *McCulloch* the unstated premise that the Court would decide if an act of Congress was "appropriate," "not prohibited," and "consist[ent] with the letter and spirit of the constitution."[9] His younger colleague on the bench, Joseph Story, in his influential 1833 *Commentaries on the Constitution of the United States*, made explicit what Marshall had left implied: that the Court was the constitutionally established "final and common arbiter . . . to whose decisions all others are subordinate."[10] By the late 1840s, there appeared a broad consensus among the parties in the debate over the power of Congress to prohibit slavery in the territories that the judiciary was the proper agency to answer the question.[11] Taking up the invitation in the *Dred Scott* case, Chief Justice Roger B. Taney proceeded to strike down the Missouri Compromise's prohibition of slavery in the Louisiana Purchase north of 36° 30'. Our duty, Taney explained, was to interpret the Constitution, "with the best lights we can obtain on the subject, and to administer it as we find it." The framers had decreed the constitutional protection of slave property. "No . . . change in public opinion or feeling . . . should induce the court to give to the words of the Constitution a more liberal construction . . . than they were intended to bear when the instrument was framed and adopted."[12]

Whatever the ambiguities in Marshall's position about the scope of judicial review over the actions of the coordinate branches of the national government, there was no doubt where he stood on its role vis-à-vis the states. In 1810, he assumed in *Fletcher v. Peck* that there was no possible argument about the Court's power to strike down acts of the state legislatures given a Constitution, "the supremacy of which all acknowledge, and which imposes limits to the legislatures of the several states, which none claim a right to pass."[13] In 1816, the Court affirmed in *Martin v. Hunter's Lessee* its authority to review state court decisions dealing with claims based upon federal law. "It was foreseen," Justice Story wrote,

that in the exercise of their ordinary jurisdiction, state courts would incidentally take cognizance of cases arising under the constitution, the laws, and treaties of the United States. Yet to all these cases the judicial power [of the United States], by the very terms of the constitution, is to extend. . . . It would seem to follow that the appellate power of the United States must, in such cases, extend to state tribunals.

Taking as settled the authority of the Supreme Court to declare "proceedings of the executive and legislative authorities of the states . . . found contrary to the constitution . . . of no legal validity," Story held that state judges were subject to the same check "if they should unintentionally transcend their authority, or misconstrue the constitution."[14]

The Court's exercise of judicial review did not pass without challenge. The heaviest attack was directed against its review of state court decisions.

Bills were repeatedly introduced in Congress to strip the Court of its jurisdiction to hear such appeals.[15] Adherents of the tripartite theory of constitutional interpretation similarly protested the Court's assumption of oversight
over the actions of the other branches of the national government. Thomas
Jefferson fumed that *Marbury* gave to one of the three branches "alone, the
right to prescribe rules for the government of the others, and to that one
too, which is unelected by, and independent of the nation. . . . The constitution, on this hypothesis, is a mere thing of wax in the hands of the judiciary,
which they may twist or shape into any form they please."[16] When vetoing
the recharter of the Bank of the United States, Andrew Jackson denied that
McCulloch had settled its constitutionality. "The Congress, the Executive,
and the Court must each for itself be guided by its own opinion of the
Constitution."[17] In reaction to *Dred Scott*, Abraham Lincoln warned in his
first inaugural address that "if the policy of the Government upon vital
questions affecting the whole people is to be irrevocably fixed by decisions
of the Supreme Court . . . the people will have ceased to be their own
rulers."[18]

The Court's success in winning acceptance of judicial review owed much
to the deeply ingrained American belief in natural law and natural rights:
that there were certain universal principles of right that government could
not violate. Colonial protests in the years preceding the Revolution assumed
the existence of a higher law of "common right and reason" limiting legislative power—and even suggested that such fundamental law was judicially
enforceable.[19] Further support for judicial review came from the new conception which emerged from the Revolution that a written constitution embodied the will of the sovereign people.[20] Whatever the source—the older
natural law tradition or the newer popular sovereignty model—most state
judges by the eve of the Civil War appear to have accepted the authority
(or to be more accurate, the *duty*) of the courts to intervene when the actions
of temporary popular majorities transcended "the constitutional limits of the
legislative power."[21] Perhaps most important in establishing the Supreme
Court's special position was the necessity of a single umpire to resolve the
conflicts growing out of the federal system. "So long . . . as this Constitution
shall endure," Chief Justice Taney declared for a unanimous bench, "this
tribunal must exist with it, deciding in the peaceful forms of judicial proceeding the angry and irritating controversies between sovereignties, which
in other countries have been determined by the arbitrament of force."[22]

One last factor was indispensable: the political astuteness shown by the
Court. *Marbury* set the pattern, as Marshall coupled the enunciation with
broad principles with avoidance of a direct confrontation with the executive
branch. *Dred Scott* was a misstep that made the Court the target of hostility
from the soon-to-be-triumphant Republican party. But the Republicans'
aim—notwithstanding Lincoln's remarks in his inaugural address—was to
change the membership and conduct of the Court rather than its structure

and functions.[23] Nor did the Court give further provocation that might have spurred a broader attack. The justices skirted any challenge to the government's conduct of the Civil War.[24] In the war's aftermath, the Court under Chief Justice Salmon P. Chase's leadership artfully avoided conflict with Congress over its southern reconstruction program while simultaneously taking the opportunity in other areas to lay down precedents aggrandizing its power.[25] Starting in the 1890s, and picking up momentum in the progressive era, dissenters unhappy with what appeared the Court's too tender solicitude for property rights launched a renewed attack upon its having final say on constitutional questions.[26] New York governor (and future Chief Justice) Charles Evans Hughes, however, expressed what had become the dominant view with blunt candor: "We are under a Constitution, but the Constitution is what the judges say it is, and the judiciary is the safeguard of our liberty and property under the Constitution."[27]

The question thus became, for what purposes did the Court exercise its power? Over the course of the Supreme Court's history, different themes have appeared to predominate in its decision-making. During the period of the ascendancy of Chief Justice John Marshall, the Court gave allegiance to three interrelated values: the expansion of its own power; the supremacy of the national government over the states via a broad interpretation of the commerce and necessary-and-proper clauses; and the protection of property rights largely though not exclusively through the contract clause. Under his successor Roger B. Taney, the Court was more respectful of state autonomy, less respectful of established vested rights. During and after the Civil War, the justices grappled with the issues arising out of that conflict: the scope of presidential and congressional war powers; the transformed relationship between the states and the national government; and the Reconstruction-era legislation for the protection of black rights. From roughly the mid-1880s on, the dominant issue became how far business should be protected against government regulation—with the years 1921 through 1937 marking the high point of the enshrinement of laissez-faire as the law of the land.[28]

The confrontation between the justices and the New Deal—climaxing in Franklin D. Roosevelt's Court-"packing" plan—forced the Court to beat a strategic retreat that was turned into a rout by the new Roosevelt appointees to the bench. The upshot was to give a virtually free sway to government economic regulation.[29] But simultaneously the Court undertook as its new major role "to protect against hasty and prejudiced legislation the citizen's freedom to express his views," to uphold "the right to a fair trial," and "to give voice to the conscience of the country . . . against local prejudice and unfairness."[30] The Modern Court has become pre-eminently a "civil rights court." Of the 160 decisions with written opinions in the 1935–1936 term, only two dealt with civil rights and liberties. The balance shifted so rapidly that by the 1959 term 27 percent of the 117 plenary decisions dealt with such matters. By the first half of the 1970s, 43 percent of the Court's plenary decisions had as their principal issue an alleged deprivation of individual rights guaranteed by the Constitution; in addition, a large proportion of the decisions on procedural issues, statutory interpretation, and federal-state relations involved civil liberties/rights questions. Nor has the change been simply quantitative. Along with vastly expanding the scope of long-recognized freedoms, the Court "broke new ground by giving constitutional recognition to rights not previously supported by decisional laws."[31]

In 1900, the first John Marshall Harlan accused his brethren of regarding "the protection of private property . . . of more consequence than the protection of the life and liberty of the citizen."[32] And at the height of the impasse between the justices and the New Deal, the historian Charles A. Beard answered the rhetoric glorifying the Court as the shield of individual freedom with the blunt rejoinder that the Court "has not been very hot in its defense of personal liberties and rights."[33] Most commentators since have reaffirmed this negative appraisal of the Old Court's record. "[I]n the area of civil liberties," John P. Roche has written, "there has been a qualitative jump between the views of our legal ancestors and those of our contemporaries. . . . [W]hat we today think of as civil liberties largely date from definitions adopted in the 1930s."[34] Even so knowledgeable a constitutional historian as Robert G. McCloskey pictured the post-1937 Court as writing upon a nearly blank slate.

America has regarded itself as the land of the free since at least 1776, and the Constitution has been revered as the palladium of freedom since its inception. But although the literature of American democracy is rich in libertarian generalities, this rhetoric of individual rights had rarely been translated into concrete legislative prescriptions and judicial doctrines in the nineteenth or even in the early twentieth century. . . . Thus the modern Supreme Court inherited only a few scattered and incomplete theoretical and doctrinal tools to handle the problems of civil and political rights with which the justices were now confronted.[35]

Reality was more complex. When the Court made its famous switch-in-time that saved nine, there was a substantial body of case law on the books interpreting the constitutional guarantees of individual rights. Nor was that record simply one of judicial negativism. Viewed in long-term perspective, many of the expansive readings of individual rights adopted by the post-1937 Court represented incremental extensions from the existing precedents. In a number of key areas—most notably regarding the meaning of the criminal procedure guarantees of the Bill of Rights—earlier decisions continue to this day to provide the governing principles. There is no question that from a contemporary standpoint the record of the Old Court has major gaps, even blindspots. Those limitations, however, in large part reflected the dominant values and attitudes of the time—just as the new ground broken by the Modern Court has owed much to changes underway in the larger society.

As Robert H. Jackson admitted when pillorying the Old Court for its hostility to governmental regulation in the economic sphere, "the picture would not be complete if we did not acknowledge that the Supreme Court has rendered civil liberties decisions of substantial value." That "record has been a variable one," he acknowledged, since no institution can "completely escape the climate in which it lives." On balance, however, "the Court has generally been sympathetic . . . toward the older liberalism of the eighteenth century . . . embodied in the Bill of Rights."[36]

The first prerequisite for keeping in perspective the record of the Old Court is to remember how few guarantees of individual rights were included in the Constitution as drafted. The delegates at Philadelphia saw as their primary task to delineate the operating machinery of the new national government. They were not insensitive to the possible dangers to personal liberties from the abuse of governmental powers. But their major reliance for safeguarding against that threat was the diffusion of powers built in the structure of the system between the states and the national government and among the three branches of the national government. Accordingly, only a handful of explicit protections were written into the text. Article I, Section 9 stated that "[t]he Privilege of the Writ of Habeas Corpus shall not be suspended, unless when in Cases of Rebellion or Invasion the public Safety may require it" and that "[n]o Bill of Attainder or ex post facto Law shall be passed." Article III, Section 2 stipulated that "[t]he Trial of all Crimes, except in Cases of Impeachment, shall be by Jury," while Section 3 defined treason narrowly and required for conviction confession in open court or "the Testimony of two Witnesses to the same overt Act."

A second point to be kept in mind—and probably the single most important fact shaping the Old Court's approach to individual rights—was that the United States was a federal system. At least until the New Deal, the states and their political subdivisions were the agencies of government that most directly touched the daily lives of the average citizen. While the framers of the Constitution took pains to underline that the national authority when exercised within its proper sphere would be supreme, the document included few explicit restrictions upon the states. Article IV, Section 2 declared that the "Citizens of each State shall be entitled to all Privileges and Immunities of Citizens in the several States." Article I, Section 10 prohibited the states from passing "any Bill of Attainder, ex post facto Law, or Law impairing the Obligation of Contracts." But the Article IV privileges-and-immunities clause had—and continues to have—no more than "limited" importance as "a barrier against some discriminations by a state against citizens of other states."[37] And though the contract clause was of major significance in the pre–Civil War period for the protection of vested property rights, its importance had largely faded by the late nineteenth century.[38]

In *Calder v. Bull*—one of the earliest Supreme Court decisions—the Court held that the ex post facto clause was limited to retroactive changes in the criminal, not the civil, law. If that prohibition applied to civil legislation, Justice Samuel Chase explained, the accompanying clause forbidding the states to pass any laws impairing the obligation of contracts was "unnecessary ... for both of them are retrospective." And he went on to define what constituted an ex post facto law:

1st. Every law that makes an action done before the passing of of the law, and which was innocent when done, criminal; and punishes such action. 2d. Every law that aggravates a crime, or makes it greater than it was, when committed. 3d. Every law that changes the punishment, and inflicts a greater punishment than the law annexed to the crime, when committed. 4th. Every law that alters the legal rules of evidence, and receives less, or different testimony, than the law required at the time of the commission of the offence, in order to convict the offender.[39]

In the post–Civil War Test Oath Cases, however, a sharply divided Court read the clause more broadly. At issue in one case—*Cummings* v. *Missouri*—was an 1865 amendment to the Missouri constitution requiring that voters, public officeholders, lawyers, teachers, and clergymen swear a so-called iron-clad oath that they had never adhered to or sympathized with the Confederacy. The other—*Ex parte Garland*—involved a federal law requiring a similar oath as a qualification for holding federal office or practicing law in the federal courts. In support of his holding that the test oath requirement violated the ex post facto clause, Justice Stephen J. Field relied upon Blackstone's definition of punishment as including "a disability of holding offices or employments."[40]

Field gave a similarly expansive interpretation to the bill of attainder clause in what was the Court's first application of that provision. The term bill of attainder had at the common law a narrow technical meaning: a legislative condemnation to death without trial accompanied by corruption of blood—that is, "the party attainted lost all inheritable quality, and could neither receive nor transmit any property or other rights by inheritance." Lesser punishments inflicted by legislative fiat were known as "bills of pains and penalties." Typical English bills of attainder had four distinguishing characteristics: identification of the victim by name; recital of the actions deserving punishment; a declaration of guilt; and prescription of the punishment.[41] But Field, drawing upon passing *dicta* by Chief Justice Marshall, held that the bill of attainder clause in the Constitution included bills of pains and penalties. Admitting that test oaths were a recurring fact in English history without having been regarded as bills of attainder, he explained away the difference by pretending that such oaths "were always limited to an affirmation of present belief, or present disposition towards the government, and were never exacted with reference to particular instances of past misconduct." Nor did he regard lack of the typical characteristics associated with English bills of attainder as material: "A bill of attainder is a legislative act which inflicts punishment without a judicial trial." Most important, he defined punishment in sweeping terms as "[a]ny deprivation ... of the rights and privileges of the citizen."[42]

Here was a striking example of judicial amendment of the Constitution. The Test Oath Cases, however, remained isolated precedents without any significant progeny. Only one later decision found a violation of the bill of attainder clause—a two-sentence memorandum opinion striking down a West Virginia test oath similar to those in the *Cummings-Garland* cases.[43] All the later decisions finding a violation of the ex post facto clause involved criminal prosecutions in the narrow sense.[44] A 1913 decision even further narrowed the scope of the clause by excluding retroactive changes in even the criminal law by judicial interpretation.[45] The focus of inquiry was thus limited to whether a new legislatively adopted penal statute, rule of evidence, or trial procedure worked a "substantial" disadvantage to a given defendant.[46] Any increase in the punishment for an offense beyond that affixed at the time of its commission was barred.[47] But the Court upheld an habitual-criminal law imposing a more severe penalty for a third offense—even when applied to a person whose first two offenses had been committed before the statute's adoption—upon the rationale that the punishment was for the new crime only and that the legislature could legitimately take past conduct into account when fixing the penalty.[48] Changes in the rules of evidence or trial procedures were approved or disapproved on a case-by-case basis.[49] And in one of the first Sherman Antitrust Law prosecutions, the Court upheld punishment of an act begun before the law's adoption but continuing after its passage.[50]

The Constitution's major limitations upon governmental authority vis-à-vis the individual were those embodied in the Bill of Rights, or, to be more accurate, in the first eight amendments. And therein lay the nub of the difficulty. The historical record made evident that those provisions were aimed at the national government, not the states. At the time of their adoption, Congress rebuffed the proposal by James Madison for an amendment to prohibit the states from infringing the rights of conscience, free press, and trial by jury.[51] When the applicability of the Bill of Rights to the states was raised before the Supreme Court in 1833 in the famous case of *Barron v. Baltimore*, Chief Justice Marshall found the question "of great importance, but not of much difficulty": the purpose of those amendments was to guard "against the apprehended encroachments of the general government—not against those of the local governments." Had Congress, he explained, "engaged in the extraordinary occupation of improving the constitutions of the several states by affording the people additional protection from the exercise of power by their own governments in matters which concerned themselves alone, they would have declared this purpose in plain and intelligible language."[52]

The adoption of the Fourteenth Amendment in the aftermath of the Civil

War, however, reopened the question. No other provision has stirred so much debate about the intent of the framers. There are those who see as its aim to safeguard no more than the narrow range of economic and legal rights listed in the Civil Rights Act of 1866: "to make and enforce contracts, to sue, be parties, and give evidence, to inherit, purchase, lease, sell, hold, and convey real and personal property, and to full and equal benefit of all laws and proceedings for the security of person and property."[53] Others argue that the purpose was to extend the full guarantees of the Bill of Rights as limits upon the states; still others that the purpose was to incorporate an even broader range of so-called fundamental or natural rights.[54] Probably the fairest conclusion that can be drawn from the evidence amassed is that there was no consensus among those responsible for the Amendment's adoption. Even individual participants were often confused and uncertain about what they had in mind. Accordingly, the final result was couched in language that was as vague as it was broad:

No State shall make or enforce any law which shall abridge the privileges or immunities of citizens of the United States; nor shall any State deprive any person of life, liberty, or property, without due process of law; nor deny to any person within its jurisdiction the equal protection of the laws.

The question of what those words meant was first explained by the Court in 1873 in the *Slaughter-House Cases*. In March 1869, the Louisiana legislature had adopted legislation restricting the slaughter of cattle in New Orleans to the facilities of the newly incorporated Crescent City Stock Landing and Slaughter House Company. The restriction was justified as a health measure—and was in accord with developments underway in cities across the country to limit slaughtering to remote locations. The difficulty was that the Louisiana statute was the product of wholesale bribery by the company's promoters. A group of independent butchers filed suit in the state courts raising—among their arguments—the plea that "the first clause of the 14th amendment . . . prohibits the States to abridge the privileges and immunities of citizens of the United States, and secures to all protection from State legislation that involves the rights of property, the most valuable of which is to labor freely in an honest avocation." When the Louisiana Supreme Court upheld the law as a sanitary measure, appeal was taken to the United States Supreme Court. In his brief, the company's attorney warned that the broad interpretation of the Fourteenth Amendment advanced by the independent butchers would "deprive the Legislatures and State courts of the several States from regulating and settling their internal affairs."[55]

Oral argument was heard by the Supreme Court on January 11, 1872. With Justice Samuel Nelson not participating because of illness, the justices deadlocked four-to-four. On April 15, 1872, the Court ordered reargument at the next term. In November Nelson resigned, and was replaced by Ward Hunt, the chief judge of the New York Court of Appeals. Hunt had written the opinion of that court upholding a New York statute authorizing the Metropolitan Board of Health of New York to restrict the location of slaughterhouses.[56] And he supplied the decisive fifth vote for upholding the Louisiana statute. Writing for the majority, Justice Samuel F. Miller dismissed the argument that the independent butchers had been denied the right to pursue their calling. They were free to continue carrying on their trade using the company's facilities at charges fixed in the statute. And he had no difficulty in showing that control over the location of slaughtering was a long-accepted practice. He then turned to the larger constitutional issue raised. The question before the Court, he summed up, was if "the purpose of the fourteenth amendment . . . [was] to transfer the security and protection of . . . the entire domain of civil rights heretofore belonging exclusively to the States . . . to the Federal government." If so, the result would make the Supreme Court "a perpetual censor upon all legislation of the States, . . . with authority to nullify such as it did not approve as consistent with those rights."

Miller concluded that so far-reaching a departure from "the structure and spirit of our institutions"—which "radically changes the whole theory of the relations of the State and Federal governments to each other and of both these governments to the people"—should not be read into the Amendment "in the absence of language which expresses such a purpose too clearly to admit of doubt." His underlying premise was that both the states and the United States had equal places in the American scheme of government, each with independent authority within its own sphere. Accordingly, he set forth the doctrine of dual citizenship—that each person was simultaneously a citizen of the United States and of the state in which he resided. He then proceeded to limit the rights of United States citizenship protected by the privileges and immunities clause to an insubstantial handful: the right to come to the seat of government, to use the navigable waters of the United States and its sea ports, to petition for a writ of habeas corpus, to peaceably assemble and petition for redress of grievances, and to seek the protection of the federal government when abroad or on the high seas. The reverse side was that the vast majority of accepted personal rights fell within the privileges and immunities of state citizenship and thus under the exclusive protection of the state governments.[57] And despite repeated appeals since, the Court has remained firm in refusing to expand in any meaningful way the coverage of the privileges and immunities clause.[58]

The independent butchers were no more successful with their argument that the statute violated the equal protection clause. The dissenters in *Slaughter-House*—and many commentators since—could make a strong argument that historically the term privileges and immunities of citizens of the United States encompassed a far broader range of rights than what the majority allowed. But equal protection of the laws lacked any developed legal interpretation that could be used to elucidate its meaning. Read literally, the words indicated that only the application of laws must be equal, not their substance. And Justice Miller appeared to adopt an even narrower reading: "We doubt very much whether any action of a State not directly by way of discrimination against the negroes as a class, or on account of their race, will ever be held to come within the purview of this provision."[59] In its 1880 decision dealing with the exclusion of blacks from juries, the Court reaffirmed the limitation of the equal protection clause to "discrimination because of race or color."[60] In another decision that year, however, the Court took the broader position that the clause guaranteed that "no person or class of persons shall be denied the same protection of the laws which is enjoyed by other persons and other classes in the same place and under like circumstances."[61] More important, *Yick Wo v. Hopkins* in 1886 adopted the formula that "the equal protection of the laws" required "the protection of equal laws."[62]

In reviewing legislative classifications under the equal protection clause, the Court adopted a two-step test that has been termed the "unjustifiable classifications" approach.[63] The first was if the purpose of the classification represented a legitimate exercise of the state's police power to safeguard public health, safety, and/or morals. The second was to appraise the reasonableness of the classification as a means of promoting that legitimate purpose. The guarantee of equal protection was not satisfied if the legislation "deals alike with all of a certain class," the Court explained in 1897. The classification itself could not "be made arbitrarily," but must have "a reasonable and just relation" to the legislative objective.[64] That approach allowed the justices broad latitude to approve or disapprove of challenged legislation on a case-by-case basis. But the Court tended to take a permissive line regarding what constituted an acceptable legislative objective. Its touchstone was if the classification had been traditionally applied as "general usage" or was "of an unusual character, unknown to the practice of our governments."[65] Even racially based classifications were held permissible if reflecting "the established usages, customs and traditions of the people."[66] Similarly regarding means, the Court allowed the legislature "a wide scope of discretion. . . . A classification having some reasonable basis does not offend . . . merely because it is not made with mathematical nicety or because in practice it results in some inequality."[67] The upshot was that the equal protection clause remained—in the dismissive words of Justice Oliver Wendell Holmes, Jr.,—"the usual last resort of constitutional arguments."[68]

Much the same fate appeared to threaten the due process clause. In the *Slaughter-House Cases*, Justice Miller adhered to the traditional interpretation that due process involved simply procedural safeguards for criminal defendants.[69] Eleven years later in *Hurtado v. California*, the Court struck an even sharper blow to any expansive reading of that provision. The issue before the justices was whether the Fifth Amendment's requirement of an indictment by a grand jury for capital cases was binding upon the states. A seven-to-one majority—with Justice John Marshall Harlan the single dissenter—first held that the due process clauses of the Fourteenth and Fifth Amendments were identical in meaning and then went on to conclude that since the Fifth Amendment had the grand jury provision in addition to the due process clause, the framers of the Bill of Rights had not understood the right of indictment by the grand jury as included in the conception of due process or they would not have listed that guarantee separately. This argument—known as "the doctrine of nonsuperfluousness"—would appear to rule out the possibility of incorporating in the due process clause any of the guarantees listed independently in the Bill of Rights. But Justice Stanley Matthews's opinion left open a loophole by saying that the clause did protect "those fundamental principles of liberty and justice which lie at the base of all our civil and political institutions."[70]

The question, therefore, became, what were the "fundamental principles" thus protected? To most late-nineteenth-century justices, the answer that immediately came to mind was the security of property rights. Beginning in 1887, the Court transformed due process into a substantive limitation upon what government could do regardless of the procedures followed.[71] Although upholding in *Mugler v. Kansas* that state's law prohibiting the manufacture and sale of alcoholic beverages, Harlan underlined that the justices would have final say if "a statute purporting . . . to protect the public health, the public morals, or the public safety, has no real or substantial relation to those objects, or is a palpable invasion of rights secured by the fundamental law."[72] Three years later, the Court in *Chicago, Milwaukee and St. Paul Railway Co. v. Minnesota* for the first time struck down a state law on substantive due process grounds, holding that a Minnesota law making rate-fixing decisions by the state railroad commission final arbitrarily deprived the companies of property in violation of the Fourteenth Amendment.[73] The culmination came in 1897 with *Allgeyer v. Louisiana*. The common-law meaning of liberty was freedom from physical restraint. Justice Rufus W. Peckham's definition was far broader in its sweep: "the right of the citizen to be free in the enjoyment of all his faculties; to be free to use them in all lawful ways; to live and work where he will; to earn his livelihood by any lawful calling; to pursue any livelihood or avocation."[74]

The premise underlying substantive due process was that freedom in the marketplace was the rule, goverment regulation the exception. Even when a business was sufficiently affected with a public interest to warrant regulation, the judiciary, not the legislature, was the final arbiter of its reasonableness (i.e., whether or not a given rate deprived a railroad of a fair return upon its investment). Similarly, "liberty of contract" presupposed that private bargaining regarding wage, hours, and working conditions should be the norm. Governmental interference was permitted only in special circumstances—with the burden of justification resting upon the government.[75] The classic expression of this laissez-faire constitutionalism was the 1905 decision in *Lochner v. New York*, invalidating that state's law prohibiting bakery workers from working more than ten hours a day or sixty hours a week as "an unreasonable, unnecessary and arbitrary interference with the right of the individual . . . to enter into those contracts in relation to labor which may seem to him appropriate." There was no evidence, Justice Peckham argued, that bakers were not as capable as men in other trades to "care for themselves without the protecting arm of the State." While paying lip service to the state's power to protect the health of its citizens, he concluded that "almost all occupations more or less affect the health. . . . [A]re we all, on that account, at the mercy of legislative majorities?"[76]

Not surprisingly, the Court's first acceptance of a separately listed guarantee of the Bill of Rights as included within the due process clause came in defense of property rights. In the 1897 *Chicago, Burlington and Quincy Railroad* case, the justices unanimously agreed that states were required to pay just compensation for private property taken for public use.[77] Since the right to compensation clause existed in the Fifth Amendment independently of the due process clause, did the decision mean that the Court was abandoning the "doctrine of nonsuperfluousness"? The answer—at least when the Court came to decide *Maxwell v. Dow* three years later—appeared to be no. At issue was the constitutionality of Utah's eight-person jury system. Justice Peckham acknowledged that the Sixth Amendment required the common-law jury of twelve in federal criminal trials. With Harlan again alone dissenting, however, the eight-to-one majority relied upon *Hurtado* to deny that the Fourteenth Amendment extended this requirement to the states. Peckham went so far as to suggest that trial by jury *per se* "has never been affirmed to be a necessary requisite of due process of law." The result was to leave open whether the railroad-compensation decision was a precedent for nationalizing the Bill of Rights or simply an aberration reflecting the justices' solicitude for corporate property. *Dow*'s answer was masterfully ambiguous: the rights protected by the Fourteenth Amendment "do not necessarily include all the rights protected by the first eight amendments to the Federal Constitution."[78]

A partial clarification came in 1908 in *Twining v. New Jersey*. The question before the Court was whether the Fifth Amendment's privilege against self-incrimination applied to the states via the Fourteenth, thereby barring adverse comment by a judge or prosecutor upon a defendant's failure to testify. Justice William H. Moody laid down as the test for whether a right was guaranteed by due process: "Is it a fundamental principle of liberty and justice which inheres in the very idea of free government and is the inalienable right of a citizen of such a government?" With Harlan again dissenting, he concluded after a lengthy—if factually questionable—exegesis that the guarantee against self-incrimination did meet that test. On the other hand, he acknowledged the possibility that "some of the personal rights safeguarded by the first eight Amendments against National action may also be safeguarded against state action, because a denial of them would be a denial of due process of law." Although saying that would appear to discard the *Hurtado* nonsuperfluity doctrine, Moody failed explicitly to overrule the earlier decision. Worse, he muddied the situation further by implying that any rights covered by the due process clause would be only similar to, not identical in meaning and scope with, those in the Bill of Rights. Such rights, he underlined, were protected "not because those rights are enumerated in the first eight Amendments, but because they are of such a nature that they are included in the conception of due process of law." The Court would decide what rights met that standard via a case-by-case "process of inclusion and exclusion."[79]

Twining presented the Court with a dilemma. If due process guaranteed against state violation "the fundamental and inalienable rights of mankind," why should its scope be limited to economic liberties? The first breakthrough toward a broader view came in 1923 in *Meyer v. Nebraska*, when a seven-to-two majority struck down that state's World War I-inspired law forbidding teaching of or in any modern language other than English through the eighth grade in all schools, public or private. While acknowledging a legislative interest in promoting "a homogeneous people with American ideals" given the "[u]nfortunate experiences during the late war," Justice James C. McReynolds found no "emergency" in the present "time of peace and domestic tranquillity" that made a child's knowledge of some other language "so clearly harmful" as to justify the law's "infringement of rights long freely enjoyed." He assimilated the ruling into the economic due process line of decisions by emphasizing how the law "materially . . . interfere[s] with the calling of modern language teachers." But perhaps reflecting judicial sensitivity to complaints that the Court was interested simply in protecting the rights of employers and property owners, he defined liberty in expansive terms as the freedom "to acquire useful knowledge, to marry, to establish a home and bring up children, to worship God according to the dictates of his own conscience, and, generally, to enjoy those privileges long recognized at common law as essential to the orderly pursuit of happiness by free men."[80]

Most accounts see a more important breakthrough coming two years later in *Gitlow v. New York*. Up to that time, the Court had rebuffed all bids to extend the First Amendment to the States via the Fourteenth. The first such attempt appears to have been made by the attorneys for the defendants in the famous Haymarket bombing case. Arguing that the Fourteenth Amendment incorporated the entire Bill of Rights, they raised—among other issues—that the defendants' punishment for "mere general advice" violated their freedom of speech. But a unanimous Court dismissed the argument with a curt reaffirmation that the Bill of Rights applied simply to the national government.[81] In 1907, Justice Oliver Wendell Holmes, Jr., when upholding a state contempt-of-court conviction of a Colorado publisher, expressly left "undecided the question whether there is to be found in the Fourteenth

Amendment a prohibition similar to that in the First."[82] While not referring to the First Amendment by name, Justice Joseph McKenna in *Gilbert v. Minnesota* in 1920 did assume—at least for "the purposes of this case... without so deciding"—that freedom of speech and press was among the "natural and inherent" rights protected by the due process clause. But he simultaneously underlined that such freedom "is not absolute, it is subject to restriction and limitation"—and proceeded to uphold Minnesota's sedition law as a legitimate "exertion of the police power."[83] The following year, Justice Mahlon Pitney refused even to concede the principle that the Constitution "imposes upon the States... the right of free speech."[84]

A founder of the Communist Labor party, Benjamin Gitlow, had been convicted under New York's criminal anarchy law making it a felony for any person to advocate, advise, or teach "the doctrine that organized government should be overthrown by force, violence or any unlawful means." Undeterred by the Court's past refusals to incorporate the First Amendment into the Fourteenth, Walter Pollak of the American Civil Liberties Union contended that freedom of speech and press in political matters was a fundamental principle of liberty that fitted the *Twining* standard for inclusion within the due process clause. He argued, therefore, that New York could punish Gitlow only if publication of the so-called "Left Wing Manifesto" in the newspaper of which he was business manager—the evidence against him—involved a clear and present danger of unlawful action. While sustaining the conviction, Justice Edward T. Sanford acknowledged, almost in passing, that "freedom of speech and of the press—which are protected by the First Amendment from abridgment by Congress—are among the fundamental personal rights and 'liberties' protected by the due process clause of the Fourteenth Amendment from impairment by the States." The trouble was that he couched this acknowledgment as no more than an assumption "[f]or present purposes."[85] And there is reason to conclude that he—like McKenna in *Gilbert*—was simply setting up a straw man to be knocked down by sustaining the conviction.

If the decision did represent a major breakthrough in the nationalization of the Bill of Rights, its significance appears to have attracted scant attention at the time from commentators or the bar. Nor did the justices give any indication of having laid down so important a new precedent.[86] Although in 1927 reversing in *Fiske v. Kansas* the conviction of an Industrial Workers of the World organizer for violating the Kansas criminal syndicalism law prohibiting the advocacy of force, violence, or lawlessness as a means of industrial or political change, Sanford ignored the free speech issue.[87] In his concurrence the same year upholding the conviction of Charlotte Anita Whitney under California's criminal syndicalism law for her role in founding that state's Communist Labor party, Justice Louis D. Brandeis did affirm that free speech was one of the "fundamental rights" guaranteed by the due process clause. But Sanford's majority opinion in *Whitney v. California* did no more than allude in backhand fashion to "the freedom of speech which is secured by the Constitution."[88] In his 1928 opinion upholding New York's law requiring Ku Klux Klan members to register, Justice Willis Van Devanter acknowledged in similar backhand fashion that the right of association was among the liberties protected by the due process clause. But he did not mention the First Amendment—and took pains to add the familiar qualifying formula that one's "liberty in this regard, like most other personal rights, must yield to the rightful exertion of the police power."[89] The following year the Court summarily dismissed an appeal from defendants convicted for violating Pennsylvania's sedition law for "want of a substantial federal question."[90]

Formal incorporation of the First Amendment into the Fourteenth came only in 1931 at the hands of the newly appointed Chief Justice Charles Evans Hughes. In *Stromberg v. California*, a seven-to-two majority overturned the conviction of a counselor at a Communist Party youth camp for violating the state law barring display of the "red flag." Hughes simply assumed—without discussion of or even evidence of much thought about the implications— that *Gitlow*, *Fiske*, and *Whitney* had "determined that the conception of liberty under the due process clause of the Fourteenth Amendment embraces the right of free speech."[91] He made the same assumption about "the liberty of the press" to strike down in a decision handed down two weeks later a Minnesota law authorizing a court injunction to prohibit publication of a "malicious, scandalous and defamatory newspaper."[92] The climax of the incorporation process came in 1937 in *De Jonge v. Oregon* when a unanimous bench joined in holding that the "right of peaceable assembly is a right cognate to those of free speech and free press and is equally fundamental." Those rights were thus not simply protected by the First Amendment against abridgement by the federal government, but "cannot be denied without violating those fundamental principles of liberty and justice which lie at the base of all civil and political institutions,—principles which the Fourteenth Amendment embodies in the general terms of its due process clause."[93]

The federal system not only complicated definition of the rights guaranteed individuals by the United States Constitution, but exacerbated the problem of what mechanisms were available for protection against their violation. Article III, Section 1 provided that the "judicial Power of the United States, shall be vested in one supreme Court, and in such inferior Courts as the Congress may from time to time ordain and establish." Section 2 gave the Supreme Court "original Jurisdiction" in "all Cases affecting Ambassadors, other public Ministers and Consuls, and those in which a State shall be Party." But the Judiciary Act of 1789 excluded from the Court's original jurisdiction controversies "between a state and its citizens."[94] That jurisdiction was further reduced by the adoption in 1795 of the Eleventh Amendment barring suits in the federal courts against a state by citizens of other states or by foreign subjects.[95] In *Marbury*, Marshall held that Congress could not add to the Court's orginial jurisdiction.[96] And Congress parcelled out to other courts concurrent jurisdiction with the Supreme Court over much of its remaining original jurisdiction.[97] The major source of the Court's power thus lay in its "appellate Jurisdiction, both as to Law and Fact, with such Exceptions, and under such Regulations as the Congress shall make."[98]

When laying down the framework of the federal judicial system in the Judiciary Act of 1789, Congress established two tiers of federal trial courts.[99] The first consisted of thirteen district courts, one for each of the then-eleven states plus two separate districts for those parts of Virginia and Massachusetts that would become Kentucky and Maine. Each district court had its own judge. The second consisted of circuit courts, with eleven of the districts divided into three circuits. The circuit courts—which were to hold two sessions a year in each district within the circuit—were three-judge panels made up of one district judge plus two Supreme Court justices sitting on circuit.[100] The burden of circuit riding imposed upon the Supreme Court justices was reduced in 1793 by requiring only one justice on the circuit courts.[101] In 1802, Congress authorized the holding of a circuit court by a single district judge.[102] As the country grew in size, that arrangement became widely practiced. In response, Congress in 1869 authorized one circuit judge for each of what had become nine circuits while reducing the circuit-riding duties of the Supreme Court justices to attendance at one term every two years in each district of the circuit to which the justice was assigned.[103]

In a bow to states' rights sensitivities, Congress in the Judiciary Act of 1789 shied from giving the lower federal courts the full extent of the jurisdiction allowable under Article III.[104] Those courts were given concurrent jurisdiction with the state courts in diversity of state citizenship cases where the dispute exceeded five-hundred dollars—or to be more precise, in suits "between a citizen of the State where the suit is brought, and a citizen of another State"—with an accompanying provision for removal to the federal courts before trial of such actions brought in a state court. Concurrent jurisdiction with the state courts was similarly given in civil suits initiated by the United States. The lower federal courts were given "exclusive" jurisdiction over only three types of cases: (1) admiralty cases; (2) "all suits for penalties and forfeitures incurred, under the laws of the United States"; and (3) "all crimes and offences cognizable under the authority of the United States." Apart from these exceptions, no jurisdiction was given over cases arising under the Constitution and laws of the United States.[105] Although the Judiciary Act of 1801 gave the lower federal courts such jurisdiction, the statute was repealed almost immediately after the Jeffersonians took power.[106] The limited role thus allowed the lower federal courts continued until the Civil War. The result was to leave to the state courts the primary responsibility for enforcing federal law.[107]

The 1789 statute made no provision for appeal to the Supreme Court from lower federal court judgments in criminal cases. Although primarily trial courts for certain types of cases (e.g., the more serious criminal offenses), the circuit courts could review the final decisions of the district courts in civil cases where the matter in dispute was over fifty dollars. Appeal to the Supreme Court from the final decisions of circuit courts in such cases was authorized when the matter in dispute was over two thousand dollars.[108] Until 1889 appeals from the lower federal courts to the Supreme Court in criminal cases remained limited to a few statutorily defined situations—the most important when the judges of a circuit court divided in their opinions on a question of law. But otherwise the long-term trend was toward increasing the types of cases from the lower federal courts reviewable by the Supreme Court.[109] The most important part of the Supreme Court's appellate jurisdiction, however, was Section 25 of the Judiciary Act of 1789 empowering the Supreme Court to review via writ of error decisions by state courts of last resort where: (1) the state court had denied "the validity of a treaty or statute of, or an authority exercised under the United States"; (2) where the state court upheld "the validity of a statute of, or an authority exercised under any State" when challenged "on the ground of their being repugnant to the constitution, treaties or laws of the United States"; and (3) where the state court decided against a "title, right, privilege or exemption . . . claimed by either party, under . . . any clause of the constitution, or of a treaty, or statute of . . . the United States."[110]

Although Congress in 1867 when reenacting Section 25 of the Judiciary Act of 1789 left out the wording explicitly limiting Supreme Court review to state court decisions where a federal question was involved,[111] a sharply divided Court in 1875 in *Murdock v. City of Memphis* took the position that if the lawmakers had intended to reverse "the policy of the government from its foundation . . . it is reasonably to be expected that Congress would use plain, unmistakable language in giving expression to such intention." And Justice Miller in his majority opinion went on to indicate that even if a state court had decided the federal question erroneously, there could be "other points in the case" resting upon grounds of purely state law "sufficient to maintain the judgment."[112] Even when "the judgment of a state court rests upon the two grounds, one of which is federal and the other non-federal in character," the Court later elaborated, "our jurisdiction fails if the non-federal ground is independent of the federal ground and adequate to support the judgment."[113] There were two exceptions. One was when the federal right turned upon the meaning of state law—e.g., whether there was under state law a contractual obligation that had been impaired).[114] The second was when state court rules of procedure did not allow adequate opportunity for raising federal issues—or as Justice Holmes put the matter, "assertion of federal rights . . . is not to be defeated under the name of local practice."[115]

But appellate review has serious limitations as a means of adequately protecting constitutional guarantees. In its decisions, the Supreme Court lays down broad principles. Their day-to-day implementation takes place at the trial court level. And experience had shown that so long as the state courts retained the primary responsibility for enforcing federal laws, there were endless opportunities for nullifying national policies that were opposed by dominant local opinion.[116] The major change came after the Civil War. Not simply did the Civil War era Amendments vastly expand the substantive federal rights protected against the states, but the Reconstruction-era Congress made the federal courts the primary mechanism for protection of those rights. The Civil Rights Act of 1870 gave the lower federal courts exclusive jurisdiction over "all causes, civil and criminal, arising" under its provisions; the following year Congress gave those courts jurisdiction over damage suits for "deprivation of any rights . . . secured by the Constitution of the United States" by persons acting "under color of any law."[117] Most important, the Judiciary Act of 1875 gave the federal circuit courts—subject to a five-hundred dollar requirement—"original cognizance, concurrent with the courts of the several States, of all suits of a civil nature . . . arising under the Constitution or laws of the United States."[118]

When the resulting growth in the volume of business threatened to inundate the federal court system, Congress responded in 1891 with a far-reaching structural change. Circuit Courts of Appeals, consisting of three judges each, were established for the nine circuits. To man these new courts, a second circuit judge was added to each circuit. The third place would be filled by a district judge—although Supreme Court justices remained eligible to sit. An even more important innovation was the introduction of the principle of discretionary review by the Supreme Court via writ of certiorari. Direct appeal to the Supreme Court via writ of error was retained for "any case that involves the construction or application of the Constitution." But decisions of the new Courts of Appeals were made "final" in diversity cases, suits under the revenue and patent laws, admiralty cases, and criminal prosecutions except "[i]n cases of conviction of a capital or otherwise infamous crime." Further appeal of such cases to the Supreme Court was left to its discretion except that a Court of Appeals was authorized to "certify to the Supreme Court . . . any questions or propositions of law concerning which it desires . . . instruction."[119] The so-called Judges' Bill of 1925 further restricted appeals as a matter of right from the lower federal courts to the Supreme Court to two major categories: (1) suits to enjoin enforcement of a state law or an action by a state administrative officer; and (2) a decision by a Court of Appeals holding a state law unconstitutional.[120]

The 1891 legislation did not touch the rules dating from Section 25 of the Judiciary Act of 1789 governing Supreme Court review of state court decisions. A loophole in that appellate jurisdiction was the lack of any provision for review when a state court had erroneously held a state law in violation of the United States Constitution. But the 1911 decision by the New York Court of Appeals striking down that state's workmen's compensation law as in violation of the Fourteenth Amendment sparked such an outcry that Congress in 1914 permitted the high tribunal to review state court decisions invalidating a state law as repugnant to the Constitution or laws of the United States.[121] More important, the justices induced Congress in the Judges' Bill of 1925 to give the Court more control over appeals from state court decisions by reducing the number of such cases where a party had a legal right to review. The Court's obligatory jurisdiction—or review by writ of error—included cases where (1) the state court held that a law or treaty of the United States was unconstitutional, and (2) where the state court upheld a state law challenged as in violation of the Constitution or a federal law. Review by certiorari—where the Supreme Court retained a free hand to review or not—applied if (1) the state court upheld the validity of a federal law or treaty, or (2) the state court ruled a state law invalid on federal grounds.[122] And the Court adopted the policy of summarily disposing without a hearing many of the cases whose review was still technically mandatory for lack of a substantial federal question.[123]

Distinct from—though related to—the question of jurisdiction was the scope of Supreme Court review of state court decisions. The traditional view was that such review was confined to matters of law, and did not include an independent inquiry into the facts. With the development of substantive due process, however, the Court silently abandoned that limitation by assuming final say about the reasonableness of a given regulation.[124] In 1927, the Court made explicit its refusal to be bound by state court determinations of fact when overturning, in *Fiske v. Kansas*, the conviction of an Industrial Workers of the World organizer under that state's criminal syndicalism law on the ground that the record showed no evidence to support guilt. "[T]his Court will review the finding of facts by a State court where a federal right has been denied as the result of a finding shown by the record to be without evidence to support it; or when a conclusion of law as to a Federal right and a finding of fact are so intermingled as to make it necessary, in order to pass upon the Federal question, to analyze the facts."[125] Chief Justice Hughes went a step farther in 1935 by affirming the Court's power to look behind the formal record.

That the question is one of fact does not relieve us of the duty to determine whether in truth a federal right has been denied. When a federal right has been . . . claimed in a state court, it is our province to inquire not merely whether it was denied in express terms but also whether it was denied in substance and effect. If this requires an examination of evidence, that examination must be made. Otherwise, review by this Court would fail of its purpose in safeguarding constitutional rights.[126]

Major jurisdictional barriers to a federal court hearing remained, however, for defendants. Private parties initiating a civil suit had substantial leeway in electing a state court as their forum. And civil proceedings or criminal prosecutions instituted by the states would be heard in their own courts. What could be done in those situations? The answer was, not much except in cases involving diversity of state citizenship. A 1793 congressional statute forbade issuance by the federal courts of injunctions to stay state court proceedings.[127] Section 641 in the 1875 Revised Statutes did authorize removal to the federal courts of civil suits and criminal prosecutions commenced in the state courts "against any person who is denied or cannot enforce in the judicial tribunals of the State . . . any right secured to him by any law providing for the equal civil rights of citizens of the United States."[128] While upholding the principle in *Strauder v. West Virginia*, the Court in its accompanying *Virginia v. Rives* decision construed the removal authority so narrowly as to limit its application to situations where a state constitution or law on its face denied a defendant's constitutional rights.[129] And in 1894, the Court read provisions adopted in 1887–1888 authorizing removal to federal courts of civil suits "arising under the Constitution or laws of the United States" as allowing removal only when the plaintiff—not the defendant—"relied on some right under the Constitution or laws of the United States."[130]

Worse, once a court proceeding was instituted—whatever the forum—the defendant faced liability if his defense was not successful. The trick, therefore, was to block action before any proceeding was begun. The problem was, how could one do so given the principle derived from English law that the sovereign was immune from suit except with his consent?[131] Under Article III, Section 2, federal court jurisdiction included "Controversies to which the United States shall be a Party." Did that provision apply to suits where the United States was the defendant rather than the plaintiff? When *Chisholm v. Georgia* was before the Court in 1793, Chief Justice John Jay in *dicta* answered no on the ground of the practical difficulties of enforcing a judgment.[132] In 1821, John Marshall in *Cohens v. Virginia* affirmed in more *dicta* that "[t]he universally received opinion is, that no suit can be commenced or prosecuted against the United States."[133] Almost as formidable an obstacle appeared to exist regarding the states. The majority in *Chisholm* did rule that the constitutional provision extending the federal judicial power to "Controversies . . . between a State and Citizens of another State" allowed a breach-of-contract suit by an out-of-state litigant against Georgia.[134] But the angry reaction of the states led to the swift adoption of the Eleventh Amendment denying federal court jurisdiction over any suit "commenced or prosecuted against one of the United States by Citizens of another State."[135]

The barrier against suits against the United States was first breached before the Civil War by decisions allowing the circuit court in the District of Columbia to issue writs of mandamus against individually named federal officers—that is, a court order requiring the officer affirmatively to take an action. The rule adopted limited such orders to instances where the action was ministerial (i.e., where specific duties were required by law), not discretionary.[136] The question of the issuance of injunctions to restrain action by a federal official did not arise until after the Civil War. Then, the Court rebuffed bids by the southern states to restrain enforcement of the Reconstruction Acts on the grounds of their unconstitutionality.[137] Once Reconstruction was out of the way, however, the Court adopted the so-called nominal party rule opening the door for such injunctions so long as an individual officer rather than the United States was named. The leading case was *United States v. Lee* in 1882. Although that decision involved a suit against federal officers for recovery of illegally taken land, Justice Miller for the narrow five-to-four majority affirmed in sweeping terms the principle of allowing suits against federal officers proceeding under an unconstitutional law or in excess of their statutory authority. "[T]here is," he reasoned, "no safety for the citizen, except in the protection of the judicial tribunals, for rights which have been invaded by the officers of the government, professing to act in its name."[138]

Given his wish to make the national judiciary a bulwark for the defense of property rights, John Marshall had adopted the same device to circumvent, at least for injunctive actions, the Eleventh Amendment by allowing suits against state officials as individuals even when those officials were acting under the authority of state law. The Court followed this tack up to the mid–1870s.[139] In a series of cases involving challenges to defaults of southern state debts, however, the Court retreated from the Marshallian tradition in face of the practical difficulties of forcing payment. In 1887, *In re Ayers* appeared to repudiate the nominal-party rule by holding that an injunctive proceeding against a state attorney general was in fact a suit against a state prohibited by the Eleventh Amendment.[140] And three years later, *Hans v. Louisiana* went beyond the literal wording of the Amendment to bar suits against a state by its own citizens.[141] But the barrier thus raised to federal court suits by private citizens against state violations of constitutionally guaranteed rights did not stand long. The Court continued to hold that the Eleventh Amendment's immunity from suit did not apply to counties, cities, or other political subdivisions of the states.[142] More important, the anxiety of late nineteenth-early twentieth century justices to protect corporate property rights led the Court to reopen the door to federal court injunctions against enforcement by state officials of regulatory laws.[143]

The climax came in 1908 in *Ex parte Young*, upholding a federal court injunction restraining Minnesota's attorney general from instituting court action to enforce that state's railroad rate regulations. In his rationale for the eight-to-one majority, Justice Rufus W. Peckham laid down what became known as the "stripping doctrine." An unconstitutional law was void; therefore, action by a state officer to enforce such a law was "an illegal act... and he is in that sense stripped of his official or representative character and is subjected in his person to the consequences of his individual conduct. The State has no power to impart to him any immunity from responsibility to the supreme authority of the United States."[144] A decade later, the Court took the further step of holding that the federal courts could enjoin further prosecution in the state courts of a proceeding begun in violation of a previous injunction.[145] And in 1932, Chief Justice Hughes ruled for a unanimous bench in *Sterling v. Constantin* that even the governor of a state was not immune from a federal court injunction to restrain actions in violation of the Constitution.[146] The one unsettled question was if the state legislature was within the reach of the federal courts' injunctive powers. In 1917, Virginia asked the Supreme Court to order the legislature of West Virginia, collectively and as individuals, to pass an appropriation act to pay a judgment of the Court. Although postponing issuance of the asked-for order, the justices strongly implied their power to do so[147]—with the result that West Virginia took the hint and paid.

What made the injunction so formidable a weapon was the federal courts' broad power to punish for contempt of court.[148] There were two types of contempt. "Direct" contempt was when the act occurred in the courtroom or so near its vicinity as to obstruct the course of justice. "Indirect" or "constructive" contempt involved an act occurring outside the courtroom, typically disobedience to a court order such as an injunction. A second line of distinction—fuzzy in theory and fuzzier still in practice—was between civil and criminal contempt. In principle, the distinction rested upon the purpose of the punishment rather than the nature of the contumacious act. If the purpose was remedial—that is, to secure obedience to the court's order—the contempt was civil. If the purpose was to punish, the contempt was criminal.[149] Whether civil or criminal, however, the judge could fine or imprison those guilty. And the Supreme Court went so far as to hold that a court could punish for disobedience a person not expressly named in an injunction so long as he knew of its existence.[150] The major difference was that paradoxically the judge's power was even more formidable when dealing with civil than with criminal contempt. Upon the theory that civil contempt was to protect the rights of a private party, the judge could imprison the recalcitrant party indefinitely until he agreed to comply with the court's order—the judicial rationale being that the prisoner had the keys to the jail in his own pocket.[151]

The Judiciary Act of 1789 as amended in 1831 authorized federal judges to "inflict summary punishments" for not simply direct contempt but "disobedience or resistance" to court orders.[152] The Supreme Court rested such authority upon a more exalted basis:

The power to punish for contempts is inherent in all courts; its existence is essential to the preservation of order in judicial proceedings, and to the enforcement of the judgments, orders, and writs of the courts, and consequently to the due administration of justice. . . . It has always been one of the attributes—one of the powers necessarily incident to a court of justice—that it should have this power of vindicating its dignity, of enforcing its orders, of protecting itself from insult, without the necessity of calling upon a jury to assist it in the exercise of this power.[153]

The most notorious example of federal court exercise of the contempt power was the sweeping injunction issued against the 1894 Pullman strike applying to the named defendants, those joining with the named defendants, and "all other persons whomsoever." When the same judge sentenced strike leader Eugene V. Debs to prison for its violation, the justices unanimously dismissed the resulting Sixth Amendment challenge to the lack of a jury trial with the rationale that "[i]n order that a court may compel obedience to its orders it must have the right to inquire whether there has been any disobedience thereof. To submit the question of disobedience to another tribunal, be it a jury or another court, would operate to deprive the proceeding of half its efficiency."[154]

Punishment of direct contempt attracted scant attention except when the target was a newspaper whose criticisms struck a too-tender judicial nerve.[155] Objections even to summary handling of violations of court orders centered upon its application to labor disputes. As a result, there was not sufficient pressure to impose meaningful restraints upon federal judges' contempt powers. Section 19 of the Clayton Act of 1914 limited the binding force of injunctions to the named parties and those who knowingly and actively conspired with them to violate the order.[156] Beating a strategic retreat, the Supreme Court discovered that this limitation accorded with the "established principles of equity jurisprudence."[157] Congress in 1932 imposed a further restriction in the Norris-LaGuardia Act by requiring jury trial in contempt proceedings growing out of labor disputes.[158] And in the name of due process, the Court gave a defendant accused of out-of-court contempt the right to a hearing after due notice, to call witnesses, to offer testimony in his own behalf, and to be represented by counsel. Apart from these exceptions, the power of federal court judges to punish contempt remained untrammeled. The Court did suggest that when the contempt involved "the element of personal criticism or attack," the preferred course was to have another judge handle the proceeding—but even that was not required.[159] Nor could the invalidity of an order be raised as a defense for its violation. The rule was that the order must be obeyed until revoked by a higher court on appeal.[160]

Given the powers enjoyed by the federal courts via the injunction, *Ex parte Young* drew heavy attack from defenders of states' rights and the reform-minded. Much of the criticism was directed against how a single federal judge could grant an interlocutory (temporary) injunction holding up enforcement of state law before any final determination of its constitutionality—in short, for an extended time. In response, Congress in 1910 required that a special court of three judges (including at least one Supreme Court or Court of Appeals judge) pass upon applications for an interlocutory order restraining enforcement of a state law on grounds of its unconstitutionality with a right of direct appeal to the Supreme Court. In 1913 the three-judge device was extended to temporary orders restraining enforcement of the orders of state administrative boards and commissions; the Judges' Bill of 1925 applied this same procedure to hearings for a permanent injunction.[161] More important, the Court itself imposed major limitations that kept the decision's impact within relatively narrow bounds. *Dicta* in *Young* indicated that the federal courts could not "interfere in a case where the proceedings were already pending in a state court."[162] And the justices went on to restrict issuance of injunctions against enforcement of state laws to "extraordinary circumstances where the danger of irreparable loss is both great and immediate."[163]

The result was to foster interest in the declaratory judgment as an alternative procedure for challenging an allegedly unconstitutional law or administrative decision in advance of its attempted enforcement. A declaratory judgment is a conclusive judicial determination of the rights of the parties without an accompanying decree compelling any particular action.[164] Although a number of states authorized issuance of declaratory judgments by their courts, the stumbling block at the federal level was a 1911 Supreme Court decision interpreting the case or controversy provision of Article III of the Constitution as barring suits "to determine the validity of legislation."[165] But the Court in 1933 accepted for review a state court declaratory judgment with the explanation that federal court jurisdictional requirements were satisfied if the litigation involved a "real and substantial" controversy between adversary parties.[166] Given this green light, Congress adopted legislation the following year that authorized the federal courts to issue declaratory judgments in "cases of actual controversy," gave "such declaration ... the force and effect of a final judgment," and provided for "[f]urther relief based on a declaratory judgment ... whenever necessary or proper."[167] In 1937, the Court unanimously upheld the constitutionality of this major new addition to the arsenal of federal judicial power.[168]

2 The Scope of Constitutionally Protected Rights

In laying down what the Constitution means, the Supreme Court has broad latitude since except in rare cases its dictates are not self-evident. At times, the justices profess to find guidance by examining "the intention of the framers." But the historical record is full of gaps and ambiguities. And given the complexity of the adopting process, whose "intention" should be deemed binding? The drafters? Those voting to submit the provision for ratification? Those doing the ratifying?[1] Still more latitudinarian is the scope for judicial decision-making when the justices look to the underlying "purpose" of a constitutional provision to deal with a situation that was not foreseen and could not have possibly been foreseen when adopted. Each provision of the Constitution, the historian Charles A. Beard has observed, "covers some core of reality and practice on which a general consensus can be reached. But around this core is a huge shadow in which the good and wise can wander indefinitely without ever coming to any agreement respecting the command made by the 'law.' Ever since the Constitution was framed, or particular amendments were added, dispute has raged among men of strong minds and pure hearts over the meaning of these cloud-covered words and phrases."[2] The first Justice John Marshall Harlan put the matter more cynically: "[I]f we don't like an act of Congress, we don't have much trouble to find grounds for declaring it unconstitutional."[3]

Perhaps no question has been more hotly debated than what substantive limits the First Amendment places upon governmental authority. At one end of the spectrum is the view that the framers accepted the Blackstonian definition of freedom of expression as simply precluding prior restraint, censorship in narrow and traditional sense, not subsequent punishment for utterances that legislatures and/or courts found harmful.[4] At the opposite extreme was the position that the amendment's purpose was to give absolute protection to what is nowadays termed "pure" speech.[5] The major focus of the debate has centered upon the question of whether the framers intended to bar prosecutions for seditious libel: "the intentional publication, without lawful excuse or justification, of written blame of any public man, or of the law, or of any institution established by law."[6] That question continues to divide historians to this day—with inconclusive results.[7] And as Kent Greenawalt has observed, there was a long tradition in Anglo-American law making liable to punishment those who successfully incited criminal action. "Even if it is granted that the First Amendment was meant to abolish seditious libel...that position cannot tenably be used to construct a historical intent argument against statutes that penalize encouragements to specific crimes."[8]

In his influential *Freedom of Speech* (first published in 1920), Harvard Law School Professor Zechariah Chafee, Jr., fostered the mistaken assumption that free speech became a major legal issue only with World War I.[9] The first major debate on the proper limits of freedom of speech and press came in the 1790s and first decades of the nineteenth century over the law of seditious libel. The social unrest and radical agitation in the generation before the First World War raised the question anew. A substantial number of cases directly raising the First Amendment or analogous provisions of state constitutions came before the courts; others, while not explicitly based upon those guarantees involved questions that present-day judges would treat as free-speech issues. The near-universal response by the courts was that freedom of expression must be exercised responsibly. While paying lip service to its importance, judges hastened to add that "license" or "abuse" were not protected. The prevailing doctrine was that the possible "bad tendency" of speech justified punishment whether or not the action advocated was actually committed. The New York Court of Appeals put this position in starkly blunt terms: "The punishment of those who publish articles which tend to corrupt morals, induce crime or destroy organized society, is essential to the security of freedom and the stability of the state."[10]

Two opinions by Justice Oliver Wendell Holmes, Jr.—long extolled as the exemplar of civil libertarianism—graphically showed how the Supreme Court shared this restrictive interpretation of the scope of free speech. In 1907, he spoke for the eight-man majority in *Patterson v. Colorado* upholding the state contempt-of-court conviction of a Colorado newspaper publisher for articles criticizing judicial behavior on the ground that such criticisms "tend to obstruct the administration of justice." Even if the First Amendment applied to the states through the Fourteenth—a point that he expressly left undecided—Holmes held that the guarantee barred simply prior restraint upon publication not "the subsequent punishment of such as may be deemed contrary to the public welfare." And that subsequent punishment even "may extend as well to the true as to the false."[11] Eight years later, he sustained the conviction of a defendant responsible for an article urging a "boycott" against those interfering with nude bathing under a Washington state law making it a gross misdemeanor to publish, edit, or circulate written matter "advocating, encouraging or inciting, or having a tendency to encourage or incite the commission of any crime . . . or which shall tend to encourage or advocate disrespect for law." While acknowledging that a law could not "prevent publications merely because they tend to produce unfavorable opinions of a particular statute or of law in general," he concluded that the article "by indirection but unmistakably . . . encourages and incites . . . an actual breach of law," i.e., "persistence" in violating "the state laws against indecent exposure."[12]

Although governmental restrictions upon free expression antedated World War I, that conflict brought the issue to the forefront. The existence of extensive opposition to American involvement spurred repression of dissent along a broad front. Private and semi-official vigilantism against those suspected of pro-German sympathies or even insufficient enthusiasm for the war effort was rife. After the Bolshevik Revolution, the same tactics were applied to "reds." A number of states had adopted before 1917 so-called criminal anarchy, criminal syndicalism, or sedition laws, partly in reaction to the assassination of President William McKinley, partly in response to the activities of the Industrial Workers of the World; the war and the postwar red scare led most of the rest to enact similar legislation. Although the exact phraseology varied, these laws generally prohibited, and penalized, the advocacy of violent and unlawful means to bring about political and economic change.[13] At the national level, the major weapon at the disposal of the federal authorities for striking at wartime dissent was prosecution under Title I, Section 3 of the Espionage Act of 1917 punishing by fines up to $10,000, two years' imprisonment, or both:

Whoever . . . shall willfully make or convey false reports or false statements with intent to interfere with the operation or success of the military or naval forces of the United States or to promote the success of its enemies and whoever . . . shall willfully cause or attempt to cause insubordination, disloyalty, mutiny, or refusal of duty, in the military or naval forces of the United States, or shall willfully obstruct the recruiting or enlistment service of the United States.[14]

The first of the Espionage Act cases to come before the Court—*Schenck v. United States*—was decided in early 1919. Charles Schenck, the general secretary of the Socialist party, and his fellow defendants had been convicted for sending out 15,000 leaflets to men subject to military service, attacking the draft as a capitalist plot with an accompanying call "to assert your opposition." With the justices unanimous in sustaining the conviction, Holmes laid down as the test for judging governmental restrictions upon free expression the so-called clear-and-present danger rule: "The question in every case is whether the words used are used in such circumstances and are of such a nature as to create a clear and present danger that they will bring about the substantive evils that Congress has a right to prevent." Abandoning his position in *Patterson*, he conceded that "[i]t may well be that the [First Amendment's] prohibition of laws abridging the freedom of speech is not confined to previous restraints." He even acknowledged that "in ordinary times the defendants in saying all that was said in the circular would have been within their constitutional rights." But, he underlined, "the character of every act depends upon the circumstances in which it is done. . . . The most stringent protection of free speech would not protect a man in falsely shouting fire in a theatre and causing a panic. . . . It is a question of proximity and degree. When a nation is at war many things that might be said in time of peace are such a hindrance to its effort that . . . no Court could regard them as protected by any constitutional right."[15]

Much ink has been spilled about the source from which Holmes derived the clear-and-present-danger standard.[16] The likeliest answer appears from the law of criminal attempts. As he wrote in 1901 while still Chief Justice of the Massachusetts Supreme Judicial Court, "[P]reparation is not an attempt. But some preparations may amount to an attempt." The line was "a question of degree": how "near" the preparation came to "the accomplishment of the act."[17] More important, the test as applied in *Schenck* continued the "bad tendency" approach of his prewar decisions. In the first place, he adhered to the common-law principle of constructive or presumptive intent: "the document would not have been sent unless it had been intended to have some effect, and we do not see what effect it could be expected to have upon persons subject to the draft except to influence them to obstruct the carrying of it out." Second, he denied "that success alone warrants making the act a crime."[18] And he went still farther the following week in *Frohwerk v. United States* sustaining the conviction of the editor of a German-language newspaper that had published articles questioning justification for the war and constitutionality of the draft. The evidentiary basis was weaker than in *Schenck*. No special effort had been made to reach men subject to the draft; nor was there any direct call for resistance. But Holmes found that the articles "might be taken to convey an innuendo" in support of such resistance. Not even mentioning the words "clear and present danger," he warned how "a little breath would be enough to kindle a flame."[19]

The issues were most sharply joined in the appeal by Socialist party leader Eugene V. Debs turned down the same day. Debs's counsel argued strongly that to allow punishment of speech because of its possible "indirect effect" would be to reduce the First Amendment to a nullity. A supporting *amicus curiae* brief warned that "[o]nce this court says that public discussion of the measures of government can be punished because of any *intent* which a jury may find caused the discussion, or because of any result which a jury may think will follow such discussion, then the free speech and free press of the Constitution is destroyed." Holmes brushed aside those arguments. He found Debs's praise for those who had been convicted of draft law violations sufficient evidence to warrant the jury's concluding that his words "had as their natural tendency and reasonably probable effect to obstruct the re-cruiting service." And construing the tendency of language as proof of the speaker's intent was a "principle too well established and too manifestly good sense to need citation of the books."[20] This reasoning drew a sharp attack from University of Chicago political scientist Ernst Freund. "[T]o be permitted to agitate at your own peril, subject to a jury's guessing at motive, tendency and possible effect," he admonished in the *New Republic*, "makes the right of free speech a precarious gift."[21] But Holmes remained unmoved. The law was full of instances, he reaffirmed, " 'where a man's fate depends on his estimating rightly, that is, as the jury subsequently estimates it, from matters of degree.' "[22]

By the end of 1919 in *Abrams v. United States*, Holmes did shift to a more expansive view of the protections that should be accorded free speech. Partly he was moved by the arguments against his former position by Freund, Zechariah Chafee, Jr., and Federal District Judge Learned Hand; partly by his revulsion against the excesses of the post-Armistice red scare; partly by his feeling that the defendants' activities presented no serious danger. They were Russian immigrants who had been convicted under the 1918 amend-ment to the Espionage Act for conspiring and attempting to harm the prose-cution of the war by publishing and distributing leaflets in English and Yiddish assailing United States intervention in Russia after the Bolshevik Revolution and urging a general strike in protest. Holmes now repudiated the doctrine of implied intent: "a deed is not done with intent to produce a consequence unless that consequence is the aim of the deed." Thus, the fact that the leaflet might have as its "indirect" effect interference with the war effort was "by no means enough to show an attempt to produce that effect." At the same time, he resurrected and strengthened the clear-and-present-danger standard to require an "imminent" threat of resulting "substantive evils." But he could not carry his colleagues—except for Brandeis—with him. Con-cluding that the "obvious effect" of the called-for strike would be "defeat of the war program of the United States," Justice John H. Clarke for the seven-man majority reaffirmed that "[m]en must be held to have intended, and to be accountable for, the effects which their acts were likely to produce."[23]

In follow-up cases upholding convictions under the Espionage Act, the majority—over the dissents of Holmes and Brandeis—continued to hew to the bad or dangerous "tendency" approach without even referring to the clear-and-present-danger test.[24] And when Walter Pollak argued that Gitlow could not be convicted unless New York proved that his statements had created a clear and present danger of unlawful conduct, Justice Sanford read *Schenck* narrowly as providing a special rule only for situations, as under the Espionage Act, where the question was if the language had a sufficient relation to the conduct prohibited (i.e., interference with the draft) to justify its punishment. Here, he explained for the seven-man majority, the legislature itself had determined that "utterances advocating the overthrow of organized government by force, violence and unlawful means . . . involve such danger of substantive evil that they may be penalized in the exercise of its police power." Repeating the familiar judicial bromide about every presumption in favor of the validity of a legislative action, he declared that the Court's only function was to decide if the legislative action was "arbitrary" or "unreasonable." And in this area at least, he was willing to grant a wide latitude to legislative judgment:

> The State cannot reasonably be required to measure the danger . . . in the nice balance of a jeweler's scale. A single revolutionary spark may kindle a fire that, smouldering for a time, may burst into a sweeping and destructive conflagration. It cannot be said that the State is acting arbitrarily or unreasonably when . . . it seeks to extinguish the spark without waiting until it has enkindled the flame or blazed into the conflagration.[25]

Holmes dissented on the ground that even the legislature was barred from proscribing speech "too remote from possible consequences."[26] But the most thoroughgoing attack upon the *Gitlow* approach came from Justice Louis D. Brandeis in *Whitney v. California*. Brandeis's contribution lay in formulating a rationale for free expression more appealing than Holmes's. Ever the skeptic, Holmes justified free speech on Social Darwinist grounds: truth was simply whatever ideas won out in the competition of the free market. Brandeis wished to place the issue on a higher ground to make free expression the rule, its limitation the exception. The difficulty that he had to circumvent was his own long-standing argument in economic regulation cases that the Court should defer to the legislative judgment so long as its means were reasonably related to a legitimate goal. Why should a stricter standard apply to free expression? In the first place, he answered that free expression was indispensable for the fullest development of each individual's faculties. Even more crucial was his identification of freedom of speech as essential to the functioning of democratic government by making possible change by lawful and peaceful means rather than by violence. The founding fathers recognized, Brandeis eulogized,

> that the greatest menace to freedom is an inert people; that public discussion is a political duty; and that this should be a fundamental principle of the American government. They recognized the risks to which all human institutions are subject. But they knew that order cannot be secured merely through fear of punishment for its infraction; that it is hazardous to discourage thought, hope and imagination; that fear breeds repression; that repression breeds hate; that hate menaces stable government; that the path of safety lies in the opportunity to discuss freely supposed grievances and proposed remedies; and that the fitting remedy for evil counsels is good ones.[27]

Accordingly, Brandeis laid down two alternative tests for when free expression could legitimately be restrained. One—borrowed from Learned Hand's opinion in the 1917 *Masses* case—was if there was direct "incitement" to lawless action. The second was a more stringent exegesis of the clear-and-present danger standard: first, that the danger threatened must be "serious" not "trivial"; second, that "the incidence of the evil apprehended must be so imminent that it may befall before there is an opportunity for full discussion.... Only an emergency can justify repression." Whitney's participation in founding the California Communist Labor party had brought her afoul of that state's law against "[a]ny person who... [o]rganizes or assists in organizing, or is or knowingly becomes a member of, any organization... advocating... unlawful acts of force and violence... as a means of... effecting any political change." And though concurring in upholding her conviction, he did so on the narrow ground that she had not raised the clear-and-present danger issue at her trial. The trouble was that Brandeis did not speak for the Court. In his majority opinion, Sanford relied upon *Gitlow*—even using the same language—to uphold the reasonableness of the legislature's prohibiting "the combining with others in an association for... the advocacy and use of criminal and unlawful methods." As a matter of fact, he concluded, "such united and joint action involves even greater danger to the public peace and security than the isolated utterances and acts of individuals."[28]

The one successful free speech challenge during the 1920s—the Court's reversal of the IWW organizer's conviction for violating Kansas's criminal syndicalism law—was of limited precedential significance. The decision rested upon the ground that the principal evidence against him—the preamble to the constitution of the Industrial Workers of the World—did not advocate force, violence, or other unlawful means for bringing about political change.[29] And while Hughes in the 1930s led the Court toward a more stringent review of state sedition laws, even he preferred to rest the decisions upon relatively narrow grounds. Although Stromberg's counsel raised the clear-and-present-danger argument, Hughes relied upon the common-law principle that a crime cannot be defined in vague or indefinite terms: that the California red-flag law was an invalid restriction on free speech because its sweeping and ill-defined phraseology could be construed to prohibit lawful opposition to the government.[30] Similarly, in his 1937 *De Jonge v. Oregon* opinion, the Chief Justice drew upon another traditional criminal law principle—that guilt must be personal—to reverse De Jonge's conviction under Oregon's criminal syndicalism law for speaking at a Communist-sponsored rally. While affirming that the state could prohibit incitement to violent overthrow of the government, he ruled that the state could not make "mere participation in a peaceable assembly and a lawful public discussion...basis for a criminal charge."[31]

Only that same year in *Herndon v. Lowry* did a majority of the justices resurrect the clear-and-present-danger standard as a protection for free expression. Negro Communist party organizer Angelo Herndon had been sentenced to eighteen to twenty years in prison for violating a post–Civil War Georgia anti-insurrection statute punishing "[a]ny attempt, by persuasion or otherwise, to induce others to join in any combined resistance to the lawful authority of the State." The Court's decision overturning the conviction could have been rested simply on the long-established criminal law principle that the statute was so vague and indefinite as to provide no reasonably ascertainable standard of guilt. Why Justice Owen J. Roberts for the five-to-four majority went beyond this relatively narrow ground is not definitively answerable: what appears likely is that Chief Justice Hughes wished to blunt FDR's Court-"packing" bid by showing that the Court's solicitude was not limited to property rights. Taking a broad stand, the opinion denied that speech could be punished simply "by reason of its supposed dangerous tendency even in the remote future." Required was evidence of a "clear and present danger of forcible obstruction." Along with the repudiation of the "bad tendency" approach, the decision accepted Brandeis's "preferred position" theory. "The power of a state to abridge freedom of speech and of assembly is the exception rather than the rule and . . . must find its justification in a reasonable apprehension of danger to organized government."[32]

With *Herndon*, the liberal view of free speech had triumphed. But there was a larger degree of consensus among the Court's liberals and conservatives than appears at first glance. The liberals were as hostile as the conservatives to what is nowadays fashionably termed direct action—or what Robert M. Cover more accurately calls the "politics of the streets."[33] Their differences revolved around the question of how close a relationship must exist between spoken or written words and unlawful action to justify their punishment. The nearest approach to an objective standard for answering that question was the direct incitement test. But opinions will differ over when advocacy turns into incitement depending partly upon the individual, partly upon the circumstances. Any test—such as the clear-and-present danger standard—that looked to the effects of the language was inevitably still more a matter of subjective judgment. That problem was not eliminated by adding such qualifiers as imminent and serious. Even Brandeis in *Whitney* acknowledged that there were circumstances justifying repressive action. As Learned Hand perceptively observed, "Once you admit that the matter is one of degree . . . you give to Tomdickandharry, D.J., so much latitude that the jig is at once up. Besides their Ineffabilities, the Nine Elder Statesmen, have not shown themselves wholly immune from the 'herd instinct' and what seems 'immediate and direct' to-day may seem very remote next year."[34]

Similarly, legend has exaggerated the scope of the liberty of the press afforded by *Near*.[35] The target of the injunction against further publication was an anti-Semitic Minneapolis scandal-sheet; its instigator the local county attorney stung by accusations that he was in collusion with the city's Jewish-run gambling syndicate. Hughes did find the injunction—along with the law authorizing its issuance—an unconstitutional previous restraint. And going beyond the necessities of the case, he rejected the Blackstonian definition of freedom of the press as limited "exclusively" to immunity from prior restraint. But he simultaneously acknowledged that "the protection even as to previous restraint is not absolutely unlimited." He deemed beyond "question" that "a government might prevent actual obstruction to its recruiting service or the publication of the sailing dates of transports or the number and location of troops." Another exception was that the "security of community life may be protected against incitements to acts of violence and the overthrow by force of orderly government." He likewise sanctioned censorship to safeguard "the primary requirements of decency . . . against obscene publications." More important, he emphasized that immunity against prior restraint did not bar "[s]ubsequent punishment for such abuses as may exist." On the contrary, he explicitly affirmed that public officials "find their remedies for false accusations in actions under libel laws providing for redress and punishment." The "common law rules that subject the libeler to responsibility for the public offense, as well as for the private injury," he underlined, "are not abolished."[36]

Under English common law, libel was defined as a publication that "robs a man of his good name."[37] Any libel—whether the target was a private individual or a public official—was regarded as a crime punishable by a severe penalty. The rationale was that libels of even private individuals tended to result in retaliatory breaches of the peace. The most controversial aspect of the law of criminal libel was the concept of seditious libel. The major complaint before the Revolution lay not so much against the principle as against how the law was enforced. In the first place, truth was not a defense on the ground that true criticisms could be as damaging as false ones to public authority. Second, the jury decided only if the defendant had published the statement while the judge decided if the material was libelous. And even before independence, the colonists had largely succeeded in making truth a defense and the jury, rather than the judge, the determiner of the criminality of the words. What spurred a more far-reaching attack that denied any power in government to punish verbal attacks as distinguished from "overt acts" was when the Federalists struck at their Jeffersonian rivals by adopting the Sedition Act of 1798.[38] But the controversy—at least regarding prosecutions for seditious libel by the national government—faded rapidly. The Sedition Act expired in 1801. And the Supreme Court's decision eleven years later that the federal courts lacked any common-law criminal jurisdiction barred prosecutions there for seditious libel.[39]

Prosecutions for criminal libel were still possible in the state courts. And the governing rules remained stringent. In most states, the only defense was truth or, more restrictive still, truth plus "good motives" and "justifiable ends." With the acceptance in the Jacksonian era of the legitimacy of party conflict as the mainspring of the democratic process, however, criminal prosecutions for libel became rare, and remained so. The typical libel action became a civil suit for damages to one's reputation.[40] While truth was an "absolute justification" in civil libel actions even under the English common law, the protection afforded thereby was more limited than might appear at first glance. In the first place, the author/publisher of a defamatory statement had the burden of proving its truthfulness. Second, the rule was that every single particular had to be shown true. Most important, strict liability applied to libelous false statements whether the result of an innocent mistake or not.[41] The application of such strict liability to the defamation of private individuals did not provoke much controversy. Libel suits by private individuals were the exception. The majority involved political or public libels— that is, suits filed by public officials or political candidates. Exponents of an expansive scope for freedom of the press favored granting a "qualified privilege" that would immunize even false statements on matters of public interest when not motivated by "express malice" (i.e., a deliberate intent to inflict injury by falsehood). But that position was adopted by only a minority of states. Although recognizing the defense of fair comment for expressions of pure opinion, most state courts continued to apply to public libels the doctrine of strict liability for misstatements of fact.[42]

No more than a handful of civil libel actions came before the Supreme Court. In dealing with the libel of a private individual, the Court followed the strict liability doctrine of the common law: anything "which is calculated to make him infamous, odious, or ridiculous, is *prima facie* a libel, and implies malice in the author and publisher. . . . Proof of malice, therefore, . . . can never be required of the party complaining."[43] But the Court took the liberal side in the dispute over the rule that should apply in public or political libels. In 1845, Justice Peter V. Daniel ruled in *White v. Nicholls* that comment upon public officials was "privileged." Accordingly, the burden of proof shifted to the complainant to show "express malice," i.e., not simply "falsehood" but "the absence of probable cause."[44] Although that case had involved a letter from a group of District of Columbia residents to the president complaining about the political activities of the local collector of customs, the Court in 1912 in *Gandia v. Pettingill* extended the same "express malice" standard to newspaper comment on and reporting about public officials.[45] Although Hughes did suggest in *Near* that state libel rules must "be consistent with constitutional privilege,"[46] he failed to spell out what those limitations were. And he probably had in mind at most the *White/Gandia* approach. Libel was simply not a major issue, even for most publishers. Suits were relatively few, significant damage awards rarer still. So staunch a defender of a broad reading of the First Amendment as Zechariah Chafee, Jr., found the existing "main rules of libel . . . intelligent attempts to adjust conflicts between the need for an unblemished reputation and the need for frank discussion of important topics."[47]

The safeguards afforded by the First Amendment remained limited in other ways. "[B]lasphemous or indecent articles, or other publications injurious to public morals" were not protected.[48] Judges could punish for contempt out-of-court statements having the tendency to incite disobedience to court orders.[49] And when upholding an injunction against the American Federation of Labor barring its publicizing a boycott, the Court made a distinction between normal speech and "verbal acts" that had "a force not inhering in the words themselves."[50] Most important, the existing precedents allowed a broad range of indirect restrictions upon the means of dissemination. A long line of rulings upheld the power of the federal government to exclude publications from the mails upon the rationale that access was a privilege subject to whatever restrictions Congress imposed.[51] Access by would-be speakers to public property—such as parks and highways— was similarly held "subject to such regulations as the legislature in its wisdom may have deemed proper to prescribe."[52] In 1936, however, the Court took its first step toward a harder line on such indirect restraints by striking down a special Louisiana tax upon publications having a circulation of more than 20,000 per week. Technically, Justice George Sutherland's opinion for the unanimous Court rested upon the narrow ground that such a tax was historically among the English abuses against which the First Amendment had been directed. But he went on to proclaim in broad terms that the Amendment "was meant to preclude . . . any form of previous restraint . . . to limit the circulation of information."[53]

The status of the new nonprint media remained more ambiguous—not simply legally, but in public attitudes. A broad consensus approved the federal government licensing of radio broadcast stations instituted by the Radio Act of 1927 and Federal Communications Act of 1934. Radio came directly into the home; the number of frequencies was limited; and the electromagnetic spectrum was public property.[54] There was similarly wide support for censorship of motion pictures, given the industry's excesses. The typical mechanism was state laws or local ordinances requiring that films be submitted to and approved by an administrative official or board before exhibition. When a challenge to Ohio's law reached the Court in 1915, the justices unanimously ruled that motion pictures were not covered by the constitutional guarantees of freedom of speech and press. In his opinion, Justice Joseph McKenna labelled the exhibition of motion pictures "a business pure and simple, originated and conducted for profit . . . not to be regarded . . . as organs of public opinion." But his major emphasis was upon their power for "evil" through the excitement of "prurient interest"—a power the more dangerous because movies were shown to mixed audiences that included women and children. But he qualified his approval of movie censorship by assuming that the standards applied would involve mere "whim" or "caprice" but would "get precision from the sense and experience of men." And he pointedly noted that the Ohio law provided for court review of decisions by the the board of censors. The trouble was that the lower courts shied from substituting their judgment for those of the censors. The

resulting limitation of their review to the narrow issue of whether the cen-
soring authority had acted arbitrarily or in bad faith allowed censors an almost
free hand to bar not simply the morally and sexually offensive but to impose
their own racial, religious, and political biases.[55]

Inconclusive as is the evidence about what the framers meant by the First
Amendment's guarantee of freedom of speech and press, still murkier is the
intent behind its accompanying proviso that "Congress shall make no law
respecting an establishment of religion, or prohibiting the free exercise
thereof."[56] The Philadelphia convention had put into Article VI of the Constitution a bar against any religious test for federal office—thus eliminating
one of the most potent instruments for religious discrimination. And in one
sense, the First Amendment simply restated what everyone was agreed upon:
that Congress could not interfere with the existing state arrangements dealing
with religion. But what more was involved remains a matter of dispute—
pitting those who see its purpose to forbid any aid to religion against those
who find the more limited aim of barring favored treatment of any single
denomination.[57] The most recent, and thoroughly researched, examination
concludes that a broad consensus had emerged by the time of the Amendment's adoption on two key propositions. One was that government had no
power to prohibit the free exercise of religion so long as peaceable. The
second was that financial support of religion and churches should be voluntary. While there was more disagreement over the second point than over
the first, nine of the eleven states that ratified the First Amendment had
taken the position that any governmental support for churches constituted
an establishment of religion and violation of its free exercise.[58]

There were no more than a handful of Supreme Court decisions touching
upon the free exercise clause.[59] And despite *dicta* that religious freedom was
among the fundamental liberties protected against state infringement by the
Fourteenth Amendment's due process clause,[60] the Court had never directly
so ruled. The existing precedents gave narrow scope to the protection afforded vis-à-vis even the federal government. The problem was that the first
free exercise cases grew out of one of the most emotionally explosive issues
in nineteenth-century America—the laws against plural marriages directed
against the Mormons. At first Mormon leaders took the absolutist position
that since polygamy was God's commandment, its practice was protected by
the free exercise clause of the First Amendment. By the 1870s, however,
they had retreated to a second line of defense. Admitting the power of
Congress to legislate for the protection of society's morals, they argued that
federal prohibition of polygamy could be justified only if its harm to others
could be shown beyond a reasonable doubt. But that argument ran up against
the widespread conviction that polygamy was a "twin relic" (with slavery)
of barbarism: a threat to the sanctity of the family and thus to the basis of
civilized society. A congressman in 1860 expressed the dominant popular
attitude toward polygamy in graphic terms:

I charge it to be a crying evil; sapping not only the physical constitutions of the people practicing it, dwarfing their physical proportions and emasculating their energies, but at the same time perverting the social virtues, and vitiating the morals of its victims. . . . It is often an adjunct to political despotism; and invariably begets among the people who practice it the extremes of brutal blood-thirstiness or timid and mean prevarication. . . . It is a scarlet whore. It is a reproach to the Christian civilization; and deserves to be blotted out.[61]

The issue came before the Supreme Court in 1879 in what Mormon leaders intended as a test case when George Reynolds, Brigham Young's personal secretary, appealed his conviction for violating the federal law prohibiting bigamy in the territories. The Court divided five-to-four in the conference in upholding Reynolds's conviction—with Chief Justice Morrison R. Waite among the dissenters. The disagreement among the justices was not over the freedom of religion issue but over the procedural irregularities in his trial raised in the appeal. Waite, however, overcame his doubts and brought his fellow dissenters, except for Justice Stephen J. Field, with him. And he devoted the major thrust of his opinion in *Reynolds v. United States* to "whether religious belief can be accepted as a justification of an overt act made criminal by the law of the land." He laid down as the governing principle what became known as the belief/action distinction: "Congress was deprived of all legislative power over mere opinion, but was left free to reach actions which were in violation of social duties or subversive of good order." Suppose one believed human sacrifice was part of his religious faith, Waite asked, "would it be seriously contended that the civil government under which he lived could not interfere to prevent a sacrifice?" That distinction in a sense begged the question since religious belief almost always involved action of some kind. Waite was on stronger ground in denying that religious motivation could exempt a person from an otherwise valid general law. "To permit this," he warned, "would be . . . in effect to permit every citizen to become a law unto himself. Government could exist only in name under such circumstances."[62]

Although the Court continued to pay lip service to the belief/action distinction, the later Mormon cases showed its willingness to make mere opinion—at least when involving something as "pernicious to the best interests of society" as polygamy—liable to penalty. In 1887, the justices upheld the practice by the federal district court in Utah of excluding for "actual bias" all those who believed that plural marriage was in accordance with the will of God from juries in trials of men accused of violating the federal law prohibiting cohabitation with more than one woman in the territories. Three years later, a similarly unanimous Court rebuffed a challenge to an Idaho territorial law requiring voters to take an oath that they were not members of any organization that "teaches, advises, counsels or encourages" bigamy or polygamy. Since those practices were (and deservedly so) crimes, "then to teach, advise and counsel their practice is to aid in their commission, and such teaching and counselling are themselves criminal and proper subjects of punishment, as aiding and abetting crime are in all other cases." While freedom of religion was guaranteed, "it does not follow that everything which may be so called can be tolerated. Crime is not the less odious because sanctioned by what any particular sect may designate as religion."[63] A six-to-three majority went so far as to uphold the 1887 congressional legislation disincorporating the Mormon Church and taking over all church property except that used for religious services. Even the dissenters, however, disagreed not on First Amendment grounds but rather the sufficiency of Congress's power to expropriate property. And the majority simply dismissed the religious freedom argument: "No doubt the Thugs of India imagined that their belief in the right of assassination was a religious belief."[64]

The second round of free-exercise cases involved religiously motivated objectors to military service—and all the challenges were turned down. When the question was first raised during World War I, the Court summarily rejected the argument that subjecting religious conscientious objectors to noncombatant service infringed the First Amendment.[65] Later decisions upheld the exclusion from citizenship of aliens who because of religious scruples would not pledge to bear arms in defense of the United States against all enemies.[66] The justices were unanimous in upholding the expulsion of students from the University of California for refusal to participate in the required first two years of the Reserve Officers Training Corps program. The students' freedom of religion, reasoned Justice Pierce Butler, was not violated because they were not compelled to attend the University of California. They did so voluntarily, and so had to abide by its rules.[67] The one pro–religious freedom decision was *Pierce v. Society of Sisters* in 1925, where the Court—on the basis of *Meyer*—found the Ku Klux Klan-inspired Oregon law requiring all children between ages eight and sixteen to attend only public schools up through the eighth grade in violation of the Fourteenth Amendment's due process clause. But Justice McReynolds did not make religious freedom the issue. Rather, he rested the decision partly upon the law's impairment of the property rights of private and parochial schools, partly upon "the liberty of parents and guardians to direct the upbringing and education of children under their control." The child, he underlined, "is not the mere creature of the State; those who nurture him and direct his destiny have the right, coupled with the high duty, to recognize and prepare him for additional obligations."[68]

Glosses, on and off the bench, on the meaning of the nonestablishment clause amounted to no more than passing—and what was worse, contradictory—*dicta*. In a letter dated January 1, 1802 to the Danbury Baptist Association, Thomas Jefferson described the First Amendment as "building a wall of separation between church and State."[69] But Justice Joseph Story held its purpose was to bar "a religious establishment which should have exclusive rights and prerogatives," not to forbid "aiding with equal attention the votaries of every sect." And in his influential *Commentaries on the Constitution*, he argued that when the First Amendment was adopted

the general if not the universal sentiment in America was, that Christianity ought to receive encouragement from the state so far as was not incompatible with the private rights of conscience and the freedom of religious worship. An attempt to level all religions, and to make it a matter of state policy to hold all in utter indifference, would have created universal disapprobation, if not universal indignation.[70]

Chief Justice Waite in *Reynolds* quoted the Jeffersonian wall metaphor as "an authoritative declaration of the scope and effect of the amendment." In a later Mormon case, Justice Stephen J. Field reaffirmed that the First Amendment "was intended . . . to prohibit legislation for the support of any religious tenets, or the modes of worship of any sect."[71] On the contrary side, an 1892 ruling declared that the United States was "a religious nation"— or to be more exact, "a Christian nation"—which meant that "no purpose of action against religion can be imputed to any legislation, state or national."[72]

The only point that was definitively resolved was the principle laid down in 1872 in *Watson v. Jones* of noninvolvement by the federal courts in intramural church controversies. The case—which involved a dispute over church property growing out of a membership schism—came before the Court under its diversity of state citizenship jurisdiction. In dealing with such disputes, most American courts had applied the so-called implied trust doctrine: that the donors of the property had intended their gift for the promotion of the doctrines and practices of the church at the time the contribution had been made. The inevitable result was to involve judges into ecclesiastical matters by requiring a decision about which of the contending factions stood for those doctrines and practices. Justice Miller laid down a different rule. A church was a purely voluntary association, all of whose members joined "with an implied consent to [its] government, and are bound to submit to it." Therefore, "[w]henever the questions of discipline, or of faith, or ecclesiastical rule, custom, or law have been decided by the highest . . . church judicatories . . . the legal tribunals must accept such decisions as final." Decided as a matter of federal common law in a diversity of state citizenship case, *Watson* was not binding upon the state courts. And even as regards the federal courts, Miller based the noninvolvement rule upon general policy grounds rather than the First Amendment. But his guiding principle would become a cornerstone of First Amendment jurisprudence. "The law," he underlined, "knows no heresy, and is committed to the support of no dogma, the establishment of no sect."[73]

By contrast, the rare cases where the First Amendment issue was directly raised offered scant guidance for the future.[74] *Bradfield v. Roberts*—decided in 1899—involved a taxpayer suit challenging upon First Amendment grounds a congressional appropriation for a building addition to a Washington, D.C., hospital that was run by an order of Roman Catholic nuns but was open to all regardless of religious affiliation. Although the justices were unanimous in sustaining the appropriation, the decision treated the question simply as a matter of corporation law: the hospital was not legally a "sectarian" institution, but a "secular corporation" carrying out on a nonexclusive basis the purposes stipulated by its charter. Thus, whatever the religious affiliation of "the individuals who compose the corporation . . . is of not the slightest consequence."[75] Eight years later, the justices rebuffed a challenge to payments by the federal government from Indian treaty funds to support schools operated by the Roman Catholic Church on the ground that the monies belonged to the Indians and "we cannot concede the proposition that Indians cannot be allowed to use their own money to educate their children in the schools of their own choice because the Government is necessarily undenominational."[76] In the 1918 *Selective Draft Law Cases*, the Court summarily brushed aside the argument that draft exemption for ordained ministers and theological students constituted an establishment of religion with no more explanation than that "its unsoundness is too apparent."[77]

That more establishment cases had not come before the high tribunal was not because of any lack of examples of federal government aid to religion. From the first Congress on, chaplains were provided for both houses of Congress and the armed services. The military academies had compulsory chapel services. Churches benefitted from tax exemptions; individual taxpayers were allowed tax deductions for gifts to religious organizations. There was required Bible-reading in the District of Columbia public schools. The support existing for what amounted to an informal "Protestant Establishment"[78] probably discouraged would-be litigants from pursuing likely futile litigation. More important, a unanimous 1923 decision in *Frothingham v. Mellon* raised a formidable jurisdictional obstacle by barring taxpayer suits to prevent federal expenditures on the ground that an individual taxpayer lacked the sufficient direct personal interest for standing to sue. The result was that no matter how strong a constitutional case there might be against a federal expenditure, one could not obtain a hearing unless he could show that he was adversely affected in a more individual way than simply as a taxpayer.[79] The barrier thus raised to attacks upon federal aid-to-religion practices was shown when in 1928 the Court of Appeals for the District of Columbia relied upon *Frothingham* to dismiss a suit to enjoin the payment of the salaries of the chaplains for Congress and the armed services.[80]

Most states had their own constitutional provisions analogous to the First Amendment's nonestablishment clause. Since many allowed taxpayer suits, there was thus the opportunity to litigate the issue in the state courts. The bulk of such litigation appears to have involved the practice of reading the

King James Bible in the public schools. But even such cases were relatively few. Those most likely to feel aggrieved thought their chances of success dubious or—as was the situation with Roman Catholics—withdrew their children from the public system and set up their own schools. When legal challenges were raised, the courts rarely interfered with the power of local majorities to impose their religious values upon the curriculum. In the nineteenth century only Massachusetts mandated reading of the Bible statewide; elsewhere the matter was left to local option. After the turn of the century, however, a growing number of states adopted laws requiring the practice in all public schools. And state court decisions sustaining Bible reading outnumbered the negative decisions by a wide margin. More broadly, judges allowed legislators wide latitude to prescribe the values—moral, social, and political—that should inform the school curriculum.[81] Even *Pierce*—while upholding the right of private choice in education—affirmed state authority to regulate all schools, private and public, to assure "that teachers shall be of good moral character and patriotic disposition, that certain studies plainly essential to good citizenship must be taught, and that nothing be taught which is manifestly inimical to the public welfare."[82]

The Supreme Court had never dealt with the question of whether the First Amendment's nonestablishment clause applied to the states via the Fourteenth Amendment. That few contemporaries thought so was shown by the 1876 attempt to adopt a new constitutional amendment stipulating that

No State shall make any law respecting an establishment of religion or prohibiting the free exercise thereof; and no money raised by taxation in any State for the support of public schools or derived from any public fund therefor, nor any public lands devoted thereto, shall ever be under the control of any religious sect or denomination; nor shall any money so raised or lands so devoted be divided between religious sects or denominations.

And its defeat revealed the lack of consensus over whether the states should be so limited. Nor did lawyers and state court judges of that era when dealing with issues of religious freedom in the schools suggest that the Fourteenth Amendment had extended the First Amendment provision to the states.[83] Only one case even touching upon the establishment issue had been decided by the Supreme Court—in 1930 in *Duncan v. Louisiana State Board of Education*—where the justices unanimously upheld Louisiana's provision of free textbooks in secular subjects to parochial along with public school students. Neither the challenge nor the Court's response rested upon First Amendment grounds. The issue was whether the practice constituted spending public funds for nonpublic purposes in violation of the due process clause. But Chief Justice Hughes's acceptance of the child-benefit rationale adopted by the Louisiana Supreme Court when upholding the free textbook law—that the beneficiary was the students not the schools—was widely read as sanctioning state aid to religious-school pupils.[84]

At the same time, the Court did acknowledge the existence of fundamental individual rights not explicitly listed in the Constitution. One was the right to travel freely within the United States.[85] Another—at least at the level of rhetoric—was the right to pursue any lawful calling free from "unreasonable and unnecessary restrictions."[86] Practice, however, was more complex. On the one hand, most states had accepted by the early twentieth century the so-called employment-at-will rule: that an employer could discharge an employee without notice and without cause unless the duration of his service had been specified in an employment contract. Workers were similarly free—absent a contractual agreement stipulating otherwise—to leave the service of their employers at any time. And while an employee who violated his labor contract could be sued for damages, he was not liable to criminal penalties.[87] On the other hand, state courts and even the Supreme Court—notwithstanding the widely repeated myth to the contrary—upheld the overwhelming majority of laws regulating the conditions of employment as legitimate exercises of the police power for the protection of public health, safety, and/or morals.[88] A like situation applied vis-à-vis the growing body of occupational licensing laws. In principle, the qualifications had to be reasonably related to the job.[89] But the courts tended to defer to the legislative judgment about their reasonableness.[90] The major limitation upon governmental power in this area was the requirement that a license once granted could not be revoked except for cause after a hearing giving the license holder the "opportunity to . . . vindicate his conduct."[91]

Government employees lacked that much protection. Post-Revolutionary American law denied any property right in public office.[92] The corollary was that governmental employment was a privilege subject to whatever conditions that the legislature chose to impose.[93] As Holmes put the matter in a famous epigram while still on the Massachusetts bench when upholding the dismissal of a policeman for violating a regulation restricting his political activities, "The petitioner may have a constitutional right to talk politics, but he has no constitutional right to be a policeman."[94] There was similarly no right to any government-provided benefits—those were a matter of legislative grace. Accepted doctrine went even a step further: expenditure of tax funds could be only for "a public use," not for "favored individuals . . . for purposes of private interest."[95] And governmental authorities had what appeared almost unlimited power to set the terms for the use of publicly-owned property. When upholding the conviction of a preacher for violating a municipal ordinance by giving a sermon on the Boston Common without the required permit from the mayor, the Supreme Court cited with approval Holmes's conclusion in the Massachusetts Supreme Judicial Court that

For the Legislature absolutely or conditionally to forbid public speaking in a highway or public park is no more an infringement of the rights of a member of the public than for the owner of a private house to forbid it in his house. When no proprietary right interferes, the Legislature may end the right of the public to enter upon the public place by putting an end to the dedication to public uses. So it may take the lesser step of limiting the public use to certain purposes.[96]

Voting constituted a special case. The Constitution as framed left the states a free hand to determine voter qualifications, even for federal elections. The only later restrictions imposed on the states were the Fifteenth Amendment ("The right of citizens of the United States to vote shall not be denied or abridged . . . on account of race, color, or previous condition of servitude") and the Nineteenth ("The right of citizens . . . shall not be denied or abridged . . . on account of sex").[97] A long debate has gone on whether the framers of the Fourteenth Amendment had intended to include the right to vote among the privileges and immunities of citizens of the United States guaranteed against state abridgment. In 1875, however, a unanimous Supreme Court answered with an unqualified no when faced in *Minor v. Happersett* with the question if state exclusion of women from the ballot violated their privileges and immunities as citizens of the United States. While acknowledging that women were citizens, Chief Justice Waite pointed out that historically voting was never co-extensive with citizenship. More important, suffrage was granted by the states: "the Constitution of the United States does not confer the right of suffrage upon any one." And the Fourteenth Amendment "did not add to the privileges and immunities of a citizen. It simply furnished an additional guaranty for the protection of such as he already had."[98]

The Court, however, did go on to acknowledge that once the state granted the right to vote, Congress could protect its free exercise under its authority in Article I, Section 4 to regulate the "Times, Places and Manner of holding Elections for Senators and Representatives." The federal government could punish official misconduct, such as ballot-box stuffing or falsification of election returns.[99] In principle—if rarely in practice—that power extended even to action by private individuals.[100] And while the states retained a free hand to determine procedures for choosing presidential electors,[101] the Court in 1934 held that Congress had implied authority under the "necessary and proper clause" to safeguard the integrity of the presidential selection process.[102] But there were counterbalancing restrictions. In the first place, congressional authority was limited exclusively to federal elections, not state and local elections.[103] An even more important limitation was the Court's narrow definition of "Elections." In a series of decisions, the justices refused, on one ground or another, to interfere with state voter registration practices.[104] And the 1921 decision in *Newberry v. United States* left open the question if Congress could regulate state-sponsored nominating primaries even for national offices. At issue was the conviction of Senator Truman Newberry for violating the limits imposed by the Corrupt Practices Act of 1911 upon expenditures in congressional elections in the 1918 Michigan Republican senatorial primary. The justices split four-to-four over whether or not a primary was an election within the meaning of the Constitution.[105]

A different, but related, question was the basis upon which representation was allocated. There was no question that Congress could, under Article I, Section 4, deal with congressional malapportionment; the lawmakers even included in several acts reapportioning seats in the House of Representatives the stipulation that the resulting districts should be compact, contiguous, and as equal in population as practicable. Not until 1932 did the issue come before the Supreme Court. Population disparities among Mississippi congressional districts were challenged as violating the Reapportionment Act of 1911, Article I, Section 4, and the Fourteenth Amendment's equal protection clause. Speaking for the five-man majority, Chief Justice Hughes refused to deal with the constitutional issues. Instead, he dismissed the injunction granted by the federal district court against the state districting law on the ground that Congress's failure to include the 1911 equal-population requirement in the 1929 reapportionment statute meant there was no federal standard to apply. But he added in *dicta* that the remedy for congressional malapportionment lay with Congress, not the courts. Concurring in the result, the other four justices—the so-called liberal bloc of Brandeis, Harlan Fiske Stone, and Benjamin Cardozo plus Owen J. Roberts—went still further: the Court should not have decided the case on its merits but should have refused to become involved for "want of equity"—that is, because the subject was not a matter with which the Court should deal.[106]

At the state level, substantial equality of population in the districts for both houses of the legislature was never the general practice; the existence of nonpopulation factors in apportionment appeared to rest upon solid popular acceptance; and even in states having equal apportionment provisions in their constitutions, courts typically shied from ordering the legislatures to reapportion.[107] Nor was the Supreme Court willing to entertain attacks upon how the states structured their governments. That principle was laid down in the famous 1849 case of *Luther v. Borden*, which grew out of a dispute over which of two rival governments in Rhode Island exercised legal authority within the state. The constitutional issue raised was whether the Court could decide the question on the basis of the so-called guarantee clause of Article IV, Section 4 ("The United States shall guarantee to every State in this Union a Republican Form of Government").[108] The negative answer given then was reaffirmed in 1912 when the Court unanimously refused to hear a challenge to Oregon's initiative and referendum procedures as violating the guarantee clause. For the Court to deal with such "purely political" matters, Chief Justice Edward D. White warned, would constitute an "inconceivable expansion of the judicial power" by requiring the courts to determine the legality of an existing state government—and worse still, to build a new one "upon the ruins of the previously established government."[109]

The Constitution made no mention, direct or indirect, of political parties.

On the contrary, the framers were deeply suspicious of, and hostile to, parties as "factions" motivated by self-aggrandizement and thus inimical to the common good. The view that the citizen should loyally support the government short of a gross abuse of power lingered on long after parties had become firmly established. Not until the Jacksonian period did parties achieve full legitimacy as a positive and beneficial part of a free government.[110] In defining their legal status, the courts assimilated parties into the broader law of voluntary associations.[111] Neither national nor state constitutions referred in so many words to the right of association; the nearest approximation was the more limited concept of the right of assembly. But the courts held that individuals had a natural right freely to join others for lawful purposes.[112] As the California Supreme Court declared in 1900:

No one can be so ignorant as not to appreciate the value, indeed, the necessity, of opposing political parties in a government such as ours. . . . No statement is needed in the declaration of rights to the effect that electors holding certain political principles in common may freely assemble, organize themselves into a political party, and use all legitimate means to carry their principles of government into active operation through the suffrages of their fellows. Such a right is fundamental. It is inherent in the very form and substance of our government, and needs no expression in its constitution.[113]

A corollary was that voluntary associations—including political parties—had an inherent right to manage their own affairs as long as there was no violation of the fundamental principles of justice.[114] In the latter years of the nineteenth century, however, complaints about abuses by so-called party bosses resulted in the adoption of an ever-expanding body of legislation regulating party nominating procedures, internal structure, and even criteria for participation in party affairs. When those laws were challenged in the state courts, the uniform response was to uphold the principle—if not always the details—of such legislation as a legitimate exercise of the police power given how the functions performed by parties affected the electoral process. The legitimacy of state regulation of parties was so strongly accepted that no case directly challenging that power came to the Supreme Court.[115] Rather the question of the state/party relationship reached the Court in the context of racial discrimination—whether the exclusion of blacks from the Texas Democratic primary by vote of the party's state convention contravened the equal protection clause of the Fourteenth Amendment. The question thus became whether the existence of an elaborate set of state regulations governing primary elections had transformed the party from a private voluntary association into a public agency.[116] A unanimous bench in *Grovey v. Townsend* held that at least in the Texas situation—where the party itself paid for the primary, furnished the ballots, and counted the votes—the convention's vote to limit party membership to whites was private, not state, action.[117]

While state regulation of political parties became the rule, the extent of governmental authority over other voluntary associations was more ambiguous. The bulk of the litigation was over laws forbidding student membership in fraternities or other secret societies in public schools and colleges. State courts invariably upheld such laws as reasonable disciplinary regulations—as did the Supreme Court in the one such case that came before the justices.[118] The only other case on the issue decided by the high tribunal involved a challenge to a New York law aimed at the Ku Klux Klan providing that, with the exception of labor unions, student fraternities and societies, and benevolent orders, all oath-bound organizations having more than twenty members had to file an annual registration statement that included a list of officers and members. The "main contention" was not the right of association as such, but rather that the distinction between types of associations violated the equal protection clause. Justice Van Devanter disposed of that argument by finding that the legislature had "a real and substantial" basis for the distinction given the evidence of the Klan's "manifest tendency . . . to make the secrecy surrounding its purposes and membership a cloak for acts and conduct inimical to personal rights and public welfare." But he simultaneously upheld the reasonableness of the regulation upon a second ground that had far broader implications: "that the State within whose territory and under whose protection the association exists is entitled to be informed of its nature and purpose, of whom it is composed and by whom its activities are conducted."[119]

Labor unions constituted a special problem within the law of associations. Unions were regarded under the common law as criminal conspiracies in restraint of trade. Beginning with the famous 1842 ruling by Chief Justice Lemuel Shaw of the Massachusetts Supreme Judicial Court in *Commonwealth v. Hunt*, however, unions as such gained recognition as legitimate.[120] But union activities remained narrowly circumscribed by court interpretations under the so-called illegal purposes doctrine. On the one hand, strikes against an employer for direct benefits—such as higher wages, shorter hours, and improved working conditions—were legal. On the other hand, most state courts held that the closed shop (i.e., where union membership was required as a condition of employment) and thus union activities directed toward its attainment were illegal as a denial of the right of all workers to dispose of their labor. Most courts similarly deemed illegal sympathy strikes, secondary labor boycotts (e.g., refusal by workers to handle the products of a nonunion firm), and even union-organized consumer boycotts. The rationale was that the involvement of outsiders not having a direct economic stake in a conflict with an employer constituted a tort—that is, an intentionally inflicted harm without justifiable cause.[121]

The attitude of the United States Supreme Court toward labor unions was the mirror image of the position taken by most state courts. Union activities aimed at inducing workers to break what were called yellow-dog contracts (i.e., agreements by which workers promised not to join a union as a condition of employment) were illegal—and thus could be restrained by the federal courts.[122] And in the heyday of substantive due process, the justices struck down state and federal legislation outlawing yellow-dog contracts as violative of the liberty of contract protected by the Fourteenth and Fifth Amendments.[123] The most sensitive issue was the applicability of the federal antitrust laws to labor unions. The Court acknowledged that unions as such were lawful.[124] So were strikes against an employer for direct economic benefits.[125] But the Court read into the antitrust laws much the same restrictions upon union activities as the state courts had done under the illegal purposes doctrine.[126] The major target of the political counterattack by organized labor was the enforcement of those restrictions by court-issued injunctions. In response, Congress adopted in 1932 the Norris-LaGuardia Act narrowly limiting the power of the federal courts to issue injunctions against those "participating or interested" in a labor dispute. The act's key provision was its broad definition of who constituted legitimate participants:

persons who are engaged in the same industry, trade, craft, or occupation; or have direct or indirect interests therein; or who are employees of the same employer; or who are members of the same or an affiliated organization of employers or employees.[127]

Up to that time, picketing had been dealt with under the law of torts.[128]Historically, the courts had regarded any picketing as illegal because inherently threatening and intimidating. By the 1920s, however, most had come to accept the legitimacy of peaceful picketing for a lawful purpose. The difficulty was that judges were inclined to allow no more than nominal picketing as peaceful.[129] And in practice what constituted a lawful purpose tended to be confined to a strike by employees of a firm for direct economic benefits. Only a few courts had suggested that picketing was protected by the constitutional guarantee of freedom of speech. The first hint of willingness by the Supreme Court to apply the free speech analogy to picketing came in the 1937 *Senn* case.[130] At issue was a challenge to the constitutionality of Wisconsin's "little Norris-LaGuardia Act" barring state court injunctions against so-called stranger picketing—that is, picketing against an employer by others than his own employees. A narrow five-to-four majority held that a state could allow stranger picketing in the exercise of its police power. Justice Brandeis included in the majority opinion the cryptic statement that "[m]embers of a union might, without special statutory authorization by a State, make known the facts of a labor dispute, for freedom of speech is guaranteed by the Federal Constitution."[131]

Just as unions belonged to a special category of voluntary associations, women were in a different class from men. Although in the colonial period women with sufficient property were technically eligible to vote on local issues, all the state constitutions adopted after the Revolution—with the shortlived exception of New Jersey's—excluded women from the ballot. Nor was women's second-class status limited to denial of the vote. Under the English common law, not only were women barred from certain occupations (such as law), but a married woman lacked any separate legal existence apart from her husband and thus could not sell, sue, or contract without his approval. Although the states beginning in the 1830s liberalized these restrictions by allowing married women to own property, conduct businesses and retain their earnings, women still continued to suffer from a broad range of legal disabilities. Hopes that the downfall of slavery would open the door for women to join black men in the "kingdom of equality" proved stillborn. The congressional debates over the Reconstruction-era amendments show that their authors had no wish to change the *status quo* in this area. The Fourteenth Amendment contained the only instance in the Constitution of an explicit sanction for differential treatment on the basis of sex: Section 2's provision for reducing the representation in Congress of states abridging the right to vote of "male" citizens. And when woman's rights activists turned to the courts to make the general language of Section 1 into a vehicle for their purposes, the result was failure.[132]

The first test came in 1873 when Myra Bradwell challenged the refusal of the Illinois Supreme Court to admit her to the bar. After studying law under the direction of her attorney husband, Bradwell began publishing in October 1868 the weekly *Chicago Legal News*. The following September she applied to the Illinois Supreme Court for admission to the bar. The Court denied her application on the ground that as a married woman she was legally disabled from entering into contracts with or in behalf of her clients. When she in rebuttal pointed out that before starting her publication she had successfully petitioned the legislature for a special act authorizing her to transact business independently of her husband, the court unanimously took the broader ground of ruling that all women, regardless of marital status, were barred from admission to the bar. While admitting that the statute regulating admission to the bar did not explicitly exclude women, the court held that the legislature had never intended to admit women. In carrying appeal to the United States Supreme Court, her attorney raised the same question that was involved in the *Slaughter-House Cases* brought to the Court one month before her case was docketed—whether freedom to pursue one's chosen occupation was a privilege and immunity of United States citizenship protected by the Fourteenth Amendment against state restriction. With the justices split four-to-four on *Slaughter-House*, final action on *Bradwell* was postponed until a decision could be reached on that case. Although there appears to have been no significant disagreement on the result, the theoretical basis for the decision was seen as depending upon the *Slaughter-House* outcome. When the newly appointed Justice Ward Hunt cast the decisive fifth vote against an expansive reading of the privileges and immunities clause, the decision in *Bradwell* was handed down the day after the announcement of *Slaughter-House*. The vote was eight-to-one against Bradwell—with only Chief Justice Salmon P. Chase dissenting without opinion.

Justice Miller's brief majority opinion relied upon the narrow definition of the privileges and immunities clause in *Slaughter-House* to hold that regulation of admission to a state bar was not "one of those powers . . . transferred for its protection to the Federal government." Justice Joseph P. Bradley— joined by two of his fellow dissenters in *Slaughter-House*—opted for a rationale based upon "the law of the Creator." While favoring a broad interpretation of the rights guaranteed males, he justified differential treatment of women on the ground of their different roles in life. Given the legislative "prerogative . . . to prescribe regulations founded on nature, reason, and experience for the due admission of qualified persons to professions and callings demanding special skill and confidence," a state could limit occupations—such as the law—requiring manly skills to men only. "[T]he civil law, as well as nature herself," he argued, "has always recognized a wide difference in the respective spheres and destinies of man and woman. . . . The constitution of the family organization, which is founded in the divine ordinance, as well as in the nature of things, indicates the domestic sphere as that which properly belongs to the domain and functions of womanhood." While there were unmarried women, "these are exceptions to the general rule. The paramount destiny and mission of woman are to fulfil the noble and benign offices of wife and mother." That role differentiation was in turn rooted in biology: "The natural and proper timidity and delicacy which belongs to the female sex evidently unfits it for many of the occupations of civil life."[133]

The two-sphere approach would run through later Court decisions on woman's rights. When upholding exclusion of women from the ballot in *Minor v. Happersett*, Chief Justice Waite went beyond simply denying that voting was among the privileges and immunities of national citizenship. He acknowledged that "women have always been considered as citizens the same as men." But he then went on to underline how women historically belonged along with children in a special category of nonvoting citizens.[134] When *Strauder v. West Virginia* ruled that official exclusion of Negroes from jury service violated the Fourteenth Amendment's equal protection clause, an accompanying *dictum* explicitly recognized that the states could continue to restrict jury service to males.[135] A unanimous Court in 1894—when rebuffing Belva A. Lockwood's challenge to her denial of bar admission by the Virginia Supreme Court of Appeals—left to the state courts final say on whether the word "person" in a statute governing bar admission should be limited to men only.[136] Paradoxically, the Court's most explicit affirmation of women's innate differences from men, and thus their different legal status, came in a highly praised bow to reform. When Oregon's ten-hour law for women workers was challenged on liberty of contract grounds, Louis D.

Brandeis in his famous brief in support of the law emphasized woman's "special physical organization," her weakness compared to men "in all that makes for endurance," and her child-bearing and -rearing functions.[137] Following that lead, Justice David J. Brewer for a unanimous court in *Muller v. Oregon* sustained the law on the rationale of the "inherent difference between the two sexes," their "different functions in life," and the public interest in preserving the health and welfare of future generations. History, he elaborated,

discloses the fact that woman has always been dependent upon man. . . . As minors, though not to the same extent, she has been looked upon in the courts as needing especial care that her rights may be preserved. . . . Though limitations upon personal and contractual rights may be removed by legislation, there is that in her disposition and habits of life which will operate against a full assertion of those rights. . . . Differentiated by these matters from the other sex, she is properly placed in a class by herself, and legislation designed for her protection may be sustained, even when like legislation is not necessary for men and could not be sustained.[138]

The first departure from the Court's approach of differential treatment of men and women came—similarly paradoxically—in a decision that was hotly assailed by contemporary liberals: the five-to-three decision in *Adkins v. Children's Hospital* in 1923 striking down the District of Columbia minimum wage law for women. After relating "the great—not to say revolutionary— changes which have taken place . . . in the contractual, political and civil status of women, culminating in the Nineteenth Amendment," Justice George Sutherland concluded that "the ancient inequality of the sexes" had been reduced "almost, if not quite, to the vanishing point." Therefore, there was no longer any justification for "the old doctrine that she must be given special protection or be subjected to special restraint in her contractual and civil relationships." In dissent, Holmes sarcastically retorted: "It will need more than the Nineteenth Amendment to convince me that there are no differences between men and women, or that legislation cannot take those differences into account."[139] The reversal of *Adkins* fourteen years later in *West Coast Hotel v. Parrish* was sex neutral—the substance of the Court's ruling was to approve hour and wage regulation for men as much as for women.[140] But the Court's continued acceptance that women still remained in a special category was shown by its reaffirming—as late as 1947—their exclusion from jury service as not contrary to "the textual or customary law of the land."[141]

Aliens constituted another special category.[142] The Constitution says little about citizenship and nothing about aliens. The document that came from the Philadelphia convention referred to United States citizenship only as a qualification for the presidency and for service in Congress, and referred to state citizenship only in the provision that citizens of each state were entitled to the privileges and immunities of citizens in the several states. While Congress was authorized to establish uniform rules of naturalization, the text was silent about whether its relatively few guarantees of individual rights applied exclusively to citizens or to all persons living within the jurisdiction of the United States. The Bill of Rights was similarly ambiguous on this question. The Fourth and Ninth Amendments spoke of "the people," the Fifth protected "any person." The Fourteenth Amendment's privileges and immunities clause was limited to "citizens." But its due process and equal protection clauses applied to "any person." And the Supreme Court in *Yick Wo v. Hopkins* held that their safeguards were "not confined to the protection of citizens. . . . These provisions are universal in their application, to all persons within the territorial jurisdiction [of the United States], without regard to any differences of race, of color, or of nationality."[143] And a later decision affirmed that aliens facing criminal prosecution were covered by the procedural guarantees of the Bill of Rights.[144]

At the same time, the Court proceeded to build upon an extra-constitutional foundation a complex of rules that sharply distinguished between aliens and citizens. The power to control immigration was not among the enumerated powers given Congress. At first, the Court rested such control upon the power of Congress to regulate foreign commerce.[145] In the 1889 *Chinese Exclusion case*, however, the Court substituted a new theory—that Congress as an incident of sovereignty had plenary power to bar from entry any alien deemed unsuitable.[146] The corollary was that the lawmakers could adopt for implementing their policies whatever procedures desired unlimited by the due process requirements of the Constitution. A six-to-three majority went so far as to hold that a would-be entrant who claimed American citizenship was not entitled to a judicial review *de novo* of the administrative decision regarding his claim.[147] Aliens were excluded on the basis of race and/or national origin starting with the first Chinese Exclusion Act of 1882 and culminating in the quota system adopted in the 1920s. Also barred from entry were persons having unwanted personal characteristics—those with physical or mental defects; those deemed morally unsound (e.g., prostitutes, procurers, and polygamists); those liable to become public charges; and illiterates. In the aftermath of the assassination of President William McKinley, Congress imposed a political test by excluding "anarchists, or persons who believe in or advocate the overthrow by force or violence of the Government of the United States or of all government or of all forms of law."[148] When that restriction was challenged upon First Amendment grounds, Chief Justice Melville W. Fuller replied that "those who are excluded cannot assert the rights in general obtaining in a land to which they do not belong."[149]

While the children of aliens born in this country were automatically citizens under the Fourteenth Amendment,[150] Congress could "grant or withhold the privilege of naturalization upon any grounds or without any reason, as it sees fit."[151] The naturalization act of 1790 limited naturalization to "free white" persons.[152] Although an 1870 amendment made aliens of African descent eligible,[153] an 1882 statute explicitly excluded Chinese from acquiring citizenship.[154] And on the basis of the 1790 statute, the courts added to those excluded from naturalization Japanese, Hindus, Afghans, Burmese, Koreans, and Filipinos[155]—with the Court in 1934 reading the law as denying naturalization "if the strain of colored blood . . . is a half or a quarter, or, not improbably, even less, the governing test always . . . being that of common understanding."[156] A 1906 statute further required an applicant for naturalization to declare that "he is not a disbeliever in or opposed to organized government, or a member of or affiliated with any organization or body of persons teaching disbelief in or opposed to organized government."[157] The same bar was extended to pacifists when beginning in 1922 applicants were asked to affirm their willingness to bear arms in defense of the United States. Although the question was introduced by administrative regulation rather than by act of Congress, the Court upheld denial of citizenship to conscientious objectors on the rationale that persons not willing to serve in the country's armed forces could not take without mental reservations the required oath to support and defend the Constitution.[158]

The power to deport aliens was "as absolute and unqualified as the right to prohibit and prevent their entrance into the country."[159] And Congress made the same political tests for admission grounds for deportation.[160] Although aliens facing criminal charges had the same due process rights as citizens, the Court adopted the fiction that deportation was not a punishment for a crime. A person threatened with deportation who claimed to be a citizen had a right to a judicial trial on that question.[161] Except for Chinese, the burden of proof for showing alienage was upon the government. But the presumption of citizenship was not as strong as the presumption of innocence in a criminal case.[162] Where citizenship was not at issue, an alien facing deportation was entitled to no more than an administrative hearing that was not "manifestly unfair."[163] He had no right to a jury trial; he was subject to retroactive application of new grounds for deportation; he could be arrested and held in custody without probable cause; he was not protected by the right to compulsory processes for the attendance of witnesses on own behalf or by the privilege against self-incrimination.[164] Nor was naturalization final. The 1906 law providing for revocation of naturalization if procured "illegally" or by "fraud" was unanimously sustained by the high tribunal.[165] And a federal district court held that membership in the Industrial Workers of the World at the time of naturalization was sufficient proof that the alien had lied when professing allegiance to the principles of the Constitution—although the Court of Appeals turned down a denaturalization bid against another IWW activist who had joined after receiving his certificate of naturalization.[166]

Even aliens legally resident within the United States remained under a complex of legal disqualifications. From its famous 1813 ruling in *Fairfax's*

Devisee v. Hunter's Lessee on, the Court hewed to the English common law rule that alien ownership of real property existed only upon legislative sufferance.[167] Twentieth-century decisions went a step farther by upholding state laws directed against the Japanese barring aliens ineligible for citizenship from acquiring any interest in land, whether by lease, a sharecropping arrangement, or even ownership of corporate stock.[168] The situation regarding aliens' right to occupational liberty was more complex. In *Yick Wo v. Hopkins*, the Court found in violation of the Fourteenth Amendment's equal protection clause discriminatory application to Chinese laundrymen of a San Francisco licensing ordinance.[169] Then in 1915 the tribunal struck down an Arizona statute requiring that the work force of employers of five persons or more be at least 80 percent citizens. In his opinion, however, Justice Charles Evans Hughes recognized the right of the states to bar aliens from particular businesses where such exclusion could be justified by a "special public interest."[170] And in practice, the justices proved willing to accept the legislative judgment so long as not "plainly irrational."[171] Not even that limitation applied to the exclusion of aliens from public employment: state power to do so was constitutionally untrammeled.[172]

3 The Dilemma of Race

There is no question that the complex of decisions giving government of-
ficialdom sweeping and arbitrary power over immigrants reflected—and accorded with—the suspicion felt by a large segment of the American public
toward the newcomers flocking to America's shore. After the turn of the
century, anxiety over the danger of contagion from foreign-spawned radi-
calisms loomed large in respectable circles. But the animus lay deeper. The
immigrants from southern and eastern Europe that came in ever-growing
numbers beginning in the latter nineteenth century were widely regarded
as too religiously and culturally different to be assimilated—or worse, as a
degraded, even innately inferior, race threatening to swamp the Anglo-Saxon
in his own land.[1] No group was more irrevocably fixed with the outcast brand
than the Chinese. They were the target of the first step in closing what had
been an open door. The Chinese Exclusion Act of 1882 in turn gave rise to
the landmark ruling affirming the near-absolute power of Congress over
immigration.[2] The decision's author, Justice Stephen J. Field, made no secret
when writing to a friend of his motivations:

The manners, habits, mode of living, and everything connected with the Chinese
prevent the possibility of their ever assimilating with our people. They are a different
race, and even if they could assimilate, assimilation would not be desirable. If they
are permitted to come here, there will be at all times conflicts arising out of the
antagonism of the races which would only tend to disturb public order and mar the
progress of the country. . . . I belong to the class, who repudiate the doctrine that
this country was made for the people of *all* races. On the contrary, I think it is for
our race—the Caucasian race. We are obliged to take care of the Africans; because
we find them here, and they were brought here against their will by our fathers.
Otherwise, it would be a very serious question, whether their introduction should
be permitted or encouraged.[3]

Field hit the nub of the dilemma presented by the Negro to white Americans of his generation. And as Justice Samuel F. Miller pointed out in *Slaughter-House*, "the one pervading purpose" of the Civil War era amendments was "the protection of the newly-made freeman and citizen from the oppressions of those who had formerly exercised unlimited dominion over them."[4] Alongside the Fourteenth Amendment, the Thirteenth Amendment provided that "[n]either slavery nor involuntary servitude, except as a punishment for crime whereof the party shall have been duly convicted, shall exist within the United States" and the Fifteenth that "[t]he right of Citizens of the United States to vote shall not be denied or abridged by the United States or by any State on account of race, color, or previous condition of servitude." Those amendments raised for the Court two distinct, though intertwined, questions. One was their direct force. The other was the scope of the power granted Congress to "enforce" each amendment "by appropriate legislation." That second issue revolved in turn around the criminal penalty provisions of the Civil Rights Acts of 1866, 1870, 1871, and 1875 plus the so-called Ku Klux Klan Act of April 20, 1871, punishing denial of Negro rights by private action, not simply action "under color of any law."[5]

Much criticism has been directed against the post-Civil War Supreme Court for its role in nullifying the guarantees of black rights by the Reconstruction-era amendments and congressional enforcement statutes.[6] The simple explanation is that the Court shared the prevailing racism of the day. If by racism one means that the justices, like most Americans of the time, shied from accepting full social equality, the charge cannot be denied. Illustrative was the unanimous 1883 decision—joined in even by the first John Marshall Harlan, the Court's most stalwart champion of Negro rights—in *Pace v. Alabama*. At issue were two Alabama laws: the first making fornication or adultery between persons of the same race punishable by a $100 fine and up to six months in jail; the second imposing a penalty of two to seven years in jail for persons of different races who intermarried, lived in adultery, or fornicated. A Negro man and white woman sentenced to two years' imprisonment under the second law appealed on the ground that the differential treatment of interracial sexual relations violated the Fourteenth Amendment's equal protection clause. Noting how the Negro man and white woman had received the same sentence, Justice Stephen J. Field denied that there was any discrimination. "The two sections of the code cited are entirely consistent. The one prescribes, generally, a punishment for an offence committed between persons of different sexes; the other prescribes a punishment for an offence which can only be committed where the two sexes are of different races. There is in neither section any discrimination against either race."[7]

There are those who see the crucial turning point the death in May 1873 of Chief Justice Salmon P. Chase and his replacement by Morrison R. Waite. Chase was the justice most philosophically sympathetic to the Radical Republicans' equalitarian aspirations. But the Court's restrictive interpretation of the new amendments antedated Chase's death. And the Waite Court decisions that have drawn the sharpest attack were by decisive margins. Field was a Democrat; but all except one of the brethren at the time Waite took the center seat were Republicans.[8] Nor were they outside the mainstream of the party's thinking. Rather, the problem was that they shared the same tensions and cross-purposes that had bedevilled the Republican approach to Reconstruction from the start. On the one hand, the Republicans were committed to assuring the former slaves the fundamental rights belonging to free men. There was no universally accepted definition of what those rights should be. The minimum was what may be termed economic rights: to contract, to sue and be sued, to give evidence, and to purchase, sell, and inherit real and personal property. Others wished to include the guarantees of the Bill of Rights; Congress would come to add—whether from conviction or expediency—the vote. On the other hand, most Republicans were simultaneously wedded to a "State-centered nationalism" that saw the states as retaining the primary responsibility for regulating men's day-to-day activities.[9] There was, Justice Miller explained to a Texas kinsman, "a large class of republicans"—himself included—who had no wish to "risk what we are risking, the eventual destruction of some of the best principles of our existing constitution; But who are still unwilling to trust you, I mean the Southern people, with full power over the negro, and the Union man of the South."[10]

The Republican hope was that the southern states would do the job of protecting all their citizens' rights. After experience proved that hope illusory, Congress moved reluctantly to supply federal protection via the Civil Rights Act of 1866, the Fourteenth and Fifteenth Amendments, and the follow-up enforcement statutes. When the constitutionality of those statutes was challenged, nearly all lower federal court and even most state appellate court judges upheld congressional power. The question first arose regarding the Civil Rights Act of 1866. The statute made a federal crime the deprivation under the color of law or custom of a citizen's right to enter into legally binding contracts, to own and dispose of property, to sue or be sued, to testify, and to enjoy equal protection of personal rights under the law. Section 3 gave the federal courts jurisdiction over "all causes, civil and criminal, affecting persons who are denied or cannot enforce" in the state courts those rights.[11] The rationale adopted by the courts in upholding this legislation was that the Thirteenth Amendment had not simply abolished chattel slavery but had given all Americans the status of freemen and thus all the rights belonging to freemen—that is, the natural rights of life, liberty, and property. Accordingly, the Amendment authorized Congress to protect those natural rights not simply against state but private violations. Lower court interpretation of the Fourteenth Amendment followed the same reasoning: the privileges and immunities of citizens of the United States were the natural rights of freemen (typically identified as those listed in the Bill of Rights) that Congress could safeguard against invasion whether by state or private action.[12]

The Supreme Court, however, failed to hand down a definitive ruling on the scope of those amendments until the practical difficulties of implementing national protection of civil rights in the South had become painfully apparent. White hostility went beyond evasion and obstruction to organized paramilitary resistance that plunged large areas of the South into near-anarchy. Even in the period of military rule in the South, there were too few federal troops and Freedmen's Bureau agents to police what was happening outside of the larger towns. Although the Ku Klux Klan Act of 1871 authorized the president to suspend the writ of habeas corpus in areas where local officials could or would not maintain law and order because of terrorist activities,[13] President Ulysses S. Grant exercised that power only once—for nine South Carolina counties.[14] And the Supreme Court's 1866 *Milligan* ruling prohibiting the trial of civilians by military tribunals in areas where the civil courts were functioning placed the full burden of enforcement upon the regular federal courts.[15] The magnitude of the task was beyond the capacity of the federal judicial system. Local United States Attorneys labored under crushing workloads, faced bitter local community hostility, and were too often no match for the legal talent on the defense side. The number of courts was too few and their sessions too brief. Not all those representing federal authority were committed to vigorous enforcement. And those who were had to struggle to find witnesses who would testify and juries willing to convict. This situation made the more remarkable the high conviction rate in completed prosecutions. But the volume of pending cases was threatening to swamp the courts. The Supreme Court itself faced the same problem. Even apart from the enforcement cases, the aftermath of the Civil War witnessed a major increase in the business of the federal courts. By 1872, legal journals—along with justices—were complaining about the backlog of cases on the Court's docket.[16]

In 1870, Congress moved to improve the enforcement process by expanding the Attorney General's office into the new Department of Justice. But the lawmakers balked at voting the funding required to meet the escalating costs of civil rights enforcement in the South. Although the Attorney General, Amos T. Akerman, was a Georgia Republican personally committed to vigorous civil rights enforcement, budgetary constraints coupled with the case load burden facing the federal courts led him in late 1871 to shift from trying to prosecute all offenders to a policy of selective prosecution aimed simply at the leaders and those guilty of more heinous crimes. Akerman's resignation shortly thereafter aggravated the situation. His successor, George H. Williams, was a hack Oregon Republican politician without any strong feelings for the protection of black rights. Pleading lack of sufficient funding, he began placing ever tighter restrictions upon federal civil rights prosecutions. By April 1873—when the Supreme Court handed down its ruling in *Slaughter-House*—the Justice Department had virtually abandoned civil rights prosecutions except in token cases where there was a flagrant violation and a high probability of conviction. The budgetary problems facing the Department were substantial; but more was involved in this retreat. By 1872, the Grant administration was on the political defensive for its extravagance, venal partisanship, and corruption. Most important, the North was losing interest in reconstructing the South. Continued turmoil was hurting business. Many, perhaps most, Northerners had never been more than lukewarm toward Negro rights. And the Liberal Republican movement of 1872 showed that the costs of upholding those rights had disillusioned even many former supporters. Simultaneously, the transformation of most of the western states into Republican strongholds reduced the importance of the South in party leaders' calculations.[17]

The delay before the Supreme Court made its definitive ruling on the scope of the amendments was due partly to the failure of administration officials to push for a speedy test. Successful in the lower courts, they saw no advantage in running the risk of a possibly adverse Supreme Court holding. The Court itself was even more reluctant to become involved in so politically controversial an issue. In March 1872, the justices, eight to one, in *United States v. Avery*, took advantage of technical grounds to avoid a decision on the merits regarding the constitutionality of the Civil Rights Act of 1870.[18] The second enforcement act case to come before the Court— *Blyew v. United States*—involved a challenge to prosecution in the federal courts under Section 3 of the Civil Rights Act of 1866 of two white men for the murder of several members of a Negro family, but the Court disposed of the case on narrow procedural grounds. The government's argument in support of federal court jurisdiction was that black victims were parties in the case and that, given how Kentucky law barred Negroes from giving evidence in any case in which whites were a party, they could not secure their rights in the state courts. When on circuit, Justice Noah H. Swayne had in another case upheld that position.[19] But a six-to-two majority relied upon an 1826 precedent to hold that the only parties to a criminal prosecution for a public offense were "the government and the persons indicted." Ergo, black victims would have to depend upon local law enforcement officers and courts to punish the whites responsible. If federal jurisdiction could be invoked simply because a potential witness was excluded from giving evidence because of race or color, Justice William Strong reasoned, "there is no cause either civil or criminal of which those courts may not at the option of either party take jurisdiction."[20]

The result was that the Court did not explicate the scope of the post–Civil War amendments until there was no doubt that Reconstruction was running out of steam. Power realities weighed with special force upon the justices. The still-fresh memories of the debacle of the *Dred Scott* decision underlined the dangers of taking a stand that would not be politically sustainable. From the mid–1870s on, the Court adapted to the practical difficulties of forcing repayment of defaulted Southern state debts after the restoration of local self-rule by retreating from the Marshallian position regarding state immunity from suits under the Eleventh Amendment.[21] Its parallel retreat on black rights represented a similarly pragmatic adjustment to the difficulties in the way of their implementation. Worse, their reluctance to become embroiled in the political storm over Reconstruction policy led the justices to pick as their instrument for dealing with the larger constitutional issues at stake a case dealing not with rights of blacks, but with those of southern white butchers. And the way the butchers' counsel formulated the issue meant acceptance of their position would have drastically restricted—if not totally eliminated—exercise by the states of their police powers to regulate economic activities at the time when rapid industrialization and urbanization were leading many in the North to demand such regulation. Accordingly, Justice Miller in *Slaughter-House* read the Thirteenth Amendment narrowly as forbidding no more than formal slavery or its near-equivalent. He simultaneously gutted the privileges and immunities clause of the Fourteenth Amendment by limiting the privileges and immunities of national citizenship to an insignificant handful. The upshot—as he explicitly acknowledged—was that the bulk of substantive rights enjoyed by individuals remained "left to the State governments for security and protection."[22]

With the major bulwark for safeguarding black rights reduced to the equal protection clause, the next step was to limit its applicability to state—as distinct from private—action. Such an interpretation would accord with a literal reading of the text—the Fourteenth and the Fifteenth Amendments referred in so many words to "State" denial.[23] Adding to the attraction of taking advantage of this opening was the justices' sensitivity to what the federal courts could and could not do. A strong argument has been made that the framers had intended to authorize Congress to act to protect constitutional rights if the states failed to do so.[24] But state inaction was elusive to define. And its remedy would involve the courts in the day-to-day supervision of a host of local officials. Most important, how could the line be drawn to prevent Congress from absorbing all the police functions of the states? The Court's resolve to uphold state authority for the preservation of the federal system was manifest even before *Slaughter-House*. In 1871, an eight-to-one majority in *Collector v. Day* barred federal taxation of the salaries of state officials on the ground "that the means and instrumentalities employed for carrying on the operations of [state] governments, for preserving their existence, and fulfilling the high and responsible duties assigned to them in the Constitution, should be left free and unimpaired."[25] In a six-to-three decision a month before *Slaughter-House*, Justice Strong upheld a Pennsylvania gross receipts tax applied to an interstate railroad incorporated there with the explanation that "the Federal Constitution ought not to be so construed as to impair, much less destroy, anything that is necessary...to the healthy existence of the State governments."[26]

The way these influences shaped legal doctrine explains what otherwise appears the Waite Court's strange twistings and turnings on the protection of black rights.[27] On one side, that tribunal took an expansive view of what constituted state action prohibited by the Fourteenth Amendment. There could be no question, a six-to-two majority held, that discriminatory action by a state or one of its political subdivisions in their corporate capacity—in this instance a state law restricting jury service to white male persons—was forbidden by the Fourteenth Amendment.[28] But was the exclusion of Negroes from juries by a local official despite a state law that was neutral on its face state action? The same majority turned down the argument by the official's counsel that the Amendment applied exclusively to the states as states—that is, to state laws. Pointing out that "the abstract thing denominated a State" could act only through its officers, the Court ruled that "[w]hoever...acts in the name and for the State, and is clothed with the State's power, his act is that of the State."[29] Similarly within the ban of the Fourteenth Amendment was discriminatory enforcement by a state or local official of a facially neutral law. Even if the law "be fair on its face and impartial in appearance," wrote Justice Stanley Matthews for his unanimous brethren in *Yick Wo v. Hopkins*, its application "by public authority with an evil eye and an unequal hand, so as practically to make unjust discriminations between persons in similar circumstances...amount[s] to a practical denial by the State of...equal protection of the laws."[30]

Even applied to state action, however, the Court bent its affirmations of federal authority to the pragmatic exigencies of the situation in the South. Barring discriminatory enforcement against Chinese laundrymen of a San Francisco licensing ordinance—the issue in *Yick Wo v. Hopkins*—was one thing. Although public opinion in California was strongly anti-Chinese, the Court could rely upon the backing of powerful elements in the local power structure. Protection of Negro rights in the South was a far different matter given the evasions and obstructionism of local officials along with the all-too-likely potential of violent resistance. The Court's resulting adjustment of principle to realities was strikingly revealed in the area of black service on juries. The same term that the justices took a stand against official exclusion of blacks from juries a unanimous bench in *Virginia v. Rives* turned down an appeal by two blacks found guilty of murder by an all-white jury in a county where no Negro had ever sat on a jury. No one had a right to serve on the jury, reasoned Justice William Strong. Nor was the absence of blacks on the jury sufficient proof of discrimination. Rather, he piously expressed his confidence that Virginia's courts could be relied upon "when a subordinate officer of the State, in violation of State law, undertakes to deprive an accused party of a right." And *Neal v. Delaware* the following year underlined how all that was necessary to keep Negroes off juries was to avoid open, public discrimination.[31]

At the same time, the Court narrowly circumscribed federal intervention against private violations of black rights. The steps in this process can be traced through the man who was its probably most intellectually acute member—Justice Joseph P. Bradley. Nor was it simply coincidence that Bradley was the key figure in the Court's simultaneous retreat from the Marshallian tradition to immunize the southern states from suits over their defaulted bonds.[32] In 1871, Bradley affirmed that the Fourteenth Amendment authorized Congress to protect "the citizen's fundamental rights" not simply against hostile state legislation, but "state inaction or incompetency. . . . [A]nd as it cannot compel the activity of state officials, the only appropriate legislation it can make is that which will operate directly on offenders and offenses."[33] In his dissent in *Blyew*, he upheld the power of Congress to protect against the violation of a citizen's rights where "the mischief consists in [state] inaction or refusal to act, or refusal to give requisite relief."[34] And in *Slaughter-House*, he gave an expansive reading of the privileges and immunities clause as including "every right and privilege belonging to a freeman"—the rights to life, liberty, and property, the right to choose an occupation, and the guarantees of the Bill of Rights. "[T]o say that these rights and immunities attach only to State citizenship, and not to citizenship of the United States, appears to me to evince a very narrow and insufficient estimate of constitutional history and the rights of men, not to say the rights of the American people."[35]

By 1874, however, Bradley shifted his ground. He still affirmed that Congress could under the Thirteenth and Fifteenth Amendments act against private violations of the rights thereby granted. "[N]ot merely a prohibition against the passage or enforcement of any law inflicting or establishing slavery," the Thirteenth Amendment was "a positive declaration that slavery shall not exist." Accordingly, the Amendment gave Congress "the power to give full effect to this bestowment of liberty." The Fifteenth Amendment similarly "confers a positive right which did not exist before"—"a right not to be excluded from voting by reason of race, color or previous condition of servitude." Congress could therefore "pass laws to directly enforce . . . that right not only as against the unfriendly operation of state laws, but against outrage, violence, and combinations on the part of individuals." But he hedged those affirmations with the qualification that Congress was not authorized "to pass laws for the punishment of ordinary crimes and offenses." Its power was limited exclusively to private actions done "on account of race." He gave the Fourteenth Amendment a still more restrictive interpretation—a "guaranty of protection against the acts of the state government itself . . . , not a guaranty against the commission of individual offenses." He continued to leave open one loophole: Congress could act when "the state fails to comply with the duty enjoined" of protecting its citizens' rights.[36] But that exception was soon abandoned. In dealing when on circuit with the removal to federal court of a prosecution against a Negro defendant under Section 3 of the Civil Rights Act of 1866, he held that the mere existence of local racial prejudice was not sufficient for removal. The petitioner must show a discriminatory state law. If removal were permitted when "one of the parties imagines, or says, that he cannot have a fair trial in the state courts," Bradley warned, ". . . it will present a powerful temptation to litigants, especially of the criminal class, and the United States courts will be flooded with [such] cases."[37]

And in 1876, Bradley joined in Chief Justice Waite's denial in *United States v. Cruikshank* that the Fourteenth Amendment had taken from the states primary responsibility for the protection of basic individual rights. Whites participating in a mob attack upon a group of Negroes that had left from sixty to over a hundred dead had been convicted under Section 6 of the Civil Rights Act of 1870 punishing conspiracies by "two or more persons . . . to prevent or hinder" any citizen's "free exercise . . . of any right . . . secured to him by the Constitution or laws of the United States."[38] While not ruling this provision unconstitutional, the Court in setting aside the convictions pulled its teeth. Waite explained that the federal government could punish private interference with the right to assemble to petition Congress for the redress of grievances "or for any thing else connected with the powers or the duties of the national government" because that was "an attribute of national citizenship." But the indictment simply charged conspiracy "to prevent a meeting for any lawful purpose." He found "even more objectionable" the charge of depriving citizens of "lives and liberty of person without due process of law." "The fourteenth amendment prohibits a State" from doing so, he explained, "but this adds nothing to the rights of one citizen as against another. . . . Certainly it will not be claimed that the United States have the power or are required to do mere police duty in the States."[39]

Congressional protection of Negro voting rights suffered the same fate. Although indicating that Congress could under the Fifteenth Amendment punish racially motivated private violations of voting rights, Waite in *Cruikshank* threw out the indictment under the general conspiracy provisions of Section 6 of the Civil Rights Act of 1870 alleging intent to deprive citizens of voting rights because of its failure to aver racial motivation.[40] More important, a seven-man majority the same term in *United States v. Reese* voided Sections 3 and 4 of that law punishing interference with voting. The state/ private action issue was not involved since the offenders were election officials who refused to allow Negroes to vote in a local election. Still, their convictions were overturned. His ruling was that the Fifteenth Amendment did not grant suffrage to anybody, but simply prohibited its denial because of race, color, or previous servitude. Because barring any interference with voting regardless of motivation, the sections were thus unconstitutional.[41]

The result was a death blow to the already faltering efforts to prosecute voting rights violations. The Court did go on to hold that Congress could under Article I, Section 4 of the Constitution protect against interference with voting in congressional elections whether by officials or private individuals and regardless of racial motivation or not.[42] But state and local elections were where the officeholders most directly affecting people's lives were chosen. And even the affirmation of congressional authority over federal elections came after white political dominance had become firmly re-established in the South.

The disputed presidential race in 1876 solidified the northern feeling that continued protection of black rights cost too high a price in terms of national stability. The deal that seated Rutherford B. Hayes peacefully in the White House included—implicitly if not explicitly—the assurance that the political branches of the federal government would refrain from further interference with southern whites vis-à-vis the Negro. The Supreme Court signalled its acceptance of this hands-off policy in 1883 in *United States v. Harris*. An armed mob of Tennessee whites had forcibly taken several arrested Negroes from the local sheriff, killing one and beating the others. The whites were arrested, indicted and convicted under Section 2 of the 1871 Ku Klux Klan Act making punishable "if two or more persons . . . shall conspire together . . . for the purpose, either directly or indirectly, of depriving any person or any class of persons of the equal protection of the laws."[43] A unanimous bench held the provision unconstitutional. The language was so broad, Justice William B. Woods explained, as to punish assaults by whites upon even whites, not simply blacks. Such power exceeded the authority given Congress by the Thirteenth Amendment; that Amendment "simply prohibits slavery and involuntary servitude." As for the Fourteenth Amendment, Congress was limited to remedying action by "the State . . . [or] one of its departments."[44]

The culmination of the Court's retreat came in the *Civil Rights Cases* of 1883, where the justices—with only Harlan dissenting—struck down Sections 1 and 2 of the Civil Rights Act of 1875 punishing denial of "equal enjoyment of the accommodations . . . of inns, public conveyances on land or water, theaters, and other places of public amusement."[45] Justice Bradley acknowledged that Congress could act directly upon private individuals for the purpose of "abolishing all badges and incidents of slavery." But he proceeded to deny that the discrimination forbidden by the Act constituted such. Treating access to public accommodations as a "social" right, he suggested in *dicta* that the Thirteenth Amendment protected simply a narrow range of legal/economic rights—to sue, contract, give evidence, and buy or sell property. "It would be running the slavery argument into the ground," he admonished, "to make it apply to every act of discrimination which a person may see fit to make as to the guests he will entertain, or as to the people he will take into his coach or cab or car, or admit to his concert or theatre, or deal with in other matters of intercourse or business." There was a time—and he left no question that he thought such time had come—after "a man has emerged from slavery . . . when he takes the rank of a mere citizen, and ceases to be the special favorite of the laws, and when his rights as a citizen, or a man, are to be protected in the ordinary modes by which other men's rights are protected"—that is, under state law.

Bradley similarly dismissed the Fourteenth Amendment as authority for the legislation. The Fourteenth Amendment simply prohibited "State action of a particular character," not "[i]ndividual invasion of individual rights." Exclusion of blacks by the operator of a public accommodation—even though licensed and/or regulated by the state—remained a private act. So long as "not sanctioned in some way by the State, or not done under State authority," the "wrongful act of an individual . . . is simply a private wrong." And the Fourteenth Amendment "does not authorize Congress to create a code of municipal law for the regulation of private rights." To read such authority into the Amendment "would be to make Congress take the place of the State legislatures and to supersede them." In a stinging dissent, Harlan protested that even if state action were required by the Fourteenth Amendment, the statute was still valid: "railroad corporations, keepers of inns, and managers of places of public amusement are agents or instrumentalities of the State, because they are charged with duties to the public." More broadly, he denied that the men who had abolished slavery meant to leave the former bondsmen "to the several States for such protection, in their civil rights, necessarily growing out of freedom, as those States, in their discretion, might choose to provide. . . . [T]he substance and spirit of the recent amendments of the Constitution have been sacrificed by a subtle and ingenious verbal criticism."[46]

The decision did not attract much attention in white circles. The law's enforcement had never been more than half-hearted and sporadic.[47] The dominant public reaction was summed up in the formerly staunchly Republican *New York Daily Tribune*:

The act, though sincerely intended, . . . had done [Negroes] more harm than good. In quarters where public opinion supports no unjust discrimination against them, no such law was needed, and it could be of no real service. In quarters where old prejudices prevailed, and public opinion sustained unjust discrimination, the law has been practically ineffective to overcome these prejudices, but has often intensified them.

Going farther, the *Nation* expressed gratification at "how completely the extravagant expectations as well as the fierce passion of war have died out." Booker T. Washington struck the same note: law "cannot make a dependent man an independent man; cannot make one citizen respect another. These results will come . . . by beginning at the bottom and gradually working up."

More militant black leaders, however, expressed outrage. "[W]e are declared to be created equal, and entitled to certain rights," fumed Negro journalist T. Thomas Fortune, ". . . but there is no law to protect us in the enjoyment of them. We are aliens in our own land." The aging Frederick Douglass protested that the decision left seven million blacks "naked and defenceless against the action of a malignant, vulgar, and pitiless prejudice." "O," he lamented, "for a Supreme Court of the United States which shall be as true to the claims of humanity, as the Supreme Court formerly was to the demands of slavery!"[48]

Worse, however, was to come. The Waite Court had hedged its affirmations of national power to safeguard black rights within the limits imposed by political realities and larger policy concerns. Its successor would turn this retreat into a surrender. Waite himself died in 1888, to be replaced as Chief Justice by Melville W. Fuller. Within a few years, there followed a large-scale turnover in the tribunal's membership. The new generation of justices belonged to a different age with different values. The moral idealism that had spurred the struggle against slavery was a spent force. Most Northerners had come to regard Reconstruction as a mistake. By the 1890's, the dominant mood was the desire for sectional reconciliation. The apprehension felt by much of the North's old-stock middle class over the influx of immigrants from southern and eastern Europe fostered sympathy with southern anxieties on the race question. Even for the reform-minded, the new problems growing out of rapid industrialization and immigration pushed the plight of the black into the background. Within the South, white rule was firmly re-established while the growing political influence of the poorer white was heightening the pressure for a harsher, more formalized caste system. These circumstances would have sufficed to militate against an activist stance by the Court in defense of black rights. But not even the inclination to do so existed. Like most Americans of the time, the justices were strongly influenced by the dominant Social Darwinist ideology that posited blacks' fundamental inferiority while simultaneously looking askance at governmental paternalism.[49]

The Fuller Court's way was smoothed because many of its predecessor's affirmations of national authority were in the form of *dicta* that could be, and were, simply ignored. *Dicta* in *Cruikshank* and *Reese* had upheld the power of Congress to reach racially motivated violations of voting rights—whether privately or officially done—in state and local elections.[50] In 1903, the Fuller Court read into the Fifteenth Amendment a state action restriction: Congress could protect against only racially motivated government, not private, interference with voting in such elections.[51] *Dicta* in *Virginia v. Rives* held that a state officer's denial of a right even when in direct contravention of state law made him "liable to punishment... under the laws of the United States."[52] A 1904 decision found that official misconduct in contravention of a state law was not state action reachable under the Fourteenth Amendment.[53] The most blatant example involved whites convicted under the 1866 and 1870 Civil Rights Acts for harassment to force Negroes out of their jobs in a lumber mill. There was no question of the race prejudice motivating the defendants. And *dicta* by Bradley in the *Civil Rights Cases* had indicated that the right to contract was among the fundamental rights distinguishing a free man from a slave that Congress could protect under the Thirteenth Amendment against private infringement.[54] In 1906, a six-to-three majority held in *Hodges v. United States* that denial of the right to contract—the most generally accepted traditional civil right—did not reduce blacks to a condition of slavery or its sufficiently near-equivalent to trigger the power of Congress. The result was to leave the Thirteenth Amendment an almost dead letter.[55]

In dealing with the direct force of the post–Civil War Amendments, the Fuller Court's approach to what the states could or could not do was as permissive as its treatment of the scope of national power was restrictive. The *Rives-Neal* decisions pointed the way to dealing with the question of the exclusion of blacks from juries. The rule became that the defendant bore the burden of proving discrimination, with the justices routinely accepting state court denial that such discrimination had taken place at face value.[56] The exceptions where convictions were reversed came when the state courts failed even to consider the discrimination claim.[57] The Waite Court had struck down in *Hall v. DeCuir* a Louisiana law forbidding segregation on public carriers as an unconstitutional burden upon interstate commerce.[58] The Fuller Court turned down a challenge on the same ground to a Mississippi law requiring railroads to furnish separate cars for whites and blacks. The difference, Justice David J. Brewer rationalized, was that the state's highest court had construed the law as applying only to intrastate travel. The decision, however, rested upon narrow grounds. The Court expressly left open the question of whether or not passengers themselves could be required to use such separate accommodations.[59] That issue came before the justices in 1896 in *Plessy v. Ferguson* when the Louisiana separate car act of 1890 was challenged. That statute not simply required railroads to provide "equal but separate accommodations" for black and white passengers, but stipulated that no passengers "shall be permitted to occupy seats in coaches other than the ones assigned to them on account of the race they belong to"—with accompanying criminal penalties for anyone "insisting on going into a coach or compartment to which by race he does not belong."[60]

In what was an arranged test case, Homer A. Plessy was asking the Court to block his trial in state court for violating the statute on the ground of its unconstitutionality. He had purchased a ticket for travel within Louisiana. And the state's supreme court had limited its application to intrastate passengers. Thus, the question before the justices focused on whether the statute violated the Fourteenth Amendment.[61] A seven-to-one majority— with Harlan alone in angry dissent—sustained the Louisiana statute as a "reasonable" exercise of the police power. In a striking example of formalistic legal reasoning, Justice Henry Billings Brown found that a "statute which implies merely a legal distinction between the white and colored races . . . has no tendency to destroy the legal equality of the two races." To require separation of the races did not "imply the inferiority of either race to the other" unless "the colored race chooses to put that construction upon it." What gave the decision its larger significance was its underlying sociological assumptions. The first was that the state legislatures were best suited to dealing with the race problem given their knowledge of "the established usages, customs and traditions of the people." The second—and capstone— was the judicial equivalent of William Graham Sumner's warning that laws cannot change "folkways":

The object of the [Fourteenth] Amendment was undoubtedly to enforce the absolute equality of the two races before the law, but in the nature of things it could not have been intended to abolish distinctions based upon color, or to enforce social, as distinguished from political equality, or a commingling of the two races upon terms unsatisfactory to either. . . . If the two races are to meet upon terms of social equality, it must be the result of natural affinities, a mutual appreciation of each other's merits and a voluntary consent of individuals. . . . Legislation is powerless to eradicate racial instincts or to abolish distinctions based upon physical differences, and the attempt to do so can only result in accentuating the difficulties of the present situation.[62]

Few decisions have drawn heavier fire from later commentators.[63] But those condemnations are exaggerated. A long debate has raged over whether the framers of the Fourteenth Amendment had intended to bar state-mandated racial segregation. No conclusive answer is possible. The question was never squarely faced in the debates in Congress at the time. When Democrats accused the Amendment's sponsors of that aim, the Republicans evaded the issue by resorting to vague generalities.[64] The weight of the evidence, however, indicates that the Amendment was not meant to bar racial segregation in the schools.[65] Even Senator Charles Sumner of Massachusetts hedged when asked if his March 1867 proposal to make readmission of the former Confederate states depend upon their establishment of free public schools "open to all without distinction of race or color" would require mixed schools.[66] His later repeated bids to end segregation in the District of Columbia schools were rebuffed by his colleagues. And when approving the equal accommodations provisions of the Civil Rights Act of 1875, the lawmakers struck out the section prohibiting racial segregation in public schools.[67] Nor did even the most radical Republicans dare to speak out against anti-miscegenation laws.[68] Over half the thirty states ratifying the Amendment had school segregation or anti-miscegenation laws.[69] More ambiguous is the situation regarding public transportation—the issue immediately before the Court in *Plessy*. Before adoption of the Fourteenth Amendment, Congress had voted to forbid segregation on street car lines in the District of Columbia. But a substantial number of Amendment supporters in the debates preceding adoption of the Civil Rights Act of 1875 favored the separate-but-equal approach.[70]

Whatever the intention of the framers of the Fourteenth Amendment, *Plessy* represented no new departure in the case law. As Brown underlined in his opinion, "[l]aws permitting, and even requiring, [the races'] separation in places where they are liable to be brought into contact... have been generally, if not universally, recognized as within the competency of the state legislatures in the exercise of their police power."[71] Although later commentators have demonstrated how Brown was guilty of the familiar judicial trick of a selective reading of precedents, there is no question that his major thrust was correct.[72] Brown relied heavily upon the 1849 ruling by Chief Justice Lemuel Shaw of the Massachusetts Supreme Judicial Court in *Roberts v. City of Boston* rebuffing a challenge to a separate school regulation by the Boston school committee. The Massachusetts Constitution declared that "All men are born free and equal"; another section prohibited grants of special privilege. Shaw agreed that those provisions meant that "all persons without distinction of age or sex, birth or color, origin or condition, are equal before the law." But he denied that this principle barred classifying students by race any more than by sex or age. Underlining that the facilities afforded Negro students were equal to those for white students, he found the school committee's decision that the good of both races would be promoted by separate education to rest "on just grounds of reason and experience." And he dismissed the argument that separate schools fostered racial antipathies with the reply that the prejudice which existed "is not created by law, and probably cannot be changed by law." On the contrary, such prejudice would probably be aggravated "by compelling colored and white children to associate together in the same schools."[73]

While *Roberts* antedated the Fourteenth Amendment by two decades, the preponderance of case law after its ratification continued to uphold the separate-but-equal principle.[74] By the 1880s, the common law of common carriers accepted the legitimacy of railroad-imposed regulations separating passengers by race provided substantially equal accommodations were furnished those paying the same fare.[75] Although the Interstate Commerce Act of 1887 forbade railroads to subject any person to "any undue or unreasonable prejudice or disadvantage," the Interstate Commerce Commission ruled that segregation—so long as the two races were provided "equal accommodations"—did not constitute "undue prejudice."[76] Lower federal and state courts dealing with segregation in public accommodations and the schools took the same line. Many federal judges read the Civil Rights Act of 1875 as requiring separate-but-equal rather than identical accommodations.[77] Of the seventy-five decided cases dealing with racial discrimination in schools filed between 1834 and 1903, blacks won 55 percent. But most rested upon state laws and constitutions. Blacks lost nearly three-fourths of the cases where the decision turned upon the Fourteenth Amendment. And in only one—an obscure 1881 ruling by a local Pennsylvania judge—did a court find that the Fourteenth Amendment outlawed segregated schooling as such.[78] In 1895, the influential constitutional law commentator Thomas M. Cooley summed up the case law as holding that "no [Fourteenth Amendment] right is violated when colored pupils are merely placed in different schools, provided the schools are equal, and the same measure of privilege and justice is given to each."[79]

The Waite Court's *Pace* ruling upholding Alabama's anti-miscegenation law confirmed that racially based classifications as such were not constitutionally prohibited.[80] And in 1885 *Barbier v. Connolly* underlined that the Fourteenth Amendment was not "designed to interfere with the power of the State, sometimes termed its police power, to prescribe regulations to promote the health, peace, morals, education, and good order of the people."[81] Although that power had its limits, courts from the Supreme Court down continued into the 1890s—and beyond—to take a permissive attitude to state regulations.[82] Brown himself was among the more willing of the justices to sustain such measures when he could find a reasonable basis given social and economic facts. In an opinion delivered shortly before *Plessy*, he affirmed in sweeping terms that "whatever is . . . inimical to the public interests is subject to the police power of the State, . . . and in the exertion of such power the legislature is vested with a large discretion" so long as "exercised *bona fide* for the protection of the public."[83] He couched the issue in *Plessy* in those same terms: "the case reduces itself to the question whether the statute of Louisiana is a reasonable regulation."[84] With the question framed thus, the answer was simple. Not simply popular thought but the dominant scientific opinion of the time accepted the existence of inborn racial instincts and antipathies. Ergo, a law requiring racial separation of railroad passengers would promote good order and public safety by reducing the frictions and hostilities arising from the commingling of the races.[85]

The decision's practical significance has similarly been exaggerated.[86] Racial segregation—*de facto* or legally mandated—had long been in place. Restricting blacks to separate facilities was the norm in the northern states before the Civil War. Although successfully attacked in some locales, that practice survived throughout much of the North after the war.[87] In the South, the caste system based upon slavery made the maintenance of a physical separation between the races appear not as urgent. But there was no lack of informal and formal mechanisms for limiting contact.[88] In the immediate aftermath of the war, the white-dominated regimes installed under the aegis of President Andrew Johnson included segregation provisions in their "Black Codes." More important, segregation was the rule in education, public and private welfare facilities, and public conveyances even during the period of radical Republican rule. Only two states—South Carolina and Louisiana— included in their constitutions explicit prohibitions against separate public schools. In South Carolina, that prohibition remained a dead letter. Only

New Orleans experienced substantial desegregation; even there, however, a majority of the city's school children still attended separate schools. The restoration of white rule led to the adoption in most of the southern states of constitutional provisions or laws requiring segregated public schooling. The first wave of separate railroad car laws similarly antedated *Plessy*. And while the Supreme Court's stamp of approval legitimized the ever-more-inclusive network of segregation laws passed in the years that followed, its direct influence upon their adoption was marginal.[89]

Given white attitudes, integration was simply not a live option at the time. Where the Supreme Court may be more properly faulted was its failure to uphold the equal side of separate-but-equal. Although *Plessy* did not explicitly say so, the opinion's emphasis upon that aspect of the Louisiana statute implied that the provision of equal facilities was required for segregation laws to pass constitutional muster. Practice, however, became increasingly unequal. Nowhere were the results more damaging than in education. A study of five southern states finds that between 1890 and 1910 expenditures on teacher salaries per black pupil declined in real terms while spending per white pupil rose dramatically.[90] But the Supreme Court refused to intervene. This hands-off attitude was first signalled in *Cumming v. Richmond County Board of Education*, handed down in 1899. The county had maintained along with two public high schools for whites a public high school for blacks. In 1897, however, the school board voted to turn the black high school into a primary school for Negroes not served by the existing facilities. The Negro plaintiffs did not challenge directly the practice of maintaining racially segregated schools. Rather, they asked for an injunction to block spending tax funds on the white high schools unless the black school was kept open. Even Harlan joined the unanimous bench in turning down the suit. Writing the opinion for the Court, Harlan took the position that the fact that whites received a disproportionate share of public benefits was not in violation of the equal protection clause unless black challengers could prove "bad faith," i.e., "hostility to the colored population because of their race."[91]

Plessy had read the Fourteenth Amendment as not requiring involuntary contact between the races. Twelve years later, the Supreme Court found in the Amendment no bar to legislation penalizing even voluntary association. Berea College was a tiny private school in the Kentucky hills that had been founded in 1858 by radical abolitionists for "the co-education of the (so-called) 'races.' " Although its major focus had shifted to the recruiting of Appalachian whites, the continued presence of approximately one hundred and fifty black students—roughly one-seventh of the total—attracted the bitter hostility of surrounding white society. In 1904, the Kentucky legislature adopted a law forbidding "any person, corporation or association of persons" from operating "any school, college or institution where persons of the white and negro races are both received as pupils for instruction." Teaching of both races was permitted only if the institution maintained a "separate and distinct branch . . . in a different locality, not less than twenty-five miles distant, for the education exclusively of one race or color." The Kentucky Court of Appeals denied any violation of the equal protection clause. The law "applies equally to all citizens. It makes no discrimination against those of either race." The court similarly rebuffed the plea that the statute violated the freedom of speech and religion guaranteed by the state's Bill of Rights. At stake was a vital societal interest: "the preservation of the identity and purity of the races" against the danger of "amalgamation."

When appeal was brought to the Supreme Court, Justice Brewer speaking for himself and four of his brethren evaded these larger issues by seizing upon a rationale that the Kentucky court had added almost as an afterthought: the reserved power of the state over its corporations. Although holding that the twenty-five-mile distance between branches was unreasonable, that court had found the law otherwise within the legislature's power. Brewer acknowledged that a state could not alter a corporate charter in such a way as to "'defeat or substantially impair the object of the grant,' " i.e., "'the education of all persons.' " But he reasoned that the law did not prevent Berea from continuing to teach students of both races at the same place at different times or at different places at the same time. "[A]n amendment to the original charter," he concluded, "which does not destroy the power of the college to furnish education to all persons, but which simply separates them by time or place of instruction, cannot be said to 'defeat or substantially impair the object of the grant.' " And while the law applied not simply to corporations but to all persons and associations of persons, he side-stepped that difficulty by finding those provisions "separable." Justices Oliver Wendell Holmes, Jr., and William H. Moody concurred with the result—probably upon broad police power grounds. "Have we," Justice Harlan lamented in his dissent, "become so inoculated with the prejudice of race that an American government, professedly based on the principles of freedom, and charged with the protection of all citizens alike, can make distinctions between such citizens in the matter of their voluntary meeting for innocent purposes simply because of their respective races?"[92]

During and immediately after Reconstruction, Negro political influence had been curtailed by extralegal methods—violence, economic coercion, and fraud. But large numbers of blacks continued to vote into the 1890's, when the southern states began adopting new legal devices to exclude blacks from the ballot without openly contravening the Fifteenth Amendment. After the Republicans had gained control of both houses of Congress in the 1888 elections, Henry Cabot Lodge of Massachusetts steered through the House of Representatives a bill for federal supervision of congressional elections. Although this so-called Force Bill failed to come to a vote in the Senate in face of a southern filibuster, the measure aroused grave apprehensions among southern whites.[93] Many such whites had grown fearful lest the extralegal methods directed against blacks become a permanently corrupting feature of southern politics. And the extension of such tactics to dissident whites during the agrarian revolt appeared to threaten the entire social fabric. Worse, the division among whites—with the accompanying struggle for the Negro vote—raised the specter of a possible return of black political influence. Mississippi led the way when adopting its new state constitution in 1890. Under the spur of turbulent events of the 1890's, most of the other southern states followed its example. The key elements in this strategy were more stringent residency requirements, disqualification for petty crimes, payment of a poll tax as a prerequisite for voting, and a literacy or understanding test that gave local election officials leeway to admit most whites while excluding most blacks.[94]

The congressional architects of Reconstruction had seen the ballot as the most important instrumentality by which the Negro could protect his interests after the return to local self-government. And black voting strength remained sufficiently powerful even after the overthrow of the radical regimes to act as a buffer against the worst excesses of white supremacy.[95] But the disenfranchisement movement that swept the region after 1890 failed to spark much outside resistance. Not simply was sectional reconciliation the motto of the day, but with the Spanish-American War the United States assumed the white man's burden of benevolent rule over darker skinned peoples overseas. On the same day that the formal declaration of war was announced, the Supreme Court handed down its approval of the Mississippi plan. A black challenged his murder conviction with the argument that since Mississippi law restricted jury service to qualified voters, its requirement that applicants for the franchise pass a literacy test to the satisfaction of local election officials effectively barred blacks from juries. For a unanimous bench, Justice Joseph McKenna held that the law was not discriminatory because the literacy requirement applied equally to whites and blacks. And refusing to look behind the text to its actual workings, he found no evidence of its "evil and discriminating administration." He even went beyond the issues raised to deliver in *dicta* approval of the poll tax: its exclusion from voting "can be prevented by both races by the exertion of that duty which voluntarily pays taxes."[96]

A direct challenge to the new political order came in 1903 in *Giles v. Harris*. The Alabama constitution of 1901 required that newly registering voters meet a stiff property or literacy test. A Negro turned down by a registration board asked the federal courts to order his registration. Justice Oliver Wendell Holmes, Jr., spoke for a six-to-three majority in upholding the refusal of the lower federal court to do so. A Social Darwinist who opposed judicial interference with predominant community opinion in the economic sphere, Holmes applied the same approach to race relations. One reason he gave for not issuing the order was a technical legal point. The suit was based upon the assumption that the registration scheme was "a fraud upon the Constitution" and therefore void. If that were true, Holmes rationalized, "how can we make the court a party to the unlawful scheme by accepting it and adding another voter to its fraudulent lists?" His more important reason was a frank admission of the limits of the Court's power. If "the great mass of the white population intends to keep the blacks from voting," putting "a name on a piece of paper will not defeat them." "[R]elief from a great political wrong, if done, as alleged, by the people of a State and the State itself," he concluded accurately if cynically, "must be given by them or by the legislative and political department of the government of the United States."[97]

Disenfranchisement came to the South under the guise of a progressive reform.[98] And even in the North reform was largely for whites only.[99] The excesses of turn-of-the-century racism, however, produced stirrings of conscience that led to the founding in 1910 of the National Association for the Advancement of Colored People. Along with its educational activities, the NAACP undertook a campaign of court litigation to test the racially discriminatory laws and practices that had mushroomed throughout the country.[100] At the same time, the Court itself was becoming more sensitive toward such issues despite the death of John Marshall Harlan in 1911. Three justices played key roles in the Court's changed attitude. Coming from a strongly anti-slavery family background, William R. Day had shown himself since his 1903 appointment the Fuller Court justice—next to Harlan—most sympathetic to Negro rights. Former New York governor Charles Evans Hughes—appointed in 1910—brought to the bench a new voice more willing than most of his brethren to look behind the forms of the law to their actual results. Probably the most important change was the elevation of Edward D. White from Associate to Chief Justice after Fuller's death in July 1910. A Confederate veteran, a leader in the fight to redeem his home state of Louisiana from Reconstruction, and a former Democratic Senator, White had supported every decision rebuffing black appeals. But his new position at the center seat strengthened his latent nationalist sympathies while simultaneously leading him to take a broader view of the Court's role as the custodian of constitutional principles.[101]

The White Court's first major contribution to Negro rights was not recognized as such at the time because occurring in a nonracial context: its return to a broader definition of what constituted state action after the 1904 decision in *Barney v. City of New York* that action by state officials contrary to state law was "not action by the State . . . within the intent and meaning of the Fourteenth Amendment."[102] That reading appeared to place actions by state officers not authorized by formal law beyond the reach of federal authority. Although not explicitly overruling *Barney*, *Home Telephone and Telegraph Co. v. City of Los Angeles* amounted to a silent reversal. At issue was whether or not a federal court could restrain enforcement of a local ordinance fixing telephone rates before the state courts had decided if the ordinance violated the state constitution and thus if the rates were authorized by state law. A unanimous Supreme Court held that accepting such an interpretation would make the state courts the primary reliance for protecting Fourteenth Amendment rights. "[T]he theory of the Amendment," the new Chief Justice explained,

is that where an officer or other representative of a State in the exercise of an authority with which he is clothed misuses the power possessed to do a wrong forbidden by the Amendment, inquiry concerning whether the State has authorized the wrong is irrelevant and the Federal judicial power is competent to afford redress for the wrong by dealing with the officer and the result of his exertion of power.[103]

The implications of the decision for black rights were not recognized until later.[104] Of more immediate benefit were the so-called peonage cases. In 1867, Congress had adopted legislation—aimed at the peonage system in New Mexico—forbidding "any attempt . . . to establish, maintain, or enforce, directly or indirectly, the voluntary or involuntary service or labor of any person as peons, in liquidation of any debt or obligation" and imposing penalties upon whomever "shall hold, arrest, or return . . . any person or persons to a condition of peonage."[105] The law, however, remained dormant until the Theodore Roosevelt administration began an active enforcement drive. Its target was the widespread practice in the South of holding workers in what amounted to forced labor until they had paid off their debts—real and fictitious—to an employer. In many instances, the debt resulted from an advance paid by the employer; in others, the employer had arranged with the local authorities to pay the fine levied upon a black for a petty offense in return for his working off the money owed.[106] The first case that reached the Supreme Court involved the operator of a Georgia turpentine still who had dragged back at gunpoint and in handcuffs two former black employees he claimed had left owing him money. When he appealed his conviction under the 1867 law, the Fuller Court upheld its constitutionality under the Thirteenth Amendment. But the decision defined peonage narrowly as "a status or condition of compulsory service, based upon the indebtedness of the peon to the master. The basal fact is indebtedness." Worse, the majority proceeded on hair-splitting technical grounds to reverse the conviction.[107]

In 1911, however, *Bailey v. Alabama* for the first time gave teeth to the Thirteenth Amendment. At issue was an Alabama statute establishing a presumption of fraud if a person obtained money under a written contract of employment but did not perform the work or offer to return the money. At the same time, the state's rules of evidence prevented the defendant from rebutting that presumption by testifying "as to his uncommunicated motives, purpose or intention." A black farm laborer named Alonzo Bailey who had been paid a $15 advance upon wages and then failed to perform the work was found guilty of violating the law and fined $30 plus costs. In default of payment, he was required to serve 136 days at hard labor. Bailey's plight caught the attention of Booker T. Washington of Tuskegee Institute.

Although wary of appearing publicly as an agitator, Washington was more active behind-the-scenes in defending black rights than his detractors, then or since, recognized. Washington arranged for financing and legal representation to carry an appeal to the Supreme Court. But what proved decisive was not so much the racial aspect as the law's conflict with freedom of contract principles. At least Hughes emphasized that issue in his opinion for the five-to-two majority holding the statute unconstitutional. "The provisions designed to secure . . . freedom of labor," he underlined, ". . . would soon become a barren form if it were possible . . . to hold over the heads of laborers the threat of punishment for crime...merely upon evidence of failure to work out their debts."[108]

In *Bailey*, the Court barred the states from criminalizing failure to perform a voluntarily agreed-to contract. Three years later, the Court struck down in *United States v. Reynolds* another Alabama law aimed at keeping the Negro under tight control while simultaneously assuring white employers an ample and cheap labor supply. The statute provided that a person guilty of an offense could have his fine and costs paid by another person in return for the convicted party contracting for labor over a certain period—typically longer than the jail term for nonpayment. If the laborer defaulted, he could be convicted for violating the contract and forced to enter into a longer period of service with another surety. The case grew out of an indictment obtained by federal authorities against two such sureties for violating the 1867 anti-peonage law. The trial court judge had thrown out the indictment; a unanimous Supreme Court reinstated the indictment on the ground that the Alabama law was constitutionally invalid and thus offered no protection. While acknowledging that the state could impose compulsory labor as punishment for a crime, Justice Day ruled that the Thirteenth Amendment forbade imposing such compulsory service for the benefit of private parties. Labor performed under the threat of rearrest and conviction amounted to a coercion "as potent as it would have been had the law provided for the seizure and compulsory service of the convict." Anyone caught in the law's toils faced recurring, ever longer terms of forced labor, "chained to an ever-turning wheel of servitude."[109]

That same year, a five-to-four majority took the first step toward requiring that separate facilities for blacks in public accommodations be equal by holding that the clause in the Oklahoma railroad segregation law authorizing the railroads to provide Pullman cars for whites without supplying any for blacks constituted a denial of equal protection of the laws. For the majority, Hughes brushed aside as "without merit" the argument that black demand was so minimal that the railroads would suffer heavy financial losses if forced to provide separate Pullman cars for blacks. The "volume of traffic" argument, he admonished, made "the constitutional right depend upon the number of persons who may be discriminated against, whereas the essence of the constitutional right is that it is a personal one. . . . [I]f facilities are provided, substantial equal treatment of persons traveling under like conditions cannot be refused. It is the individual who is entitled to the equal protection of the laws." But even Hughes shied from attacking segregation as such. The Court was unanimous in denying that the Oklahoma statute—apart from the Pullman car clause—violated the Fourteenth Amendment.[110] And a six-to-three bench went on in 1920 to uphold the application of a Kentucky statute requiring separate accommodations to a street railway running from Covington, Kentucky, across the Ohio River to Cincinnati on the ground that the law "affects interstate business incidentally and does not subject it to unreasonable demands."[111]

The White Court gave a mixed reception to renewed bids to punish violations of voting rights even in elections for federal offices. Much of the problem was statutory. In 1894, Congress had repealed all the provisions of the Reconstruction-era acts dealing with interference with voting. The remaining statutory basis for such prosecutions was Section 19 of the Criminal Code of 1909 punishing conspiracies against the exercise of rights secured by the Constitution or federal laws.[112] Whether that provision—which was derived from Section 6 of the Civil Rights Act of 1870—had been intended to include voting rights was problematic, even dubious. And even if voting rights were included, the purpose was to protect against violent intimidation by lawless groups rather than official misconduct. Nevertheless, a seven-to-one majority in 1915 in *United States v. Mosley* gave the provision a latitudinarian reading to uphold the prosecution of two local election officials for fraudulent vote-counting in a congressional election. Although *Mosley* was not presented as a race case, most of those whose ballots had been thrown out were blacks.[113] But the Court then backtracked in a 1917 ruling that—while resting upon a technical issue of state law—hinted strongly that the power of Congress to regulate elections under Article I, Section 4 did not cover primaries.[114] And the following year, a similarly unanimous bench in *United States v. Bathgate* dismissed indictments for a private conspiracy to bribe voters in a congressional election. Since the provisions of the 1870 law expressly dealing with bribery had been repealed, Section 19 did not apply given the policy adopted by Congress "not to interfere with elections within a State except by clear and specific provisions."[115]

In 1915, however, the Chief Justice lined up a unanimous bench to give renewed life to the Fifteenth Amendment by invalidating in the *Guinn* case the so-called "grandfather clause" in the Oklahoma constitution. A number of other states had adopted similar devices to ease the anxieties of poor whites lest they suffer disenfranchisement under the new literacy test requirements for excluding blacks from the ballot. The Oklahoma provision exempted from the general literacy requirement that a would-be voter read and write any section of the state's constitution all those entitled to vote under any form of government or living in any foreign country as of January 1, 1866, and their lineal descendants. The case arose out of a prosecution by the federal government under what remained of the Reconstruction-era statutes of two Oklahoma election officials for their refusal to register Negro voters. Although avoidance was possible on technical grounds, White frontally attacked the larger issue. That the provision did not explicitly refer to race made no difference; the purpose was to establish "a standard of voting which on its face was in substance but a revitalization of conditions which when they prevailed in the past had been destroyed by the self-operative force of the [Fifteenth] Amendment." Along with upholding the election officials' convictions, White added to southern disquiet by throwing out the entire literacy test requirement because invalidation of the exemption left the measure far different from the one adopted.[116] More disturbing still, White in the companion case of *Myers v. Anderson* upheld a damages award under another Reconstruction-era provision against election officials who had refused to register Negroes under an Oklahoma-type Maryland law.[117]

Probably the White Court's most important contribution to black rights came in 1917 when the justices in *Buchanan v. Warley* halted the threatened spread of a legally-formalized pattern of residential segregation. Baltimore had led the way by adopting in 1911 an ordinance prohibiting blacks from moving into homes on all-white occupied blocks.[118] Similar laws were adopted by other cities in the South and even the border states. In response, the NAACP arranged for a test case to challenge the Louisville, Kentucky, ordinance barring new black householders from residential blocks more than 50 percent white. Arrangements were made for purchase by the president of the local NAACP chapter of a lot for a house in a white block from a white real estate agent with the proviso that he would not pay unless he had the legal right to occupy the property as a residence. He then refused to pay on the ground that he could not occupy the house under the city's segregation law. The white seller thereupon sued to enforce performance. The tactic was a failure at the state court level, where the ordinance was upheld as constitutional and thus a full defense against the breach of contract suit. With blunt frankness, the Kentucky Court of Appeals openly declared that "this State is fully committed to the principle of the separation of the races whenever and wherever practicable and expedient for the public welfare."[119]

Although a collusive suit, the Supreme Court agreed to hear the appeal. The existing state court precedents were mixed. The Maryland Court of Appeals had struck down the Baltimore ordinance as an unconstitutional invasion of the right to acquire, enjoy and dispose of property. But other courts had upheld such laws, at least as applied prospectively, as legitimate exercises of the police power.[120] More important, the concept of rational control of urban land-use was in harmony with the ethos of the progressive era. Although the intellectual rationale was supplied by the emerging profession of city planning, the major support for zoning laws and subdivision restrictions governing land usage came from private real-estate interests looking to protect "good residence neighborhoods" from "undesirable" uses. And there was a powerful body of sentiment—even in the North—that favored geographical isolation of blacks to reduce racial frictions, prevent the spread of vice, crime, and disease, and safeguard the property values of the white majority. The counsel for Louisville submitted a lengthy Brandeis-type brief drawing upon a mix of scientific and pseudo-scientific authorities to defend the ordinance as a way of protecting the white race from the degeneracy accompanying the racial amalgamation that would be fostered by allowing whites and blacks to live in close proximity.[121] Acceptance of the ordinance by the Court would thus have probably led to nationwide adoption of similar legislation.

In 1915, the Court had upheld without dissent Los Angeles's pioneering use-zoning regulations. That approval was the more significant because the legislation had been applied retroactively to force the closing of a brick yard in a newly-designated residential district.[122] Most commentators accordingly were surprised, even disapproving, when the justices in *Buchanan* unanimously struck down the Louisville ordinance. Although the formal ground for the decision was the ordinance's impairment of the property rights of the white seller, Justice William R. Day strongly intimated that its racially discriminatory aspect was the decisive factor. While acknowledging that property use could be controlled in the interests of health and safety, he asked if the transfer of property could be restricted "solely because of the color of the proposed occupant of the premises?" In answering no, he emphasized how the "principal purpose" of the Fourteenth Amendment was to "extend federal protection to the recently emancipated race from unfriendly and discriminating legislation by the States." And nothing was more important to its framers than "to secure upon the same terms to citizens of every race and color . . . fundamental rights in property." Even though "there exists a serious and difficult problem arising from a feeling of race hostility," he concluded, that problem could not be solved "by depriving citizens of their constitutional rights and privileges."[123]

Whether the more liberal approach of the White Court on race issues would have survived the strains and tensions accompanying American involvement in World War I and its aftermath cannot be answered. White's death in 1921 allowed President Warren G. Harding to fulfill former president William Howard Taft's long-held aspiration for the Chief Justiceship. And there followed another large-scale turnover in the Court's membership. The new bench was more doctrinairely hostile than even the Fuller Court to government paternalism. Even its "liberal" members did not give black rights a high priority.[124] *Buchanan v. Warley* was undercut by the rapid spread of private agreements stipulating that a covered property should never be sold or leased to a black. The same property-consciousness that had worked in favor of blacks in the 1917 case worked to their disadvantage when court enforcement of such a restrictive covenant was challenged in 1926. A unanimous bench ruled in *Corrigan v. Buckley* that not simply the agreement but its court enforcement transgressed no "constitutional or statutory right."[125] A similarly agreed Court next year rebuffed a suit by a Chinese parent in Mississippi for admission of his daughter to the local white rather than black school. Although the issue was the legitimacy of her classification as colored, Taft took the opportunity to affirm the constitutionality of school segregation. "Were this a new question," the Chief Justice wrote, "it would call for very full argument and consideration, but we think that it is the same question which has been many times decided to be within the constitutional power of the state legislature to settle without intervention of the federal courts under the Federal Constitution."[126]

Alarmed by the threat presented by *Guinn* to the complex of devices adopted to nullify Negro political influence, southern white leaders placed heavy emphasis upon the importance of the so-called white primary—the more so because the 1921 decision in *Newberry v. United States* was widely read as holding that primaries were not elections within the meaning of the Constitution and thus beyond the power of Congress to reach.[127] When adopting the direct primary, each of the southern states had given the parties the authority to establish their own membership qualifications for participation. The tacit understanding was that blacks would thereby be excluded from the only meaningful vote in most of the South without raising the constitutional problems that direct state action would involve. The Texas law of 1905 authorized the county Democratic executive committees to establish the qualifications for voting in primary elections. But a substantial number of blacks continued to cast votes in those elections. Texas had a relatively large group of well-organized and urban-based educated and economically independent black businessmen and professionals. More important, the rampant factionalism in Texas Democratic politics resulted in rival factions bidding for Negro support. Complaints from the losers in such contests struck a responsive chord in the aftermath of World War I with the rise of the Ku Klux Klan to become a major force in state politics. In response, the legislature approved in 1923 legislation openly barring Negroes from voting in the state's Democratic primaries. A test case challenging the new law by an El Paso Negro physician, Dr. Lawrence A. Nixon, was initiated by the local NAACP chapter with the backing of the national office.[128] With the justices still divided over the legal status of primaries, the Supreme Court sidestepped the question of whether the Texas law contravened the Fifteenth Amendment. Instead, Holmes, speaking for a unanimous bench in *Nixon v. Herndon*, struck down the statute as a violation of the equal protection clause of the Fourteenth Amendment. "States may do a great deal of classifying that is difficult to believe rational, but there are limits."[129]

Encouraged by this victory, NAACP legal strategists decided to challenge the state laws authorizing the parties to determine primary voter qualifications. Test cases were initiated in Virginia, Florida, and Arkansas. The litigation was successful in the lower courts in the first two cases, but failed to reach the Supreme Court for a definitive ruling.[130] Texas provided that opportunity when the legislature in 1927 adopted a statute providing that "every political party . . . through its State Executive Committee shall have the power to prescribe the qualifications of its own members." When the Democratic state executive committee proceeded to adopt a resolution that "all white democrats . . . and none other" shall be allowed to participate in the Democratic primary, Dr. Nixon filed a new challenge that reached the Court in 1932. The justices again skirted the Fifteenth Amendment question. And they were sharply divided over even the equal protection issue. Four dissenters held that political parties were voluntary private associations that could determine their own membership rules. Speaking for the five-man majority, Justice Benjamin Cardozo explicitly reserved judgment on "[w]hether a political party in Texas has the inherent power today without restraint by any law to determine its own membership" and "[w]hether the effect" of the extensive regulations governing primaries "has been to work . . . a transformation of the concept of a political party as a voluntary association." Rather, he rested invalidation of the law upon the narrow ground that whatever inherent power a party had to prescribe membership qualifications lay in the state convention, not the state executive committee. That legislation had been thought required to give the committees that authority showed their lack of any such inherent power. "The pith of the matter," Cardozo explained, "is simply this, that when those agencies are invested with an authority independent of the will of the association in whose name they undertake to speak, they become to that extent the organs of the State itself, the repositories of official power." Accordingly, "[d]elegates of the State's power have discharged their official functions in such a way as to discriminate invidiously between white citizens and black" in violation of the Fourteenth Amendment.[131]

Cardozo strongly intimated that action barring Negro voting in the Democratic primaries by the party's state convention would raise a different issue. Taking the hint, the 1932 meeting of the Democratic state convention adopted a resolution limiting party membership to "white citizens." A group of Houston blacks led by Richard R. Grovey filed a test case without the support—and even against the advice—of the NAACP national office. Their attorney argued that extensive legislative regulation had transformed the primaries into state-conducted proceedings. And underlining how victory in the primary was in Texas tantamount to election, he had contended that the exclusion of black voters contravened the Fifteenth Amendment. In a stinging blow to supporters of Negro rights, a unanimous Supreme Court in 1935 in *Grovey v. Townsend* brushed aside the challenge. "The argument is [made] that as a negro may not be denied a ballot at a general election on account of his race or color, if exclusion from the primary renders his vote at the general election insignificant and useless, the result is to deny him the suffrage altogether." That argument, Justice Owen J. Roberts replied dismissively, "is to confuse the privilege of membership in a party with the right to vote for one who is to hold a public office." He similarly denied that the convention's exclusion of blacks from the primary constituted state action within the Fourteenth Amendment. He pointed out that in Texas the party paid the expenses of the primary, furnished the ballots, and counted the vote. He emphasized even more that the Texas Supreme Court had ruled that under state law the Democratic party was a voluntary private association whose supreme governing authority was the state convention. While "true that Texas has by its laws elaborately provided for the expression of party preference as to nominees, has required that preference to be expressed in a certain form of voting, and has attempted in minute detail to protect the suffrage of the members of the organization against fraud, it is equally true that the primary is a party primary."[132] And in 1937, the justices continued this formalist, shuttered-eye approach by reaffirming the constitutionality of the poll tax.[133]

But there was one area where the Supreme Court, beginning in the 1920s, did act in defense of Negro rights—that of criminal procedure. Reflecting his devotion to maintaining law and order against private violence, Chief Justice Taft personally was instrumental in lining up a seven-to-two majority in 1923 to overturn in response to a habeas corpus petition the murder conviction of a group of Arkansas black sharecroppers and tenant farmers in a trial held in a mob-dominated atmosphere. The same issue had arisen in 1915 in the famous Leo Frank case, where the Jewish manager and part-owner of an Atlanta, Georgia, pencil factory had been found guilty of the murder of a young girl employee on the basis of dubious testimony in a trial held under the menace of a threatening mob. A seven-to-two majority then—over the dissents of Hughes and Holmes—had refused to question the finding of the Georgia Supreme Court that no violation of constitutional rights had occurred. While shying from going so far as to hold expressly such state appellate court determinations conclusive, Justice Mahlon Pitney treated their findings as practically definitive.[134] Speaking now for the majority, Holmes held in *Moore v. Dempsey* that the federal courts had a duty to look beyond simply the formal procedures followed in state criminal trials to see if constitutional rights had been in fact violated. Equally important, he laid down the so-called "fair trial" standard as the test for whether or not a state proceeding satisfied the due process requirement of the Fourteenth Amendment. That requirement was not met when the trial was "a mask"—with "counsel, jury and judge swept to the fatal end by an irresistible wave of public passion."[135]

Under Taft's successor Charles Evans Hughes, the Court extended its scrutiny of the treatment given black defendants by the southern courts. The first landmark decision—*Powell v. Alabama* in 1932—grew out of the notorious Scottsboro boys case where a group of Negro youths were convicted of raping two white girls of doubtful reputation on even more dubious testimony. In a striking opinion, Justice George Sutherland for a seven-to-two majority reversed the convictions on the ground that the trial court's failure to afford the defendants effective assistance of counsel was a denial of due process.[136] In 1936, Chief Justice Hughes spoke for a unanimous bench in *Brown v. Mississippi* reversing the murder convictions of three black defendants based upon confessions that had been extorted by brutal third-degree methods. Few cases that reached the Court revealed a more grisly set of facts. One defendant had been twice hanged by the neck from the limb of a tree, whipped, and then beaten before confessing. The others had been forced to strip and were whipped with a leather belt to which metal buckles were attached before giving in. The police officers involved admitted at the trial what had happened. And although the Mississippi Supreme Court affirmed the convictions on the technicality that the defense had failed to move formally at the trial for exclusion of the confessions, the two dissenting judges put on the record the sordid details. While acknowledging that the states retained substantial leeway in matters of criminal procedure, Hughes underlined that such latitude was limited by the principles of due process underlying constitutional government. "The rack and torture chamber may not be substituted for the witness stand."[137]

Between came an even more epoch-making decision in the second Scottsboro boys appeal—*Norris v. Alabama* in 1935. After *Powell* remanded the defendants for retrial, their defense team headed by the famed criminal lawyer Samuel Leibowitz centered its attack upon the exclusion of blacks from Alabama juries. Witnesses testified that never in their memories had a black served on a grand or petit jury in their counties; jury selection officials admitted placing the notation "col." after the names of blacks that appeared on the preliminary lists from which the jury roll was selected; a handwriting expert found that the jury roll had been tampered with by the later addition of the names of six blacks to give the appearance of not having been racially exclusionary. This evidence had no influence in the state courts. But Leibowitz brought the jury roll books to his oral argument before the Supreme Court. As the justices peered at the added names under a magnifying glass, the staunchly conservative senior associate justice Willis Van Devanter was heard to exclaim: "Why it's as plain as punch." For a unanimous Court, Hughes had no difficulty in finding that there was overwhelming evidence of deliberate exclusion of blacks from the grand jury. Although there was not the same hard evidence about the selection of the petit jury, he concluded that the fact that no blacks had served upon such juries in anyone's memory was sufficient to infer a pattern of systematic discrimination. *Norris* marked the passing of the all-white jury as a bulwark of the South's caste system. "But it was much more," Benno C. Schmidt, Jr., has written. "It heralded a new day for the recognition of federal rights in state criminal cases."[138]

Norris was announced on April 1, 1935, the same day that the Court handed down its similarly unanimous ruling in *Grovey v. Townsend* upholding the Texas white primary. The NAACP's field secretary went so far as to suggest that the justices had "made a trade."[139] The coincidence, however, symbolized the conflicting pressures tugging at the Court at a time of transition in its, and the country's, attitude on the race question. But there were powerful forces at work during the 1930s that would inaugurate a new era for black rights—the growing Negro vote in the North; the widening split in the Democratic party between its New Deal and southern Bourbon wings; the rise of the Congress of Industrial Organizations; the priority given the black plight by the political left; the mounting attack upon the intellectual rationale for racism by social and natural scientists; and the publicity accompanying the fight for a federal anti-lynching law.[140] Working in the same direction was a heightened mood of black militancy. The NAACP's lobbying in 1930 against Senate confirmation of President Herbert Hoover's nomination of John J. Parker of North Carolina to the high court bench had for the first time made racial attitudes of a Supreme Court appointee a major public issue.[141] And in mid–1935 Charles H. Houston, the dean of the Howard University Law School, joined the NAACP staff as its new Special Counsel. Up to that time, the Association's legal efforts were more *ad hoc* responses to initiatives by individuals and local groups than a planned and organized campaign. Poor coordination, lack of adequate funding, and the difficulty of attracting the services of top-flight legal talent too often resulted in flawed presentation at the crucial trial court stage. Under Houston's direction the NAACP would launch a skillfully managed program of litigation that in the years that followed rewrote the law.[142]

4 The Criminal Defendant

Before the 1930s, the United States had developed two largely distinct and separate bodies of law in the area of criminal procedure. One was governed by the United States Constitution, Supreme Court interpretations of its provisions, and rulings by that tribunal under its extraconstitutional supervisory authority over the federal court system. The other was governed by state constitutions, statutes, and court decisions. Although the Supreme Court could, and did, review challenged state laws and procedures under the due process clause of the Fourteenth Amendment, such attacks were rarely successful.[1] The full protection afforded by the United States Constitution to the accused extended only to persons facing action under a federal statute, plus persons living in the District of Columbia, the so-called incorporated territories within the continental United States, and Alaska.[2] Those guarantees fell into three broad categories. The first were those found in the original text, i.e., the prohibitions against ex post facto laws and bills of attainder and the requirement in Article III, Section 2 that the "Trial of all Crimes, except in Cases of Impeachment, shall be by Jury." The second were the independently listed rights in the Fourth through Eighth Amendments. The third was the sweeping declaration in the Fifth Amendment that "[N]o person shall . . . be deprived of life, liberty, or property, without due process of law."[3]

The leading pre–Civil War ruling dealing with the meaning of due process laid down a two-pronged guide: "We must examine the constitution itself, to see whether [a given practice] be in conflict with any of its provisions. If not found to be so, we must look to those settled usages and modes of proceeding in the common and statute law . . . of our ancestors."[4] But the post–Civil War Court balked at including the procedural guarantees of the Bill of Rights as essential parts of due process so as not to handcuff the states via the Fourteenth Amendment. "[W]hile the cardinal principles of justice are immutable," Justice Henry Billings Brown explained, "the methods by which justice is administered are subject to constant fluctuation, and . . . the Constitution of the United States, which is necessarily and to a large extent inflexible . . . , should not be so construed as to deprive the States of the power to so amend their laws as to make them conform to the wishes of the citizens."[5] Nor were the justices willing to accept history as a definitive guide lest—as Justice William H. Moody pointed out in *Twining v. New Jersey*— "the procedure of the first half of the seventeenth century would be fastened upon the American jurisprudence like a straight-jacket."[6] Instead the Court relied upon the amorphous and flexible standard of what was variously termed "those fundamental principles of liberty and justice which lie at the base of all our civil and political institutions," "certain immutable principles of justice," or "an unchangeable principle of universal justice."[7]

At a minimum, due process required "that there be a regular course of judicial proceedings, which imply that the party to be affected shall have notice and an opportunity to be heard."[8] Notice assumed "that the indictment shall apprise him of the crime charged with such reasonable certainty that he can make his defence."[9] Related was the so-called void-for-vagueness doctrine: that a criminal statute must not be so ill-defined and uncertain that "men of common intelligence must necessarily guess at its meaning and differ as to its application."[10] But whether or not those requirements were met was a matter for *ad hoc* determination depending upon the circumstances. The vagueness rule was defined as demanding no more than "that a fair warning should be given to the world in language that the common world will understand, of what the law intends to do if a certain line is passed."[11] And a statute was not automatically invalid even if "the crime thus defined . . . contains in its definition an element of degree as to which estimates may differ."[12] Similar flexibility applied regarding the sufficiency of indictments. Although the rule-of-thumb was that when a statute defined the offense in general terms the indictment "must descend to particulars,"[13] the "true test" remained "not whether it could have been made more definite and certain, but whether it contains the elements of the offense intended to be charged."[14]

Although the Court never directly ruled on this point, various *dicta* assumed that the presumption of innocence with its corollary that the prosecution must prove guilt beyond a reasonable doubt was constitutionally protected.[15] A different—though related—issue was if punishment could be imposed without proof of criminal intent: what the common law termed *mens rea* ("guilty mind") and Blackstone more graphically called "vicious will." The Court found no constitutional bar to statutes imposing strict liability for actions—"that he who shall do them shall do them at his peril and will not be heard to plead in defense good faith or ignorance."[16] What about a statutory presumption whereby a particular inference is deemed to follow from the proof of another fact? Due process was violated when the statute set up

a so-called irrebuttable presumption—that is, made proof of one fact conclusive evidence of another fact—because the defendant was denied his right
to an assumption of innocence.[17] But a statute that simply made proof of
the first fact *prima facie* evidence of the second with the party affected given
the opportunity to rebut the presumption was permissible so long as "there
shall be some rational connection between the fact proved and the ultimate
fact presumed, and that the inference of one fact from proof of another shall
not be so unreasonable as to be a purely arbitrary mandate."[18]

Although recent decisions have linked the ban against the admission in
evidence of coerced confessions to the Fifth Amendment's privilege against
self-incrimination, the Court historically—with one exception that was never
followed up—dealt with confession cases upon independent due process
grounds.[19] At first, the Court applied the traditional common-law rule of
reliability. Even voluntary confessions had to be accompanied by independent corroboratory evidence.[20] Forced confessions were regarded as inadmissible because of their inherent untrustworthiness—that is, the strong
likelihood that the suspect had made an untrue confession simply to save
himself from further maltreatment. Accordingly, the test for the admission
of an out-of-court confession became its voluntariness.[21] A 1924 decision,
however, broadened the definition of "compulsion" to include extreme psy-
chological pressure (i.e., repeated and intensive interrogation of an ill suspect) without even raising the question of the confession's authenticity.[22]
And in 1936, the Court appeared in *Brown v. Mississippi* to adopt as the basis
for review of confessions the so-called procedural fairness standard. But the
ruling, probably because the brutality involved was so blatant as to make
the resulting confessions inadmissible whichever standard was applied, failed
explicitly to repudiate the trustworthiness/voluntariness test—a failure that
would constitute a source of much later confusion.[23]

The Supreme Court did not do much in the way of interpreting the
independently listed guarantees of the Bill of Rights until the latter years
of the nineteenth century. In the first place, there arose relatively few criminal cases in the federal courts after the Supreme Court held in 1812 that
there were no federal common-law crimes.[24] That holding left prosecutable
in the federal courts outside of the territories and District of Columbia a
narrow range of federal statutes, involving mostly white-collar crimes such
as counterfeiting, bribery, and fraud. Second, before 1889 lower federal court
judgments in criminal cases were appealable to the Supreme Court in only
a few statutory-defined situations.[25] Thus, the Court began dealing with
criminal law issues in a large way at a time when the majority of justices
were strongly imbued with safeguarding individual rights against governmental authority. And not until the adoption of national prohibition in 1919
did the federal courts have to deal with the kinds of law enforcement problems that were the staple of the state courts. At first, this experience appeared
to incline the Court to take a more permissive attitude toward law enforce-

ment practices. But the rapid disenchantment with the noble experiment led the Court to shift in favor of imposing more stringent restrictions upon police behavior.[26]

The most extensively litigated of the Bill of Rights guarantees was the Fourth Amendment. And if that Amendment is today the most confused and chaotic area of constitutional jurisprudence, the source lies in its pre-1937 development. The Fourth Amendment consists of two clauses separated by a comma: "The right of the people to be secure in their persons, houses, papers, and effects, against unreasonable searches and seizures, shall not be violated, and no Warrants shall issue, but upon probable cause, supported by Oath or affirmation, and particularly describing the place to be searched, and the persons or things to be seized." The target was the English practice of general warrants authorizing indiscriminate searches without limit as to time or objective; the most notorious example was the writs of assistance utilized by British officials to enforce the customs laws in the pre-Revolutionary period. But the debates at the time of the Bill of Rights gave scant guidance to what the Amendment's framers had substantively in mind. There were three possible interpretations of the text. One was that a search or seizure to be lawful must be made in accord with the warrant requirements of the second clause. Another is that the first clause's prohibition against "unreasonable searches and seizures" meant that some were not permitted even under warrant. The third is that the first clause authorized warrantless searches and seizures if "reasonable" in a given circumstance.[27]

In the first Supreme Court test of its scope and meaning, Chief Justice John Marshall read the Amendment broadly as applying not simply to searches for things but to the arrest of persons.[28] And while the amendment did not define who could issue a warrant, the assumption from the first was that its issuance was the responsibility of a judicial officer. The Amendment stipulated that a warrant must "particularly" describe the person, place, or articles affected. A search warrant calling for the seizure of one thing would not, therefore, authorize the seizure of something else.[29] The only exception was when the name of the person was unknown; then a warrant could be issued in a fictitious name ("John Doe") so long as accompanied by a sufficient physical description.[30] The tricky question was what constituted "probable cause." The classic definition of the Court was "if the apparent facts set out in the affidavit are such that a reasonably discreet and prudent man would be led to believe that there was a commission of the offense charged."[31] How much evidence was required for that purpose? Marshall had suggested that probable cause was satisfied by "circumstances which warrant suspicion."[32] But later decisions laid down a more stringent rule: probable cause required less that the showing of guilt beyond a reasonable doubt demanded for a conviction, but more than "suspicion." Nor was "mere affirmance of suspicion or belief" sufficient; the police officer requesting the warrant must present "adequate supporting facts."[33] A warrant issued without probable cause was not made valid by the later discovery of incriminating evidence: "A search prosecuted in violation of the Constitution is not made lawful by what it brings to light."[34]

But were all warrantless searches and seizures "unreasonable"? The Court followed the common law's more permissive approach to the arrest of persons than to the search of a place.[35] The rationale was that a suspect liable to arrest could flee while a building was stationary. An officer could make a warrantless arrest for a felony on the basis of probable cause.[36] He could arrest without warrant when a misdemeanor involving a breach of the peace occurred in his presence. The felony/misdemeanor distinction made sense at a time when the two types of offenses were sharply differentiated according to relative seriousness. Over time, however, legislatures added to the list of felonies crimes less serious than many misdemeanors and to the list of misdemeanors crimes more serious than many felonies. As a result, many jurisdictions modified the rule to permit warrantless arrest for misdemeanors occurring in an officer's presence whether or not a breach of the peace was involved. And the Supreme Court appeared to give its approval in a 1925 case involving the warrantless arrest of the driver of a car which when searched was found to contain bootleg liquor.[37] By contrast, the Court took a harder line in defense of property rights. In the first place, the Fourth Amendment was read as protecting not simply natural persons but corporations.[38] More important, the Court took the position that a warrantless search of a private dwelling or business premises—"notwithstanding facts unquestionably showing probable cause . . . that an article sought is concealed"—was "in itself unreasonable and abhorrent to our laws."[39]

Even here, however, there were exceptions. One—which Justice Holmes called "as old as the common law"—was in open fields.[40] In 1925, a seven-to-two majority in *Carroll v. United States* approved the warrantless search of an automobile moving on the highway that officers had probable cause to believe was carrying bootleg liquor. Putting heavy emphasis upon what was read as congressional authorization for such action, the Court justified the exception on the ground that if the officers had to wait for a warrant the vehicle might disappear.[41] And the same rule was applied to include the warrantless search of a parked automobile since the officers did not know when the car might be moved.[42] A third exception—accepted in 1914 in *dicta* in *Weeks v. United States*—allowed a warrantless search incident to a lawful arrest.[43] Under the common law, such a search was permitted to protect the arresting officer from concealed weapons and/or to prevent destruction of evidence. What became the focus of controversy was its scope. In 1925, the Court expanded the scope to include not simply the suspect's person but the area under his physical control.[44] The Court next appeared to allow a broader search extending to "all parts of the premises used for the unlawful purpose,"[45] but then shifted to the more restrictive position of limiting the articles liable to seizure to those "visible and accessible and in the offender's immediate custody." The result was a lack of adequate guidance to police officers on where the line must be drawn. "There is," the Court acknowledged, "no formula for the determination of reasonableness. Each case is to be decided on its own facts and circumstances."[46]

On the other hand, were all searches and seizures made upon a properly issued warrant automatically "reasonable"? In the landmark 1886 case of *Boyd v. United States*, Justice Joseph P. Bradley for a seven-to-two majority answered no. Two New York merchants in a forfeiture proceeding for violation of the customs laws had been ordered by the trial judge on the authority of an 1874 statute to produce documents from the firm's records as part of the government's case. Although a prior Supreme Court decision had ruled the Fourth Amendment not applicable to civil proceedings,[47] Bradley declared that a forfeiture proceeding "though technically a civil proceeding, is in substance and effect a criminal one." Nor was he bound by the historical meaning of search as involving a physical entry onto the premises. He rationalized that "a compulsory production of a man's private papers . . . accomplishes the substantial object of . . . search and seizure . . . in forcing from a party evidence against himself." Still more broadly, he defined the Fourth Amendment as prohibiting "all invasions . . . [of] the privacies of life." Treating the judicial order as equivalent to a search warrant, he proceeded to hold that the Amendment limited searches and seizures to so-called contraband—articles legally prohibited to the possessor and thus to which he had no property right. And he drew upon Lord Camden's 1765 opinion in the famous English case of *Entick v. Carrington* to link the Fourth Amendment to the Fifth Amendment's privilege against self-incrimination. Ergo, the search was illegal under the Fourth Amendment and the evidence thus acquired inadmissible under the Fifth.[48]

Few decisions have been more frequently cited than *Boyd*. Much of its attraction to latter-day activist-minded justices lay in Bradley's rhetoric about the duty of the courts to defend the liberty of the citizens against governmental encroachment. But another reason for that attraction—even if unconsciously so—was how Bradley's opinion represented a striking illustration of audacious judicial lawmaking. His definition of the scope of the Fourth Amendment represented a revolutionary stretching of the traditional meaning of search. He ignored the long-standing common-law rule allowing the admission of otherwise competent evidence regardless of how acquired. His linkage of the ban against unreasonable searches with the privilege against compulsory self-incrimination was historically incorrect. He misread the leading precedent upon which he relied: Camden's opinion was directed against the generality of the challenged warrant and its lack of basis in probable cause. His assumption that the records called for were the property of the defendants to which the government had no right was wrong on the facts. Under its power over foreign commerce, Congress had the authority to lay down the conditions under which imports were brought into the country.

And Congress had required importers to furnish the government essentially the same information as the documents the court ordered produced—a requirement that the defendants had not complied with. Last, the decision foreshadowed future Fourth Amendment rulings in protecting the guilty rather than the innocent.

The implications of *Boyd* were immense. One was the limitation of the articles subject to search and seizure to contraband. At first, the Court read *Boyd* narrowly as applying only to direct testimonial compulsion not to papers taken under a valid search warrant.[49] In 1921, however, the justices unanimously ruled in *Gouled v. United States* that the Fourth Amendment prohibited the search for papers or things of "evidential value only." A federal officer armed with a search warrant had taken papers showing the suspect's involvement in a conspiracy to defraud the government. The layman unattuned to the higher judicial wisdom might think that the purpose of a search was exactly that. But the Court restricted the target of any search to articles whose possession by the suspect was "unlawful"; even a warrant could not "be used as a means of gaining access to a man's house or office solely for purpose of making search to secure evidence to be used against him." *Gouled* did leave an opening permitting the seizure of legally owned articles that were an "agency or instrumentality" of a crime.[50] But later decisions drew such subtle distinctions about what constituted "instrumentalities" of a crime that law enforcement officers were left without meaningful guidance.[51] As with the ambiguity surrounding the scope of a warrantless search incident to arrest, what made this uncertainty so troublesome was that if the officer made a mistake the accused would go free thanks to another *Boyd*-derived rule: the inadmissibility of evidence acquired by an illegal search and seizure.

As late as 1904, the Court continued to adhere to the common-law principle allowing the admission of competent evidence no matter how acquired.[52] In 1914, however, a unanimous Court laid down in *Weeks v. United States* the so-called exclusionary rule forbidding admission in the federal courts of evidence found during an illegal search. In his opinion, Justice William R. Day was not explicit about whether the rule's basis was the Fourth Amendment, the Fifth, or the Supreme Court's extraconstitutional authority over the federal court system. Nor was he clear about its rationale. There was the suggestion that its purpose was to preserve the integrity of the courts by refusing to give judicial sanction to police misconduct. But what appeared his major justification was that the exclusionary rule was the only way of enforcing the Fourth Amendment: if evidence acquired through an illegal search were admissible, the Fourth Amendment would be "of no value, and . . . might as well be stricken from the Constitution."[53] And in 1920, the Court took *Weeks* a step farther by adopting what became known as the "fruit of the poisonous tree" doctrine—barring prosecution use not simply of any evidence acquired by an illegal search, but of any knowledge derived from such a search. "The essence of a provision forbidding the acquisition of evidence in a certain way," Justice Holmes declared in sweeping terms, "is that not merely evidence so acquired shall not be used before the court but that it shall not be used at all."[54]

Two possible escape hatches remained in the exclusionary rule. One was opened by the Court's controversial seven-to-two decision in 1921 in *Burdeau v. McDowell* permitting the admission of evidence acquired through private theft and then turned over to federal authorities.[55] *Weeks* left open a potentially more significant loophole by allowing the admission of evidence found by local police officers before the arrival of the federal officers on the scene despite their lack of a search warrant.[56] And that same year, the justices explicitly held that the Fourth Amendment did not apply to the states.[57] But the Court in the late 1920s narrowed this opening. In one case—*Byars v. United States*—a federal prohibition agent accompanied state officers on a search under a state warrant that did not meet federal standards. A unanimous Court agreed that because of the agent's involvement "the search in substance and effect was a joint operation of the local and federal officers." The second—*Gambino v. United States*—involved a warrantless search for liquor by New York state police of a car without probable cause. Although federal officers had not participated, the Court concluded that since New York had repealed its own prohibition law the "wrongful" actions "were made solely on behalf of the United States." As Justice George Sutherland intoned in *Byars*, the protection of the Fourth Amendment "is not to be impaired by judicial sanction of equivocal methods, which, regarded superficially, may seem to escape the challenge of illegality but which, in reality, strike at the substance of the constitutional right."[58]

The development of devices allowing eavesdropping without physical entry into a suspect's home or place of business added a further complication.[59] The first case raising the question came before the Court in 1928 as a result of the Treasury Department's reliance on telephone wiretaps in enforcing the prohibition law. The defendants in *Olmstead v. United States* had been convicted on the basis of incriminating conversations overheard by wiretaps on their phones. A five-to-four majority of the justices upheld the convictions on the ground that no physical trespass had taken place. "There was," Chief Justice Taft explained, "no searching. . . . The evidence was secured by the use of the sense of hearing and that alone. There was no entry of the houses or offices of the defendants." Nor did he find any seizure. That term applied to the taking of "material things" such as a person's papers or effects; all that was involved here was the overhearing of spoken words. And even though the wiretapping had taken place in a state where such action was illegal, he balked at extending the exclusionary rule to that situation unless Congress expressly required doing so. "A standard which would forbid the reception of evidence if obtained by other than nice ethical conduct by government officials," he concluded, "would make society suffer and give criminals greater immunity than has been known heretofore."[60]

Although expressing doubt if wiretapping came within the Fourth Amendment, Holmes waxed indignant about the "dirty business" of allowing federal officials to violate the law. "I think it a less evil that some criminals should escape than that the Government should play an ignoble part." Brandeis echoed that complaint. "Decency, security and liberty alike demand that government officials shall be subjected to the same rules of conduct that are commands to the citizen." More broadly, he argued that the purpose behind the Fourth Amendment was the protection of individual privacy: "the right to be let alone—the most comprehensive of rights and the right most valued by civilized men." Accordingly, its scope should not be limited to such past abuses as physical entry into homes, seizure of papers, and torture of suspects. "Subtler and more far-reaching means of invading privacy have become available to the Government. Discovery and invention have made it possible for the Government, by means far more effective than stretching upon the rack, to obtain disclosure in court of what is whispered in the closet. . . . [W]rits of assistance and general warrants are but puny instruments of tyranny and oppression when compared with wire-tapping." Therefore, he concluded, harking back to *Boyd*, "every unjustifiable intrusion by the Government upon the privacy of the individual, whatever the means employed, must be deemed a violation of the Fourth Amendment. And the use, as evidence in a criminal proceeding, of facts ascertained by such intrusion must be deemed a violation of the Fifth."[61]

The majority ruling was strongly attacked by most commentators. Taft himself suggested that Congress could protect the secrecy of telephone conversations by making inadmissible evidence acquired by wiretaps. And Brandeis had pointed to a provision in the Radio Act of 1927 that "no person not being authorized by the sender shall intercept any message or divulge or publish the contents, substance, purport, effect, or meaning of such intercepted message to any person" as evidence of a public policy in support of his position.[62] A similar provision was included in Section 605 of the Federal Communications Act of 1934.[63] There is no evidence that Congress when doing so had intended to bar official wiretapping. On the contrary, the lawmakers had refused to pass any of the bills introduced in the aftermath of *Olmstead* to outlaw use of wiretap evidence. In 1937, however, a seven-man majority of the Supreme Court read Section 605 expansively to accomplish that result. Holding that "no person" included federal agents, Justice Owen J. Roberts ruled that the statute prohibited the admission in federal court trials of the contents of wiretapped telephone conversations. In response to the argument that Congress had intended the ban to apply simply to private individuals not law enforcement officers, he replied that, if so, Congress should have been explicit. Given its silence, he rationalized, "Congress may have thought it less important that some offenders should go unwhipped of justice than that officers should resort to methods deemed inconsistent with ethical standards and destructive of personal liberty."[64]

Boyd had involved an expansive reading not simply of the Fourth Amendment, but the Fifth Amendment's guarantee that "[n]o person . . . shall be compelled in any criminal case to be a witness against himself."[65] Literally read, those words appeared to mean simply that a defendant in a criminal trial could not be compelled to give oral testimony against himself. A long debate has gone on among historians over whether the framers of the Bill of Rights intended the privilege to have a more latitudinarian scope.[66] The most recent, and thorough, study of the evidence concludes yes. The source of the provision was the common-law maxim *nemo tenetur seipsum prodere* ("no man is bound to accuse himself"). The development of the concept was closely linked with the seventeenth-century protests against the practice of the so-called prerogative courts of administering *ex officio* oaths whereby a person was put on oath without a charge and questioned for the purpose of finding wrongdoing. The victim was caught in a trap: to refuse to take oath or to answer after having done so made him liable to punishment for contempt; to take the oath and answer truthfully often meant to convict oneself and one's associates; to take the oath and then lie was a sin that carried the threat of eternal damnation. In 1641, Parliament prohibited ecclesiastical courts from administering oaths obliging anyone to confess a crime. By the early eighteenth century, the ban against the interrogation of suspects under oath had been extended to the common-law courts. The principle that a suspect had the legal right not to answer incriminating questions appears to have become embodied in the common law of all the states at the time of the Constitution. There is evidence that this rule applied even to witnesses in a case.[67]

Apart from this history—of which the Supreme Court remained largely ignorant[68]—the strongest argument that the clause meant more than its literal reading would indicate is that the provision would have been a nullity if limited to giving a right of silence to the defendant in a criminal trial. The common-law rule at the time the Amendment was adopted held that a party to a litigation was not a competent witness because his testimony was tainted by self-interest. The first state to allow criminal defendants to take the stand in their own defense did so in 1864; Congress did not authorize defendants in federal criminal trials to testify at their own request until 1878.[69] Opponents of such grants of testimonial competence argued that since no jury would believe the innocence of a person who refused to testify in his own defense, the defendant would be compelled to testify, making his privilege against self-incrimination worthless. In response, Congress in its 1878 legislation took pains to stipulate that a defendant's failure to testify "shall not create any presumption against him."[70] The Supreme Court read this provision as barring any comment by the prosecution or court upon a defendant's failure to testify.[71] What remained ambiguous was if the no-comment rule was constitutionally required. While *Twining* assumed for purposes of argument that comment by a trial judge on a defendant's failure to testify violated the privilege against self-incrimination, the opinion went on to add: "We do not intend, however, to lend any countenance to the truth of that assumption. . . . The authorities upon the question are in conflict."[72]

Except for one case that was never followed up, the Court did not extend the privilege of self-incrimination to cover out-of-court involuntary confessions. The broadening of the privilege came in different areas. One was its expansion in *Boyd* to apply to the compulsory production of private papers, records, and the like. The second, even more important, expansion came six years later in *Counselman v. Hitchcock* to cover witnesses before any official investigating body. Although American courts had upheld the refusal of witnesses to testify because of possible self-incrimination, they had done so on common-law, rather than constitutional, grounds. Only a few scattered precedents linked that privilege to state constitutional provisions analogous to the Fifth Amendment's. Even *Boyd* had involved defendants in what the Court defined as a criminal proceeding. *Counselman* grew out of the invocation of the Fifth Amendment by a recalcitrant witness who had been called to testify in a grand jury investigation of possible violations of the 1887 Interstate Commerce Act. The Supreme Court declared in sweeping terms:

It is impossible that the meaning of the constitutional provision can only be, that a person shall not be compelled to be a witness against himself in a criminal prosecution against himself. It would doubtless cover such cases; but it is not limited to them. The object was to insure that a person should not be compelled, when acting as a witness in any investigation, to give testimony which might tend to show that he himself had committed a crime. The privilege is limited to criminal matters, but it is as broad as the mischief against which it seeks to guard.[73]

Along with upholding the application of the privilege to such a witness, *Counselman* read its scope broadly as covering not simply testimony which was incriminating in itself but testimony which was likely to lead to finding incriminating evidence. Combined with *Boyd*'s bar against compulsory production of private papers, the result was to shackle any meaningful federal investigation of business malpractices. But political realities forced the Court to beat a retreat. One loophole was opened in 1906 when a bare five-man majority in *Hale v. Henkel* held that the privilege against self-incrimination was limited to natural persons, not corporations. Since "the corporation is a creature of the State," the state retained the right "to investigate . . . and find out whether it has exceeded its powers." Therefore, a duly authorized investigating body could compel the production of documents belonging to a corporation unless the request was so unreasonable as to paralyze the operation of the business.[74] And an officer of a corporation holding such papers in a representative capacity could not invoke the privilege on his own behalf even though the documents may disclose guilt on his part.[75] Justice Holmes went on to assume in conclusory, almost offhand fashion in *Schenck v. United States* that the same rule applied to any collective body, incorporated or not, such as a political party.[76]

Counselman left open a second loophole. The government had argued that even if the privilege against self-incrimination applied to witnesses, Counselman was still required to answer because of an immunity statute providing that "no discovery or evidence obtained from a party or witness by means of a judicial proceeding" here or abroad "shall be given in evidence, or in any manner used against him or his property . . . in any court of the United States, in any criminal proceeding, or for the enforcement of any penalty or forfeiture."[77] The question, therefore, was whether such a grant of immunity was an adequate substitute for the privilege against self-incrimination. The Court answered no because the statute left open the possibility of using the admissions of the witness as a basis for unearthing sufficient independent evidence for a prosecution. "[L]egislation cannot abridge a constitutional privilege," Justice Samuel Blatchford reasoned, " . . . at least unless it is so broad as to have the same extent in scope and effect." But he suggested that the answer would be yes if witnesses were given what is called full transactional immunity—"absolute immunity against future prosecution for the offence to which the question relates."[78] Taking the hint, Congress proceeded to enact a new immunity statute covering Interstate Commerce Commission investigations providing that "no person shall be prosecuted or subjected to any penalty or forfeiture for or on account of any transaction, matter or thing, concerning which he may testify or produce evidence."[79]

When another railroad official still balked at testifying notwithstanding the new statute, the justices were sharply divided. The dissenters in *Brown v. Walker* argued that the privilege against self-incrimination gave the witness an absolute right to silence. But Justice Henry Billings Brown for the five-man majority held "that, if the testimony sought cannot possibly be used as a basis for, or in aid of, a criminal prosecution against the witness, the rule ceases to apply." He similarly dismissed the argument that the guarantee extended to compulsory testimony that would bring a witness into disrepute:

[I]f the proposed testimony is material to the issue on trial, the fact that the testimony may tend to degrade the witness in public estimation does not exempt him from the duty of disclosure. A person who commits a criminal act is bound to contemplate the consequences of exposure to his good name and reputation, and ought not to call upon the courts to protect that which he has himself esteemed to be of such little value. The safety and welfare of the entire community should not be put into the scale against the reputation of a self-confessed criminal.

The third major argument by the dissenters was that the statute failed to provide a witness protection from prosecution in the state courts. Brown skirted the issue by reading the statute as doing so.[80] But the Court would later backtrack from that position to hold that Congress neither could nor was required to grant such immunity. The privilege was limited to compulsion to accuse oneself of crimes "arising within the same jurisdiction and under the same sovereignty."[81]

The federal rules governing the privilege against self-incrimination may be summarized as follows: A witness could not refuse to appear.[82] He simply could object to specific questions. In each instance, his claim had to be passed on by the court—the witness was not the final judge.[83] If he admitted an incriminating fact, then he was deemed to have waived the privilege regarding further questions on that matter. On the other hand, his denial of an incriminating fact, as contrasted with an affirmative admission, did not require him to answer follow-up questions.[84] In one sense, the privilege of the defendant in a criminal trial was even more extensive. He could refuse to take the stand at all. If he did testify, however, he must answer relevant questions upon cross-examination.[85] The most important limitation was that the privilege did not protect against making the defendant himself physical evidence for the purpose of identification via fingerprinting, photographs, and the like. In the leading case—*Holt v. United States*—the defendant asked to exclude the admission of testimony that a blouse put on over his protest fitted him. For a unanimous Court, Holmes replied that "the prohibition of compelling a man in a criminal court to be a witness against himself is a prohibition of the use of physical or moral compulsion to extort communications from him, not an exclusion of his body as evidence when it may be material."[86]

The first clause of the Fifth Amendment requiring indictment by a grand jury "for a capital, or otherwise infamous crime . . . except in cases arising in the land or naval forces . . . when in actual service in time of War or public danger" was not a major source of dispute. Given the explicitness of this guarantee, only two significant issues came before the Court. One was whether the same evidentiary standards applied at the grand jury level as at criminal trials. The Court's answer was no, an indictment was still valid even if supported by evidence that would be inadmissible at the trial since the grand jury simply decides if there is a *prima facie* case warranting holding the accused for trial.[87] The more troublesome question was what constituted an "infamous" crime? In the leading case, the Court rejected the common-law rule making the nature of the crime the determining factor in favor of the severity of the punishment. But the justices shied from laying down hard-and-fast guidelines so as to accommodate changes in public opinion.[88] Section 335 of the Criminal Code of 1909 defined all offenses punishable by imprisonment for a term exceeding one year as felonies, the rest as misdemeanors. And in 1930 Congress amended that section to make petty offenses not requiring a grand jury indictment those where the penalty did not exceed a $500 fine and/or six months' confinement in a common jail without hard labor.[89] But the Court held that a misdemeanor carrying a heavier penalty did not automatically involve "infamous punishment."[90]

By contrast, the Fifth Amendment's provision "nor shall any person be subject for the same offence to be twice put in jeopardy of life or limb" plunged the Court into a morass of complicated problems. The clause was a restatement of the common-law maxim *nemo debet bis vexari pro una et eadema causa* ("no one should be twice vexed for one and the same cause"). The seventeenth-century English interpretation of that principle was that no man's *life* should be placed twice in jeopardy. But the colonial courts in reaction to the severity of the criminal law extended the rule to all kinds of criminal offenses. And a majority of the states appear to have adopted this more generous interpretation, including even misdemeanors.[91] In what became the leading Supreme Court case on the issue—*Ex parte Lange* in 1874—Justice Samuel F. Miller gave the constitutional provision the same broadened scope. He simultaneously drew upon common-law precedents to hold that both former acquittal and former conviction were comprised in the protection to the accused. And he read the provision as not simply barring repeated prosecutions, but as prohibiting more than one punishment for the same offense and/or more severe punishment than the legislature had intended.[92] A 1904 ruling further expanded the privilege by liberalizing the common-law definition of when jeopardy attached. Whereas the English rule required a final verdict of guilt or innocence before jeopardy could be said to attach, the Supreme Court said jeopardy began when "a jury has been called and charged with the deliverance of the accused."[93]

Accordingly, what happened in any preliminary hearing did not matter. Even if the magistrate dismissed the suspect for lack of probable cause, he still could be later prosecuted on the same charge.[94] Similarly, if a grand jury refused to indict, the identical charge could be resubmitted to another grand jury.[95] Nor did the quashing or dismissal of an indictment preclude a later trial so long as done before the defendant had been put in jeopardy.[96] Reversing the situation, a judge's imposing a second sentence without a second trial after the first sentence had been reversed did not constitute double jeopardy since sentencing was part of the original trial.[97] And future prosecution was still possible even after the jury was impanelled and sworn if the judge had to halt the trial because of "manifest necessity" that was not the fault of the government—such as the disqualification of a juror, a defective indictment, or a hung jury.[98] If the trial court acquitted the defendant, however, then the government could not appeal the result even if errors prejudicial to the prosecution had occurred—or even if the indictment had been defective.[99] If a verdict was overturned as a result of action by the defendant, on the other hand, he was regarded as having by his appeal waived the privilege. Did this waiver reopen the whole proceeding or simply allow a retrial on the offense for which he had been convicted? The weight of authority was that when a new trial was granted the defendant was in the same position as if there had never been a first trial.[100]

The most difficult problem was what constituted more than one punishment for the same offense. Could the government after a criminal trial file a civil action against the defendant to recover a statutory penalty for the same conduct? Given the difference in the degree of proof required in civil and criminal cases, acquittal on a criminal charge did not automatically bar a civil action for the same behavior.[101] Whether such a civil proceeding amounted to double jeopardy depended on if, broadly speaking, the purpose was punitive or remedial—a distinction that was in practice more a matter of the justices' opinion regarding a given case than any meaningfully defined standard.[102] The situation was further complicated by the legislative tendency to multiply the number of offense categories covering a single act. The rule that the Court applied to overlapping offenses to determine if two different offenses were involved was if the second " 'requires proof of an additional fact which the other does not.' " Conspiracy to commit a crime, for example, was different from its commission.[103] Similarly, a defendant convicted of selling illicit liquor could be tried for illegal possession of the same liquor: "There is nothing in the Constitution which prevents Congress from punishing separately each step leading to the consummation of a transaction which it has power to prohibit and punishing also the completed transaction."[104] On the other hand, acquittal or conviction for a lesser offense included within a greater offense was held to bar a later trial for the greater offense (e.g., a conviction for illegal cohabitation prevented a later trial for adultery).[105]

The most controversial question was if a person could be prosecuted, tried, and/or convicted in two different jurisdictions for the same act. In 1820, the Court indicated that prosecution in the courts of another nation would bar prosecution in the federal courts of the United States.[106] And in an early–twentieth-century case growing out of the concurrent jurisdiction of Washington and Oregon over the Columbia River, the justices ruled that "one convicted or acquitted in the courts of the one State cannot be prosecuted for the same offense in the courts of the other."[107] But the Court applied a different rule to the relationship between the federal and state governments when in 1852 dealing with a man brought to trial in an Illinois court for violation of that state's fugitive slave law who raised as a defense that he would be also liable to punishment under the federal law. The justices—with only one dissent—agreed in *Moore v. Illinois* that no double jeopardy was involved because each citizen owed allegiance to two different sovereignties, nation and state, and thus was punishable for violation of the laws of either.[108] And *dicta* in a series of cases before and after took that same position. Thus, in 1898 the Court could declare as "settled law that the same act may constitute an offence against the United States and against a State, subjecting the guilty party to punishment under the laws of each government."[109]

But all of the cases raising the dual sovereignty issue before the adoption of national prohibition had involved potential, not actual, successive prosecutions. Accordingly, the question before the Court in those cases was whether federal authority over a subject preempted concurrent state jurisdiction. By contrast, the Eighteenth Amendment expressly granted Congress and the states "concurrent power" to enforce the Amendment. The purpose—as the chairman of the House committee responsible for inclusion of the "concurrent power" language explained—was to remove any doubt about the continued power of the states to enforce their own prohibition laws rather than to allow both state and federal governments to prosecute an offender for a single act. In 1922, however, a unanimous Court in *United States v. Lanza* ignored this legislative history and upheld a federal prosecution under the Volstead Act against defendants who had been previously convicted for the same conduct under a state prohibition law. Chief Justice Taft affirmed in sweeping terms that "an act denounced as a crime by both national and state sovereignties is an offense against the peace and dignity of both, and may be punished by each." Four years later, the justices in *Hebert v. Louisiana* sustained a Louisiana Supreme Court ruling on the basis of *Lanza* that a pending federal charge for violating the Volstead Act did not bar prosecution for the same conduct under the state's prohibition law. The Court's position was influenced by the circumstance that the cases arose in the first phase of prohibition when support for the noble experiment was still strong. More important, the *Lanza* doctrine fitted in with the Taft Court's dominant value regarding federal-state relations—the preservation of a broad area of state authority free from federal control.[110]

The protections of the Sixth Amendment applied to "all criminal prosecutions."[111] The Supreme Court defined that term much more narrowly than the "any criminal case" in the Fifth Amendment's privilege against self-incrimination clause—as applying only to actual criminal trials.[112] And the Court further narrowed the Amendment's scope by holding that actions to recover a statutory-imposed monetary penalty were "civil" and thus not covered by the Sixth Amendment's guarantees.[113] Those guarantees fell into two broad categories. The first involved the so-called venue and vicinage restrictions written into the Constitution in reaction against the British practice of removing the trial of colonial defendants outside their home colony and even back to England. Article III, Section 2 of the Constitution stipulated that the "Trial of all Crimes . . . shall be held in the State where the said Crimes shall have been committed." The Sixth Amendment added the further requirement that the trial be by jury "of the State and district wherein the crime shall have been committed," but with an accompanying provision authorizing Congress to define districts by statute. Although a substantial body of litigation under these provisions reached the Supreme Court, most involved technical issues of statutory interpretation (e.g., where a given crime had been committed). Disputes over larger constitutional issues revolved around the second group of guarantees: those covering the procedures that must be followed in criminal trials.

The right of the accused "to be informed of the nature and cause of the accusation" was treated as part of due process. Apart from the degree of particularity required in an indictment, the major issue grew out of the Constitution's silence about when the defendant must receive the information. Congress by statute required that persons accused of a capital offense receive a copy of the indictment at least two days (three in treason cases) before the trial.[114] But the government was not constitutionally bound to furnish the accused with a copy of the indictment unless he asked.[115] As for the right "to have compulsory process for obtaining witnesses in his favor," such compulsory process was provided by statute—at least in capital cases—from 1790.[116] The requirement that the accused "be confronted with the witnesses against him" was construed to mean that a defendant had the right to be present at every stage of the proceedings.[117] More important, the accused had the right to cross-examine witnesses testifying against him. In the leading case on this matter, the Court struck down an 1875 law making conviction of a person charged with stealing property from the United States "conclusive evidence" that the property had been stolen in any prosecution against an alleged receiver. The provision was found in violation of the Sixth Amendment because the accused receiver was denied the opportunity to confront witnesses to controvert a vital fact, the status of the property.[118] There were only a few exceptions where a transcript could substitute for the witness himself—when the witness died after giving testimony at a former trial where the defendant has been present, where the defendant was responsible for the witness's absence, and death-bed statements "from the necessity of the case."[119]

In recent years, the guarantee that an accused person shall have "the Assistance of Counsel for his defence" has become regarded as the most important of the Sixth Amendment's provisions. Historically, however, the clause was of secondary importance. At the time the Constitution was adopted, English law permitted representation by counsel in only misdemeanor and treason cases. In felony cases other than treason there was no legal right to counsel, although many courts of their own volition permitted an attorney's participation. Most of the states after the American Revolution adopted a more liberal approach; yet even here the right to counsel meant in most instances simply that the accused had the privilege of retaining an attorney if he could afford to do so rather than the right to have counsel provided if he could not.[120] Congress did require by statute that the federal courts appoint counsel at the defendant's request in cases of treason or other capital crimes.[121] But there was no indication before the first Scottsboro boys case in 1932 that a defendant had a constitutional right to be offered counsel or that a conviction without counsel was void.[122] And even there, Justice George Sutherland took pains to limit his ruling to the facts of the case: that due process required a state court to provide the effective assistance of counsel "in a capital case where the defendant is unable to employ counsel, and is incapable adequately of making his own defense because of ignorance, feeble-mindedness, illiteracy, or the like."[123]

Historically, trial by jury was the most important procedural guarantee to a criminal defendant. The Court read the provision in Article III, Section 2 of the Constitution that "Trial of all Crimes, except in Cases of Impeachment, shall be by Jury" as identical in meaning to the Sixth Amendment's "right to a speedy and public trial, by an impartial jury."[124] In the famous Civil War-era case of *Ex parte Milligan*, the justices held that the right to a jury trial could not be suspended even in wartime, at least for civilians in areas where the regular courts were functioning.[125] Notwithstanding the inclusive language of the provisions, the justices upheld nonjury trials for petty offenses on the ground that summary handling of such cases had been widely practiced in England and the colonies. But the boundary line was left to a case-by-case determination depending upon "the nature of the offense and the amount of punishment prescribed."[126] Given the mandatory language of Article III, Section 2, there was for a long time doubt if a defendant in a serious crime could waive jury trial, even by pleading guilty. In 1930, the Court held in *Patton v. United States* that the right to a jury trial was a privilege afforded the defendant that he could voluntarily forego. But Justice Sutherland took pains to underline that such a waiver required the defendant's "express and intelligent consent." Even then, waiver required the concurrence of the prosecution and approval of the court. At the same time, the decision made explicit what had long been assumed in *dicta*: that a jury trial within the meaning of the Constitution required the twelve-man jury and unanimous verdict of the common law.[127]

The accompanying guarantees associated with the right to jury trial received no more than passing attention. No case involving the closure of a trial appears to have reached the Court.[128] The question of how far a trial court could restrict attendance short of complete secrecy remained unsettled. Nor had the Court defined in any meaningful way "speedy": "The right of a speedy trial is necessarily relative. . . . It secures rights to a defendant. It does not preclude the rights of public justice."[129] Lower court decisions that the Court refused to review placed the burden of proof upon the defendant to show that he had asked for, but was denied, a speedy trial.[130] The most difficult issue was what constituted an "impartial jury." The Judiciary Act of 1789 simply provided that jurors in the federal courts should have the same qualifications and be selected in the same manner, "so far as . . . practicable," as jurors in the highest trial court of the state where the trial was held.[131] The result was that jury selection procedures in the federal courts depended upon improvements in the state procedures. And the Supreme

Court proved reluctant about interfering with state procedures. In *Strauder*, the Court held that the states were free to restrict jury service "to males, to freeholders, to citizens, to persons within certain ages, or to persons having educational qualifications."[132] A 1910 decision even upheld a South Carolina statute authorizing jury commissioners to pick from among persons who met certain standards those whom "they may deem otherwise well qualified."[133]

Did impartiality require that the composition of the jury accuratelty reflect the make-up of the local population as a whole? Most of the litigation touching upon that question involved challenges to the exclusion of blacks from jury service in violation of the Fourteenth Amendment—with the Court until the 1930s shying from looking behind the legal forms to the actual results.[134] The leading case dealing with the representativeness issue in a nonracial context was when Socialists appealed their conviction under the World War I draft law because the jury was composed exclusively of members of other parties and property owners. Although the decision rested technically upon due process rather than Sixth Amendment grounds, the Court laid down as the formula for judging the representativeness of juries not whether all groups were included but whether any group had been systematically excluded.[135] More attention had been paid to the problem of impartiality at the individual juror level. The Court had ruled that defendants in the federal courts had a constitutional right to the *voir dire* —that is, to question prospective jurors to gain information for possible challenges.[136] While peremptory challenges were regarded as a statutory-granted privilege,[137] challenge for cause was constitutionally protected. And in principle, a prospective juror could be challenged for cause if "[h]aving formed or expressed an unqualified belief that the prisoner is guilty or not guilty of the offence charged."[138]

What constituted the requisite impartiality of mind was debated at the treason trial of Aaron Burr. The defense took the position that jurors must be free of any opinions on the cases. Presiding on circuit, Chief Justice Marshall made a distinction between casual or lightly held opinions that still left "the mind open to a fair consideration of . . . the testimony that may be offered" and strongly held views "which will close the mind against the testimony that may be offered in opposition to them."[139] The Supreme Court formally adopted this standard in the first of the Mormon cases. But the ruling simultaneously left the decision of the trial judge on whether or not to grant the challenge practically final.[140] A special problem was if the defendant could challenge a government employee for cause because of the government's interest in the case. In 1909, the Court answered yes on the common-law principle that a master-servant relationship with one of the parties disqualified a prospective juror.[141] The difficulties that rule made in the District of Columbia led Congress in 1935 to adopt legislation making government employees eligible for jury service there. The following year, a five-to-three majority in *United States v. Wood* sustained the law, holding that actual bias must be shown, not simply inferred. "Impartiality," Chief

Justice Hughes explained, "is not a technical conception. It is a state of mind. For the ascertainment of this mental attitude of appropriate indifference, the Constitution lays down no particular tests and procedure is not chained to any ancient and artificial formula."[142]

There has been much criticism of the jury for its lack of expertise in dealing with complex, even technical, issues. The reason, however, why the founders of the republic so esteemed the right to a jury trial was their recognition that judges were as liable to abuse their power as any other mortals.[143] From this perspective, the problem has been the tendency to aggrandize the judge at the expense of the jury. The prevailing view during the first half of the nineteenth century was that the jury was the determiner not simply of the facts but the law. The jury, in other words, would decide not only if the accused committed the charged act, but if the act was criminal—that is, the substantive meaning of the statute. But this power of the jury became the target of a judicial counterattack that culminated in 1895 when the Supreme Court ruled in *Sparf and Hansen v. United States* that the jury was bound to follow the judge's instructions on all matters of law. If the judge could not instruct the jury "what the law is upon a given state of facts," Justice Harlan rationalized for the seven-to-two majority,

the result would be that the enforcement of the law against criminals and the protection of citizens against unjust and groundless prosecutions, would depend entirely upon juries uncontrolled by any settled, fixed, legal principles. . . . Public and private safety alike would be in peril, if the principle be established that juries in criminal cases may, of right, disregard the law as expounded to them by the court.[144]

In practice, trial court judges were allowed broad discretion to comment even upon the facts except in the most blatantly prejudicial circumstances—e.g., when a judge told the jury that everything the defendant said was a lie.[145] And the judge could direct a verdict of acquittal for lack of evidence. But the Court acknowledged that the right to a jury trial barred judges from directing a verdict of guilty.[146] Although judges preferred not to publicize the matter, juries thus still had the power—if not the right—to acquit against the evidence, with the prosecution barred by the double-jeopardy clause from any appeal.

The Eighth Amendment stipulation that "[e]xcessive bail shall not be required" was taken from the English Bill of Rights of 1689. But a long debate has gone on whether the purpose was to establish a blanket guarantee of bail or simply to limit the amount of bail that the courts could require in cases where Congress had authorized bail. The weight of the historical evidence is in support of the second position. English law from the Assize of Clarendon (1166) on had excluded from bail a wide range of offenses. That practice was followed by the American colonies and by the states after the Revolution.[147] The Judiciary Act of 1789 adopted contemporaneously with the Bill of Rights guaranteed bail "upon all arrests in criminal cases . . . except where the punishment may be death"—with bail in such instances left to judicial discretion.[148] While the Supreme Court failed to rule definitively upon the meaning of the bail clause, the thrust of its pronouncements touching upon the issue was to deny that bail was an absolute right. Thus, for example, the Court in *Hudson v. Parker* not only implicitly accepted the distinction dating from 1789 between capital and noncapital offenses regarding bail pending trial, but explicitly affirmed that given the absence of a statutory provision covering bail during appeal from a trial court conviction granting such bail was a matter of judicial discretion.[149] Nor did the Court lay down any meaningful guidelines on how much was "excessive." Accordingly, judges retained wide latitude as to what constituted a sufficient guarantee for the defendant's appearance.[150]

A similar looseness of definition surrounded the rest of the Eighth Amendment. The Court's elucidation of the import of the prohibition against "excessive fines" did not go beyond the vague formula "so grossly excessive as to amount to a deprivation of property without due process of law."[151] The ban against "cruel and unusual punishments" reflected an abhorrence for the barbarities of the English criminal code that found expression even in the early days of the colonial period.[152] The major question facing the Supreme Court was if the provision applied simply to the mode of punishment or imposed limitations upon the severity of the penalty relative to the crime. In dealing with the first issue, the justices did no more than lay down the vague standard that the provision forbade "unnecessary cruelty."[153] The second issue was raised in the famous 1910 case of *Weems v. United States*. A man found guilty of falsifying a public record was sentenced under a Philippine statute dating from Spanish rule to a fine, fifteen years in prison at hard labor with chains at the ankle and wrist, and permanent loss of basic civil rights. Finding the statute in violation of the Eighth Amendment, the Court held as "a precept of justice that punishment for crime should be graduated and proportioned to offense"—and went on to add that the meaning of what constituted cruel and unusual punishment was not restricted to what had been thought such at the time the Constitution had been adopted but "may acquire meaning as public opinion becomes enlightened by a humane justice."[154]

When one turns from general principles to actual cases, however, the record shows that the Court was extremely reluctant to find any sentence excessive so long as within the statutory limits.[155] At least part of the reason was that, unlike some state appellate courts, federal appeals courts had no power to reduce an excessive sentence. The only alternative was to reverse the judgment and order a new trial. Nor was the Court willing to intervene when there were disparities in sentencing for the same offense. As Justice David J. Brewer put the matter, "Undue leniency in one case does not transform a reasonable punishment in another case to a cruel one."[156] The justices allowed similar latitude to legislative judgment regarding statutory penalties. Although hinting that a cruel and unusual punishment levied by a state would violate the due process clause of the Fourteenth Amendment, the Court never ruled adversely to a state on that ground. State habitual offender laws were upheld against challenge.[157] An 1891 decision even gave the stamp of approval to solitary confinement.[158] And the Court left no question that the death penalty as such was not unconstitutional. "Punishments are cruel," Chief Justice Melville W. Fuller explained, "when they involve torture or a lingering death; but the punishment of death is not cruel, within the meaning of that word as used in the Constitution. It implies there something inhuman and barbarous, something more than the mere extinguishment of life."[159]

There was one group, however, for whom none of the Constitution's criminal procedure guarantees applied except as a matter of legislative grace: persons under military or naval jurisdiction facing court-martial. In 1858, the Court held in *Dynes v. Hoover* that court-martial verdicts were not reviewable by the federal courts unless, first, the military court "had not jurisdiction over the *subject-matter or charge*," or, second, "having jurisdiction over the subject-matter, it has failed to observe the rules prescribed by the statute for its exercise."[160] As regards jurisdiction, the Court in 1866 in *Ex parte Milligan* ruled that military courts could not try civilians even in wartime, at least in areas where the regular courts were still functioning—but added in *dicta* that persons on "actual" military or naval service were not covered by the Sixth Amendment's guarantee of jury trial.[161] More important, the Court largely forswore looking into if a court-martial had followed its own prescribed procedures: the rule became that "the civil courts exercise no supervisory or corrective power over the proceedings of a court-martial; and that no mere errors in their proceedings are open to consideration. The single inquiry, the test, is jurisdiction."[162] But this situation failed to arouse much controversy because the military services limited their jurisdiction to persons receiving pay for military service—a relatively few volunteers except in wartime. And even for military personnel, the military codes dealt for the most part with strictly military offenses.[163]

There is no question that the Old Court's interpretation of the criminal procedure guarantees of the Bill of Rights was on balance weighted on the side of the accused. The difficulty was that major responsibility for law enforcement lay with state and local governments. And the Supreme Court had stood firm in refusing to extend the criminal procedure provisions of the Bill of Rights to the states.[164] None of the decisions before 1932 where the Court had overturned a state conviction had involved an independently listed guarantee of the Bill of Rights. On the contrary, the Court had in many instances held that a practice that would have contravened one of those guarantees if done by the federal government did not violate due process when done by a state. *Hurtado* in 1884 allowed states to provide for prosecution by information—i.e., the filing of charges directly by the prosecutor—rather than by grand jury indictment.[165] In 1900, *Maxwell v. Dow* upheld the power of a state to substitute an eight-man jury for the common-law one of twelve—and went so far as to suggest in *dicta* that the states were not required to provide a jury trial.[166] There was similarly doubt if the federal rule of a unanimous jury verdict applied to the states.[167] A 1904 decision allowed use of a deposition taken in a preliminary hearing in a state court trial in lieu of an absent out-of-state witness.[168] *Twining* ruled that the state courts were free not to follow the federal court rule barring comment upon a defendant's failure to testify.[169]

Even when reviewing state practices upon independent due process grounds, the Court had shied from interfering with local autonomy so long as the defendant had been accorded the basic requirements of "reasonable notice, and reasonable opportunity to be heard and to present his claim or defence."[170] The states were deemed not constitutionally required to provide a mechanism for appealing trial court judgments.[171] How adversely this situation affected individual defendants cannot be assessed. Nearly all the state constitutions had provisions analogous to those in the federal Bill of Rights. But not much is known about how state supreme courts interpreted those guarantees. Still less is known about day-to-day practice in the trial courts. Historians have been attracted to the spectacular cases of flagrant abuse. At the same time, those were the cases most likely to be carried to the Supreme Court. As the number of such appeals reaching the high tribunal increased, the justices responded by beginning to move toward imposing tighter supervision over state practices. In 1923, the Court ruled that a trial "dominated by a mob so that there is an actual interference with the course of justice" violated due process.[172] Four years later, the justices found a like violation when the presiding judge lacked the requisite impartiality "to hold the balance nice, clear and true between the State and the accused."[173] And the first breakthrough where the Court accepted an independently listed criminal procedure guarantee of the Bill of Rights as included within the due process clause of the Fourteenth Amendment came in the 1932 Scottsboro boys case of *Powell v. Alabama.*

The nine black youths were arrested for the rape of two white girls on March 25, 1931; the county grand jury met on March 30 and next day returned formal indictments; the judge set the trial for April 6. At first, the judge assigned the entire local bar to represent the defendants. But all found excuses to withdraw. On the day of the trial, he accepted the services of two volunteers—one a local attorney, the other a Chattanooga, Tennessee, lawyer with a reputation for chronic drunkenness sent down by a group of that city's black ministers to look after the youths' interests. Their only opportunity to prepare was an interview with the defendants lasting less than a half-hour. When appeal was brought to the Supreme Court, Walter Pollak—who had been Gitlow's attorney in the 1925 free-speech case—asked for reversal on two grounds. First, that the defendants had not been given adequate opportunity to retain counsel of their own. Second, that the trial judge had erred in not properly appointing counsel. Sutherland agreed that the "failure of the court to give them reasonable time and opportunity to secure counsel was a clear denial of due process." But he rested his opinion on broader grounds: that in a situation where "the necessity of counsel was so vital and imperative" the trial court's duty was "not discharged by an assignment at such a time or under such circumstances as to preclude the giving of effective aid in the preparation and trial of the case." And in sweeping *dicta*, he suggested that the assistance of counsel was a "fundamental" right that should be accorded all defendants whatever the crime. "Even the intelligent and educated layman has small and sometimes no skill in the science of law. . . . He requires the guiding hand of counsel at every step in the proceedings against him. Without it, though he be not guilty, he faces the danger of conviction because he does not know how to establish his innocence."[174]

At the same time, Sutherland made explicit what had been implicit in *Twining*: that the doctrine of nonsuperfluity did not apply when a Bill of Rights guarantee was so "fundamental" as to be an indispensable part of due process.[175] But still left unanswered were two crucial questions. What rights belonged in that category? And did those rights have the same scope and meaning as their counterparts in the Bill of Rights? The next case raising those issues—*Snyder v. Massachusetts* in 1934—furnished scant guidance. The defendant had not been allowed, over his protest, to go along when the jury was taken to view the scene of the crime. Four of the justices agreed that the accused in a state case had as part of due process the same constitutional right to be present at all stages of the trial as the defendant in a federal case had under the Sixth Amendment. For the majority, however, Justice Benjamin Cardozo skirted the question of the applicability of the confrontation clause to the states: "For the present purposes we assume that the privilege is reinforced by the Fourteenth Amendment, though this has not been squarely held." He then proceeded to point out that the Fourteenth Amendment did not "in so many words" require that the accused must be present at all times during the trial. "Due process of law requires that the proceedings shall be fair, but fairness is a relative, not an absolute concept." Since the accused could not have gained anything by being present, he had not been denied a fair hearing. "The concept of fairness must not be strained till it is narrowed to a filament."[176]

In 1937, however, Cardozo came frontally to grips with the incorporation issue in *Palko v. Connecticut*. Frank J. Palko had been indicted for first degree murder, but because of the judge's definition of premeditation in his instructions to the jury, the jury had returned a guilty verdict only for second degree murder. The prosecution thought the instructions in error, and, acting on the basis of a Connecticut law allowing the prosecution to appeal the outcome of a criminal trial if errors prejudicial to the state had occurred, successfully asked the state's Supreme Court of Errors to order a retrial. At retrial, Palko was convicted of first degree murder. The Fifth Amendment's guarantee against double jeopardy had been read as prohibiting the federal government from appealing in such a situation. And Palko's attorney, relying heavily upon Horace Flack's 1908 study, *The Adoption of the Fourteenth Amendment*, argued that the due process clause had been intended to extend all of the Bill of Rights to the states. Cardozo gave short shrift to the claim of total incorporation. After reviewing the existing precedents, he concluded that the due process clause protected only those rights that—as he eloquently though vaguely put the matter—were "implicit in" or "the very essence of a scheme of ordered liberty," represented " 'fundamental principles of liberty and justice which lie at the base of all our civil and political institutions,' " and thus whose denial would impose "a hardship so acute and shocking that our polity will not endure it."

Cardozo affirmed that the Fourteenth Amendment prohibited the states from abridging "the freedom of speech which the First Amendment safeguards . . . or the like freedom of the press . . . ; or the free exercise of religion . . . ; or the right of peaceable assembly." The reason, however, was not their inclusion in the Bill of Rights, but because "neither liberty nor justice would exist if they were sacrificed." The only one of the criminal law guarantees that had been similarly "absorbed" into the due process clause was "the right of one accused of crime to the benefit of counsel." Although not dealing directly with the status of the provisions of the First Amendment, he underlined that the right to counsel guaranteed by the due process clause was not identical to the Sixth Amendment's. Rather, he laid down what became known as the "fundamental fairness" or "totality of circumstances" doctrine. Due process guaranteed the right to a fair trial and that, in turn, depended upon whether "in the particular situation laid before us in the evidence the benefit of counsel was essential to the substance of a hearing." Double jeopardy—or at least the kind of double jeopardy involving Palko— did not meet that standard. The state's requiring "a trial free from the corrosion of substantial legal error" was "not cruelty at all, nor even vexation in any immoderate degree." If the error had been adverse to the defendant, he could have appealed. "A reciprocal privilege . . . has now been granted to the state. There is here no seismic innovation. The edifice of justice stands, its symmetry, to many, greater than before."[177]

At the same time, how to appeal a trial court's denial of a constitutionally. protected right involved special problems for the criminal defendant. After 1916, most would-be challenges to state criminal judgments fell into the Court's discretionary jurisdiction through a petition for a writ of certiorari.[178] The situation was much the same for defendants in federal criminal proceedings. In 1889, Congress granted defendants in federal criminal capital cases the right of appeal to the Supreme Court. Two years later, this right of appeal was expanded to include any "infamous crime." When the Court threatened to become inundated because of its construction of that term to cover any offense punishable by imprisonment in a penitentiary regardless of what the actual sentence was, the lawmakers in 1897 restricted appeal by right in all except capital cases to the recently established Circuit Courts of Appeals. Appeal to the Supreme Court was made a matter of the justices' discretion. The Judicial Code of 1911 put capital cases in the same category.[179] Given the ever-rising volume of litigation, only a small fraction of criminal appeals could, or would, be given a full hearing. The other possible route for challenging a state or lower federal court judgment was via the writ of habeas corpus. Habeas corpus involved what the lawyers call a collateral attack upon a judgment—a challenge not to its substantive merits, but its legal validity.[180]

The writ was a court order requiring an official holding a person in custody to bring him before the court along with an explanation ("return"). If the judge found no legal justification for the confinement, he would free the prisoner. The Judiciary Act of 1789 provided

That all the before-mentioned courts of the United States, shall have power to issue writs of *scire facias*, *habeas corpus*, and all other writs not specially provided for by statute, which may be necessary for the exercise of their respective jurisdictions. . . . And that either of the justices of the supreme court, as well as judges of the district courts, shall have power to grant writs of *habeas corpus* for the purpose of an inquiry into the cause of commitment.[181]

The language thus left ambiguous whether the federal courts could issue the writ only as an auxiliary to cases otherwise within their statutory jurisdiction. The point was crucial because the act did not authorize Supreme Court review of lower federal court criminal judgments. In the famous 1807 case of *Ex parte Bollman*, however, Chief Justice Marshall ruled that when a person was held under the order of a lower federal court the Supreme Court could issue the writ under its appellate jurisdiction even though there was no statutory provision for appeal to the Court of a conviction.[182] Later decisions settled conclusively that the Court had appellate jurisdiction under the Constitution to issue the writ when the applicant's confinement was initiated by or has been subsequently judicially reviewed by a lower federal court.[183]

But there remained major limitations upon the habeas corpus powers of the federal courts. Historically the writ was a means of freeing prisoners held by executive authority without judicial trial. The English Habeas Corpus Act of 1679 excluded from its coverage any person convicted in a court of competent jurisdiction.[184] The Supreme Court applied that principle to the habeas corpus powers of the federal courts: the writ was not available to persons held under "the judgment of a court of record whose jurisdiction is final."[185] The Supreme Court could thus issue the writ only when the applicant was held under the judicial order of a lower federal court that was not a final judgment—an exceptional circumstance that rarely came up. More important, the Judiciary Act of 1789 in a bow to states' rights sensitivities barred the federal courts from issuing the writ to "prisoners in gaol, unless where they are in custody, under or by colour of the authority of the United States."[186] In *Bollman*, Marshall acknowledged that the power of the federal courts to issue writs of habeas corpus was not an inherent power but "must be given by written law."[187] Accordingly, the Court in 1845 ruled that

Neither this nor any other court of the United States, or judge thereof, can issue a *habeas corpus* to bring up a prisoner, who is in custody under a sentence or execution of a state court. . . . And it is immaterial whether the imprisonment be under civil or criminal process.[188]

The first step in the transformation of the writ into a meaningful postconviction remedy came when Congress in the Habeas Corpus Act of 1867 authorized the federal courts to grant the writ "in all cases where any person may be restrained of his or her liberty in violation of the constitution, or of any treaty or law of the United States." And whereas applicants were not permitted under the common law to challenge the truth of the particulars set forth in the return, the 1867 legislation allowed petitioners to present "material facts . . . to show that the detention is in contravention of the constitution or laws of the United States." A strong argument has been made that Congress did not intend to grant to the federal courts authority to issue the writ to prisoners under state court judgment but had the more limited aim of protecting blacks against the reimposition of involuntary servitude under the so-called Black Codes adopted by the Southern states immediately after the Civil War. From the start, however, the lower federal courts assumed that the statute authorized issuance of the writ to state prisoners.[189] Since Congress in 1868 barred the Supreme Court from reviewing lower federal court decisions in habeas corpus cases brought under the 1867 statute to forestall a threatened legal challenge to its southern reconstruction program,[190] the Court did not rule upon the issue until such appeals were reallowed in 1885. Then the Court in *Ex parte Royall* accepted the broader reading of the statute as making available habeas corpus relief via the federal courts to state prisoners.[191]

The next breakthrough came through a more circuitous route. The Court continued to hold that habeas corpus was not a substitute for the writ of error but was restricted to the question of whether or not the lower court had proper jurisdiction. In other words, habeas corpus could be used to challenge "only the power and authority of the court to act, not the correctness of its conclusions."[192] But the Court adopted the principle that jurisdiction was lost when a court exceeded its constitutional authority, thereby opening the door to the release of the prisoner through habeas corpus. This expansion of the reach of habeas corpus came primarily in two areas. One was where the conviction was under an unconstitutional law.[193] The other was where the attack was upon the particular sentence imposed rather than upon the conviction as such.[194] Although the Court never explained its rationale, what appeared to be the determinative circumstance was that the justices were utilizing habeas corpus as a way of dealing with cases that were otherwise not appealable.[195] After Congress provided for appellate review of federal trial court criminal judgments, the Court took a harder line regarding the availability of habeas corpus relief for federal prisoners. In 1895, the Court laid down the rule barring interference by habeas corpus with proceedings in the federal courts before their final determination.[196] And early–twentieth-century decisions made review by direct appeal rather than by habeas corpus the accepted procedure for challenging the constitutionality of federal criminal statutes.[197]

The major limitation affecting state prisoners was the restriction of judicial inquiry under habeas corpus to issues of law, not fact. In a bow to protests from the defenders of states' rights, the Court in 1891 instructed the lower federal courts not to retry the merits of federal constitutional questions that had been dealt with by the state courts. Speaking for a unanimous bench, Justice Harlan in *In re Wood* denied relief to a black petitioner convicted of murder who alleged that he had been denied due process and equal protection because of the unlawful exclusion of blacks from the jury. Since the state law governing jury selection did not discriminate against blacks, the question of whether or not the jury had been selected in conformity with state law "was a question which the trial court was entirely competent to decide, and its determination could not be reviewed . . . upon a writ of habeas corpus." Even if the court had erred, such error was reviewable only by direct appeal on a writ of error to the Supreme Court from the state court of last resort.[198] In 1915, the Court underlined in *Frank v. Magnum* that the federal courts would not intervene with state criminal proceedings via habeas corpus so long as the state provided its own adequate "corrective process." While shying from saying explicitly that state appellate court determinations of fact were conclusive, the majority opinion treated such findings as practically final.[199]

At the same time, *Frank* added a new dimension to the habeas corpus powers of the federal courts vis-à-vis state criminal proceedings. The federal courts were to consider if the applicant had been given adequate opportunity to raise his constitutional claims in the state courts.[200] The next breakthrough came in 1923 in *Moore v. Dempsey*. The facts were similar to those in *Frank*. A group of blacks had been convicted in an Arkansas court of murder in a trial held under menacing mob threats. The state high court affirmed the convictions, and the federal district court dismissed the application for writs of habeas corpus. But Holmes—who had dissented from the refusal to grant the writ in *Frank*—now spoke for a seven-to-two majority in directing the district court to hold a habeas corpus hearing and to order the release of the prisoners if there had been mob domination of the trial. His opinion left ambiguous the exact import of the ruling. There are those who argue that Holmes said no more than that the Arkansas Supreme Court's consideration of the mob domination issue had been so perfunctory—in contrast with the examination by the Georgia high court in *Frank*—as to constitute lack of an adequate state corrective procedure and thus open the door for consideration of the merits of the claim by the federal courts via habeas corpus. The more widely accepted interpretation—and the one later adopted by the Court itself—read the decision as requiring that whenever a denial of a constitutionally protected right was raised in a habeas corpus petition, the federal court judge had the "duty of examining the facts for himself."[201]

One jurisdictional barrier remained in the way of a state prisoner's challenging his conviction in the federal courts through habeas corpus. In another bow to states' rights, the Court had laid down the so-called exhaustion doctrine: that for the sake of federal-state comity the federal courts should refuse to grant the writ until the prisoner had exhausted all his available state remedies.[202] The difficulties that the exhaustion doctrine could present were strikingly illustrated by the celebrated case of Tom Mooney. A San Francisco labor organizer, Mooney had been convicted in 1917 for the bombing of a parade by preparedness advocates on the basis of what was later revealed to have been perjured testimony arranged by the prosecution. When attempts to win Mooney's release through the state courts failed, his attorneys applied to the federal district court for a writ of habeas corpus. After turndowns there and by the Court of Appeals, an appeal was carried to the Supreme Court. The justices in 1935 unanimously agreed that knowing use of perjured testimony by the state had deprived Mooney of his right to a fair trial guaranteed by the due process clause of the Fourteenth Amendment. But the *per curiam* opinion refused to free Mooney because he had not exhausted all his state remedies by trying the state's own habeas corpus procedure. The upshot was that Mooney remained in prison until receiving in 1939 a gubernatorial pardon.[203]

5 The Old Court and Individual Rights Reappraised

Simply to look at United States Supreme Court decisions does not provide a complete guide to the legal status of individual rights during the pre-1937 period. All the state constitutions included protections analogous to those in the federal Constitution. And scholars have only begun to examine state court interpretations of those provisions and their impact.[1] But there is no question that the Old Court had done more to lay the foundations of the civil rights revolution wrought by the Modern Court than has been appreciated. Its major contribution lay in opening the door for application of the limitations of the Bill of Rights upon governmental power to the states and their enforcement through the federal courts. By the time FDR's first appointee took his seat on the bench, the justices had extended to the states via the due process clause of the Fourteenth Amendment the First Amendment's rights of free speech, free press, and assembly. Freedom of religion was assumed similarly incorporated, although no decision had yet explicitly so held. The instrument for that achievement was paradoxically the favorite target of liberal critics of the Old Court—substantive due process. The crux of substantive due process was the existence of fundamental rights that government could not infringe without an exceptionally high standard of justification.[2]

As such, substantive due process represented a re-emergence of the natural law strain in American constitutional thinking.[3] The natural law tradition— a tradition whose roots can be traced back to Blackstone, John Locke, and the Magna Carta, and even beyond to the Romans and Aristotle—postulated that government rested upon a social contract embodying pre-existing fundamental rights that were entitled to protection whether or not formally stated in any written constitution.[4] As Thomas Jefferson proclaimed in the Declaration of Independence, men were "endowed by their Creator with certain unalienable Rights," and "to secure these rights, Governments are instituted."[5] Echoes of this thinking can be found in early Supreme Court decisions.[6] And while the Court came to adopt the positivist approach of tying—at least formally—limits upon governmental power to explicit provisions of the constitutional text, natural law ideas remained strongly influential. On the eve of the Civil War, the Iowa Supreme Court reaffirmed that the individual

> needed no constitutional declaration to protect him in the use and enjoyment of his property. . . . To be thus protected and thus secure in the possession of his property is a right inalienable, a right which a written constitution may recognize or declare, but which existed independently of and before such recognition, and which no government can destroy.[7]

That substantive due process was first applied to protect what might be called the liberties of the marketplace was not an accident nor an aberration. John Locke's social contract philosophy had emphasized the right of the individual to the product of his labor as the most basic of natural rights. A more immediate influence was the anti-slavery movement. From the 1830s on, abolitionists had made one of their major indictments of slavery its denial of the slave's natural right to property in his own labor. And historians have shown how the "free labor" ideology came to permeate much of northern opinion. That ideology saw as the major difference distinguishing North from South the freedom of the worker to decide for whom he labored and upon what terms and to keep the fruits of that labor. The lack of such freedom for the slaves explained the South's economic backwardness. A corollary was that the free labor system benefited not simply society-at-large but the individual: that in a dynamic, expanding economy such as the North had, every man had the opportunity for upward mobility and eventual economic independence.[8] Accordingly, when Congress in the Civil Rights Act of 1866 defined the rights of the freed slaves, the first listed was "to make and enforce contracts."[9]

The judicial apotheosis of liberty of contract in *Lochner* was one aspect of a larger natural law premise underlying the Old Court's jurisprudence: the vision of the autonomous individual free to pursue self-chosen ends. Where the Old Court followed Herbert Spencer was not in his laissez-faire dogmatism, but in his affirmation of what he called the "law of equal freedom"—the principle that *"Every man has freedom to do all that he wills, provided he infringes not the equal freedom of any other man."*[10] And the Old Court acknowledged that this concept had far broader implications than simply freedom in the marketplace. In his expansive reading of the Fourth and Fifth Amendments in *Boyd*, Justice Joseph P. Bradley pictured as an inextricably intertwined trinity the individual's "indefeasible right of personal security, personal liberty and private property."[11] Charles Warren's famous 1926 article attacking the expanded definition of liberty under substantive due process had as its major target the Court's assumption in *Gitlow* that the First Amendment's freedom of speech and press were among the fundamental personal rights and liberties protected by the Fourteenth Amendment.[12] The Modern Court has in its privacy decisions, starting with *Griswold v. Connecticut*, repeatedly cited Justice James C. McReynolds's sweeping definition of Fourteenth Amendment liberties in *Meyer v. Nebraska*.[13]

Commitment to upholding the autonomy of the individual underlay much of the Old Court's decision-making, ranging from its suspicion of labor unions, to give one illustration,[14] to its defense of the right of parents to direct the education of their children, for another.[15] Therein simultaneously lies the explanation for many of what appear blindspots in its record by present-day standards. Take, for example, its treatment of women. The justices were heirs to an an almost unbroken tradition in Western thought that deemed the male-headed family as inevitable and necessary, ordained by God and/or nature. Woman's role was defined as wife and mother, and as such, to obey her husband without question. While there were unmarried women, those were exceptions, or, to be more accurate, aberrations—and even they were likely to be under the control of fathers and brothers. Accordingly, the law took as a given that women were not fully persons but fell into a special category, destined by biology to be passive, subservient, and dependent, and thus requiring men's protection and solicitude.[16] The result was to stunt many women's potential. In the context of the time, however, the judicial willingness to approve protective legislation on the ground of women's special position benefited many others. And given the extent of occupational sex-typing, the adverse effects of such legislation upon women's job opportunities were minimal.[17]

Nor was individual autonomy an absolute even for adult males. A countervailing limitation was imposed by the common–law concept *sic utere tuo ut alienum non laedas*—use your own so as not to injure another.[18] As Chief Justice Lemuel Shaw of the Massachusetts Supreme Judicial Court explained in his much cited 1851 opinion in *Commonwealth v. Alger*:

We think it is a settled principle, growing out of the nature of well ordered civil society, that every holder of property... holds it under the implied liability that his use of it may be so regulated, that it shall not be injurious... to the rights of the community.... Rights of property, like all other social and conventional rights, are subject to such reasonable limitations in their enjoyment, ... as the legislature, under the governing and controlling power vested in them by the constitution, may think necessary and expedient.... The power we allude to is... the police power, the power vested in the legislature by the constitution, to make... all manner of wholesome and reasonable laws... not repugnant to the constitution, as they shall judge to be for the good and welfare of the commonwealth, and of the subjects of the same.[19]

Isaac F. Redfield of the Vermont high court put the matter more succinctly: "[P]ersons and property are subjected to all kinds of restraints and burdens, in order to secure the general comfort, health, and prosperity of the state."[20] Chief Justice Morrison R. Waite sounded the same note in *Munn v. Illinois*. "When one becomes a member of society," Waite pointed out, "he necessarily parts with some rights. ... This does not confer power upon the whole people to control rights which are purely and exclusively private ... but it does authorize the establishment of laws requiring each citizen to so conduct himself, and so use his own property, as not unnecessarily to injure another. This is the very essence of government."[21]

The question, therefore, became one of balancing—of deciding how far the rights of the individual may be limited for the larger community good. The governing test became what one commentator has termed the *"principle of conditions"*: whether a regulation was reasonable given existing social and economic conditions.[22] Contrary examples such as *Lochner* notwithstanding, the Supreme Court at least until the 1920s tended to defer to the legislative judgment regarding the legitimacy of restrictions upon private economic activity. Most state courts were similarly permissive.[23] Judges who were willing to approve a wide range of restraints upon individual freedom in the marketplace could hardly be expected to deny government a like power to curb the abuse of First Amendment liberties. Liberal theory historically made a sharp distinction between "liberty" and "licence"[24]—the counterpart to the distinction made by judges and legal commentators between the responsible and irresponsible exercise of freedom of speech and press. And there was a long tradition in Anglo-American law of complicity liability for "all those that incite, procure, set on, or stir up any other" to commit a felony.[25] The debate among the justices was thus over subsidiary questions: what constituted intent; if the language used actually urged criminal action; and when encouragement threatened to result in such action.[26] Holmes in *Abrams* did not question the power of Congress to pass the Espionage Act. Nor did Brandeis in *Whitney* challenge California's criminal syndicalism law as such. Their differences with their brethren were over whether the circumstances in which the activity took place involved a sufficient degree of danger to society to warrant punishment.[27]

Another influence limiting full judicial acceptance of the individual autonomy model came from the legacy of classical republican ideas transmitted through the radical Whig theorists of the so-called commonwealth tradition.[28] The classical republican conception of government held that men could not be truly free unless they actively participated in the decisions affecting their lives. But there was a qualification: the conviction that such active participation was possible only in small, relatively homogeneous communities whose members shared a morality of civic virtue that placed service to the common good above the pursuit of individual ambitions. Although the communitarian aspect had largely faded by the late nineteenth century before the ascendancy of the individualistic ethos of natural rights philosophy, the identification of republicanism with a society made up of small, homogeneous, self-governing communities retained strong vitality until the New Deal. That identification not simply provided intellectual justification for the exclusion of aliens not sharing the same skin color, religion, or values, but underlay the continued appeal of the principles of states' rights and federalism.[29] Even after the Civil War, most Americans remained wedded to a "State-centered nationalism" that left to the states major responsibility for determining what rights—such as voting—that their citizens should enjoy.[30]

The confluence of these strains of thought appears strikingly in the Old Court's worst blindspot—the Negro. The underlying premise of the Republican "free labor" ideology was that the Negro, once given the basic natural right to dispose of his labor freely in the marketplace, would have to prove himself by his own efforts. This approach militated during Reconstruction against the adoption of special paternalistic legislation such as land redistribution, then led to disillusionment at black failure to achieve the upward mobility that was assumed to reward hard work, thrift, and self-discipline. More important, the Court's limitation of the scope of the Fourteenth Amendment to remedying state, and not private, discriminatory action represented the reverse side of its liberty of contract philosophy—a point made manifest by Justice Joseph P. Bradley's heavy reliance upon contract law analogies in the *Civil Rights Cases*. At one level, Bradley saw the Civil Rights Act of 1875 as an attack upon the liberty of the public accommodations owner to set the terms for the use of his property. At a deeper level, his purpose was to preserve a realm of autonomy for individual decision–making free from governmental control. Even the Warren Court, while blurring the line between the public and private spheres, shrank from abandoning a distinction so deeply rooted in the American *mentalité*.[31]

The Court's treatment of the Negro reflected the larger currents of the time in other ways. The Waite Court had to deal with the application of the Reconstruction-era legislation at a time when political support for their enforcement had largely faded—a situation that raised in a painfully graphic way the limits of judicial power. The Fuller Court's acquiescence in the relegation of the Negro to second-class citizenship represented accommodation to the facts of life in turn-of-the-century America. The genetic determinism that dominated the social sciences from the late nineteenth century through the 1920s took as given that the Negro was inherently and permanently inferior; that he learned much more slowly than whites; and that racial amalgamation—which was thought inevitable if the races were allowed to commingle—would drag down the white race. Why should not the states be allowed to exercise their police power to prevent that danger, just as they did for other dangers when limiting liberty of contract in the economic sphere or curbing the abuse of freedom of speech and press?[32] A strong argument can be made that from the White Court on, the Court was in advance of the prevailing values and attitudes—without questions those in the South but probably those in the country at large. As Justice Holmes cynically but accurately observed about the uproar of the Sacco-Vanzetti case: "A thousand-fold worse cases of negroes come up from time to time, but the world does not worry over them."[33]

On the other hand, the Old Court laid down interpretations of the criminal law procedure guarantees of the Bill of Rights that if newly adopted today would spur loud complaints about handcuffing the police. Its most important contribution here was the adoption of the exclusionary rule as the mechanism for enforcing the ban against illegally acquired evidence, whether testimonial or physical. And its treatment of the Fourth Amendment imposed such stringent restrictions upon law enforcement officers that the Modern Court has in some areas at least—such as abandonment of the "mere evidence" rule—been driven to retreat from the earlier position.[34] A key factor in the Court's expansive reading of defendants' rights was its heavy reliance on the common law with its built-in bias in favor of protecting the individual from abuse of governmental authority as the guide to the meaning of the Bill of Rights criminal law provisions.[35] Equally important, the Court refused to accept the state of English law at the time of the American Revolution as the last word. Justice George Sutherland—otherwise no liberal hero—in *Powell* gave the right-to-counsel clause a far broader scope than its meaning at the time the Constitution was adopted. In justification, he pointed to how the "unanimous accord" that had developed among the states in requiring the appointment of counsel in at least capital cases gave "convincing support to the conclusion we have reached as to the fundamental nature of that right."[36] The duty of the Court, Sutherland reaffirmed the following year, was to re-examine the common-law heritage "in accordance with present day standards of wisdom and justice rather than in accordance with some outworn and antiquated rule of the past."[37]

The Court's devotion to procedural regularity appears the more striking given much of the opinion of the time. From the 1890s on, influential and respected voices were raised calling for doing away with outdated technical niceties that impeded the speedy and effective maintenance of law and order.[38] These demands reached their height in the 1920s in face of what appeared a worsening "crime wave." The justices were not immune to such feelings.[39] When upholding the warrantless search of automobiles, Chief Justice William Howard Taft emphasized that the Fourth Amendment should be construed in "a manner which will conserve public interests as well as the interests and rights of individual citizens."[40] Underlying his approval of wiretapping in *Olmstead* was his fear that "[w]e have a hard enough time to convict without presenting immunity to the worst and most advanced and most progressive criminals."[41] But he with his brethren on the Court's right wing tempered their support for more effective law enforcement with a recognition that official misconduct—or even toleration of private lawlessness—threatened to undermine respect for the entire legal system.[42] In an obvious reference to the mob-dominated trial in *Moore v. Dempsey*, Justice Pierce Butler told the 1923 meeting of the American Bar Association that the "overthrow of the just power of courts in the trial of cases by these forms of lawlessness is worse—if anything can be worse—than lynchings."[43] Upholding while sitting with the Seventh Circuit Court of Appeals the right of a person convicted of violating the prohibition laws to bail during appeal, Butler reaffirmed the importance of upholding the rule of law. "Abhorrence, however great, of persistent and menacing crime will not excuse transgression in the courts of the legal rights of the worst offenders."[44]

A cynic may say that the Court's application of high standards upon the federal government was largely a meaningless gesture so long as those restrictions were not placed upon the states. Without question the Court's refusal to extend the criminal procedure guarantees of the Bill of Rights to the states mitigated judicial anxiety about the possible impact upon law enforcement of a stringent interpretation of those provisions. One, however, should not underestimate the strength of the commitment to the principles of federalism. In no area was the primacy of state responsibility more widely accepted than in the administration of criminal justice.[45] At the same time, even those justices most sympathetic to states' rights underlined that local responsibility—while primary—was not final. Although the states had broad latitude regarding their criminal law procedures, Chief Justice Melville W. Fuller admonished in 1891, the due process clause of the Fourteenth Amendment protected against their "subjecting the individual to the arbitrary exercise of the powers of government unrestrained by the established principles of private right."[46] That formula would recur with growing frequency as more and more appeals from state criminal convictions reached the justices. And by the 1930s, the Court was looking beyond simply whether the proper legal forms had been followed to whether a constitutionally protected right had been in fact violated. As Chief Justice Hughes enunciated in *Norris*, "Whenever a conclusion of law of a state court as to a federal right and findings of fact are so intermingled that the latter control the former, it is incumbent upon us to analyze the facts in order that the appropriate enforcement of the federal right may be assured."[47]

Viewed in long-term perspective, the trend was toward an increasingly activist role by the Court in supervising state administration of criminal justice.[48] And while still rarely used, habeas corpus gave the federal courts the potential for still more detailed and extensive intrusion into local autonomy in this area. Prohibition did much to educate the Court into the day-to-day realities of law enforcement practice.[49] The documentation of police abuses by an offshoot of that noble experiment—the 1931 reports of the National Commission on Law Observance and Enforcement (the so-called Wickersham Commission)—would have an even longer-term impact.[50] At least as influential in sensitizing the justices to malpractices at the local level was the string of appeals dealing with the treatment of blacks in the South.[51] In *Powell*, the Court applied to the states for the first time an independently listed criminal law guarantee of the Bill of Rights. More important, *Powell* foreshadowed a shift in approach that would provide the rationale for the incorporation into the due process clause of the Fourteenth Amendment of most of the rest. Up to that time, the justices had asked if a given practice was required by fundamental principles of liberty and justice in a universal sense and answered no. When the focus of inquiry became if that practice was fundamental in the Anglo-American legal tradition, a different answer resulted.[52]

Perhaps the most important contribution of the Old Court to its successor lay in the machinery erected for enforcing its will. Whatever the twists and turns in legal doctrine over time, there has been one thread of consistency in the Court's decision-making: the aggrandizement of its own power. The 1925 legislation passed by Congress at the justices' urging gave the Court an almost free hand to control the selection of cases for its docket.[53] The Court had achieved a similarly broad latitude regarding the scope of its jurisdiction. The definition of what constituted a justiciable case or controversy under Article III of the Constitution was so open-ended as to impose no meaningful limitation except the justices' own sense of self-restraint.[54] Nor did the Court formulate "any clear test" for defining what was a federal question.[55] The Court likewise retained final say if a state court decision rested upon a sufficiently adequate independent state ground.[56] The major instruments by which the Modern Court has implemented the civil rights revolution were in place by 1937—direct appeal from the lower federal courts and state courts of final jurisdiction; habeas corpus review of state criminal proceedings; the injunction against state officers; the declaratory judgment; and a nearly unlimited power to punish for contempt. All that was required was the will, and the opportunity, for their boldly aggressive exercise.

Notes

1 Individual Rights in a Federal System

1. Philip B. Kurland, ed., *Of Law and Life and Other Things That Matter: Papers and Addresses of Felix Frankfurter 1956–1963* (Cambridge, Mass.: Harvard University Press, 1967), 94.

2. The debate is summarized in Alan F. Westin, "Introduction: Charles Beard and the American Debate Over Judicial Review, 1790–1961," in Charles A. Beard, *The Supreme Court and the Constitution* (Spectrum Book ed., Englewood Cliffs, N.J.: Prentice-Hall, 1962), pp. 1–34.

3. 1 Cranch 137, at 180, 179, 176–77 (1803).

4. Compare Frank R. Strong, "Judicial Review: A Tri-Dimensional Concept of Administrative-Constitutional Law," *West Virginia Law Review* 69 (February 1967): 119 (*Marbury* did no more than affirm the authority of the Court to review the constitutionality of acts of Congress dealing with the judicial power itself) with William W. Van Alstyne, "A Critical Guide to Marbury v. Madison," *Duke Law Journal* 1969 (January): 35–36 (Marshall did not limit himself to "the legitimacy of constitutional review used only defensively in the protection of the balance of the judicial power" but took the "more grandiose" position "that the whole business of interpreting 'law'—including the 'law' of the Constitution—is emphatically judicial business"). The Modern Supreme Court has fully embraced the judicial monopoly interpretation of *Marbury*: "This decision declared the basic principle that the federal judiciary is supreme in the exposition of the law of the Constitution...," Cooper v. Aaron, 358 U.S. 1, at 18 (1958).

5. Thomas Jefferson to Spencer Roane, September 6, 1819, in Paul L. Ford, ed., *The Writings of Thomas Jefferson*, 10 vols. (New York: G.P. Putnam's Sons, 1892–1899), 10: 142–43. The conflict between the "judicial monopoly" and "tripartite" theories of constitutional interpretation is traced in Donald G. Morgan, *Congress and the Constitution: A Study of Responsibility* (Cambridge, Mass.: Harvard University Press, 1966).

6. 1 Cranch 137, at 165–66 (1803).

7. The clause was a catch-all provision appended at the end of the listing of

the enumerated powers granted to Congress in Article I, Section 8, authorizing Congress "To make all Laws which shall be necessary and proper for carrying into Execution the foregoing Powers, and all other Powers vested by this Constitution in the Government of the United States, or in any Department or Officer thereof."

8. 4 Wheat. 316, at 407, 415–16, 421 (1819).

9. As Edward S. Corwin has observed regarding *McCulloch*, "The real question at issue when the validity of an act of Congress is challenged before the Supreme Court is *not* whether the fundamental Constitution shall give way to an act of Congress, but whether Congress' interpretation of the fundamental Constitution shall prevail or whether it shall yield to that of another human, and therefore presumably fallible, institution,—a bench of judges": Corwin, "The Supreme Court and Unconstitutional Acts of Congress," *Michigan Law Review* 4 (June 1906): 625.

10. Joseph Story, *Commentaries on the Constitution of the United States*, 2 vols. (5th ed., Boston: Little, Brown, 1891), 1: 276.

11. Wallace Mendelson, "Dred Scott's Case—Reconsidered," *Minnesota Law Review* 38 (December 1953): 16–28.

12. Dred Scott v. Sandford, 19 How. 393, at 405, 426 (1857).

13. 6 Cranch 87, at 136 (1810).

14. 1 Wheat. 304, at 342, 344 (1816). Marshall did not participate because of his personal interest in the property dispute at issue, but he followed the same line of reasoning in upholding the authority of the Court to review state criminal judgments in Cohens v. Virginia, 6 Wheat. 264 (1821).

15. Charles Warren, "Legislative and Judicial Attacks on the Supreme Court of the United States—A History of the Twenty-Fifth Section of the Judiciary Act," *American Law Review* 47 (January-February 1913): 1–34, and (March-April 1913): 161–89.

16. Jefferson to Roane, September 6, 1819, in Ford, *Writings of Thomas Jefferson*, 10: 141.

17. Andrew Jackson, "Veto Message," in James D. Richardson, ed., *A Compilation of the Messages and Papers of the Presidents, 1789–1897*, 10 vols. (Washington, D.C.: Government Printing Office, 1896–1899), 2: 582.

18. Abraham Lincoln, "First Inaugural Address," in Richardson, *Messages and Papers of the Presidents*, 6: 9.

19. Thomas C. Grey, "Origins of the Unwritten Constitution: Fundamental Law in American Revolutionary Thought," *Stanford Law Review* 30 (May 1978): 843–93.

20. Leslie F. Goldstein, "Popular Sovereignty, the Origins of Judicial Review, and the Revival of Unwritten Law," *Journal of Politics* 48 (February 1986): 51-71.

21. Wynehamer v. People, 13 N.Y. 378, at 405–06 (1856). For fuller elaboration, see William E. Nelson, "Changing Conceptions of Judicial Review: The Evolution of Constitutional Theory in the States, 1790–1860," *University of Pennsylvania Law Review* 120 (June 1972): 1166–85.

22. Ableman v. Booth, 21 How. 506, at 521 (1859). On this point, see Archibald Cox, *The Role of the Supreme Court in American Government* (New York: Oxford University Press, 1976), pp. 16–23.

23. Don E. Fehrenbacher, *The Dred Scott Case: Its Significance in American Law and Politics* (New York: Oxford University Press, 1978), pp. 450–54.

24. David M. Silver, *Lincoln's Supreme Court [Illinois Studies in the Social Sciences*, 38] (Urbana: University of Illinois Press, 1956).

25. Stanley I. Kutler, *Judicial Power and Reconstruction Politics* (Chicago: University of Chicago Press, 1968).

26. William M. Wiecek, "The 'Imperial Judiciary' in Historical Perspective," *Supreme Historical Society Yearbook 1984* (Washington D.C.: Supreme Court Historical Society, 1984), 76-79.

27. David J. Danelski and Joseph S. Tulchin, eds., *The Autobiographical Notes of Charles Evans Hughes* (Cambridge, Mass.: Harvard University Press, 1973), 144.

28. This schematic breakdown is from Richard Funston, "The Supreme Court and Critical Elections," *American Political Science Review* 69 (September 1975): 795–811.

29. This turnabout is described in the symposium "Ten Years of the Supreme Court: 1937-1947," *American Political Science Review* 41 (December 1947): 1142–81, and 42 (February 1948): 32–67; Vincent M. Barnett, Jr., "The Supreme Court and the Capacity to Govern," *Political Science Quarterly* 63 (September 1948): 342–67; Robert L. Stern, "The Commerce Clause and the National Economy, 1933-1946," *Harvard Law Review* 59 (May 1946): 645–93, and (July 1946): 883–947; and David Fellman, "Federalism and the Commerce Clause, 1937-1947," *Journal of Politics* 10 (February 1948): 155–67.

30. Edward S. Corwin, *Constitutional Revolution, Ltd.* (Claremont, Calif.: Claremont Colleges, 1941), pp. 111–12, 115.

31. *Re* the 1935-1936 term: Henry J. Abraham, *The Judicial Process: An Introductory Analysis of the Courts of the United States, England, and France* (4th ed., New York: Oxford University Press, 1980), p. 368. For the increased saliency of civil rights issues since, see Arthur D. Hellman, "The Business of the Supreme Court under the Judiciary Act of 1925: The Plenary Docket in the 1970's," *Harvard Law Review* 91 (June 1978): 1737–60.

32. Maxwell v. Dow, 176 U.S. 581, at 614 (1900).

33. Charles A. Beard, "What About the Constitution?" *Nation*, April 1, 1936, 405.

34. John P. Roche, "Civil Liberty in the Age of Enterprise," *University of Chicago Law Review* 31 (Autumn 1963): 103, 107

35. Robert G. McCloskey, *The Modern Supreme Court* (Cambridge, Mass.: Harvard University Press, 1972), 4.

36. Robert H. Jackson, *The Struggle for Judicial Supremacy: A Study of a Crisis in American Power Politics* (New York: Alfred A. Knopf, 1941), p. 71.

37. Gerald Gunther, *Cases and Materials on Constitutional Law* (10th ed., Mineola, N. Y.: Foundation Press, 1980), p. 374.

38. This story is traced in Benjamin F. Wright, Jr., *The Contract Clause of the Constitution* (Cambridge, Mass.: Harvard University Press, 1938).

39. 3 Dall. 386, at 390 (1798). The limitation of the ex post facto clause to retroactive criminal laws was reaffirmed repeatedly: Watson v. Mercer, 8 Pet. 88, at 110 (1834); Baltimore and Susquehanna Railroad Co. v. Nesbit, 10 How. 395 (1850); Carpenter v. Pennsylvania, 17 How. 456 (1855); Locke v. City of New Orleans, 4 Wall. 172 (1867).

40. Cummings v. Missouri, 4 Wall. 277 (1867); *Ex parte* Garland, 4 Wall. 333 (1867). The quote from Blackstone is at 321. For background, see Harold M. Hyman, *Era of the Oath: Northern Loyalty Tests during the Civil War and Reconstruction* (Philadelphia: University of Pennsylvania Press, 1954).

41. On the historical meaning of the term, see the dissent by Justice Samuel F. Miller in *Ex parte* Garland, 4 Wall. 333, at 387–88 (1867); and Raoul Berger, "Bills of Attainder: A Study of Amendment by the Court," *Cornell Law Review* 63 (March 1978): 355–404.

42. The Marshall *dicta* is in Fletcher v. Peck, 6 Cranch 87, at 138–39 (1810). For Field's argument: Cummings v. Missouri, 4 Wall. 277, at 318–25 (1867). As Justice Miller rightly pointed out in his dissent, this definition "would make a great number of laws, partaking in no sense of a criminal character, laws for punishment," and thus invalid under the bill of attainder and ex post facto clauses: *Ex parte* Garland, 4 Wall. 333, at 394 (1867).

43. Pierce v. Carskadon, 16 Wall. 234 (1873).

44. Dent v. West Virginia, 129 U.S. 114 (1889) (application of new qualifications for the practice of medicine applied to person who had been previously practicing not a bill of attainder or ex post facto law); Hawker v. New York, 170 U.S. 189 (1898) (statute barring convicted felon from practicing medicine applied to person convicted before its adoption not a bill of attainder or ex post facto law). The Court's treatment of the ex post facto clause is surveyed in Breck P. McAllister, "Ex Post Facto Laws in the Supreme Court of the United States," *California Law Review* 15 (May 1927): 269–88; of the bill of attainder provision in Berger, "Bills of Attainder," plus two Comments: "The Bounds of Legislative Specification: A Suggested Approach to the Bill of Attainder Clause," *Yale Law Journal* 72 (December 1962): 330–67, and "The Supreme Court's Bill of Attainder Doctrine: A Need for Clarification," *California Law Review* 54 (March 1966): 212–50.

45. Ross v. Oregon, 227 U.S. 150 (1913).

46. Kring v. Missouri, 107 U.S. 221, at 232 (1883).

47. Medley, Petitioner, 134 U.S. 160, at 167-70 (1890) (new requirement of solitary confinement before execution for murder an "additional punishment" in violation of the ex post facto law clause). But a retroactive change in the method of execution from hanging to electrocution was permissible because electrocution was more "humane": Mallory v. South Carolina, 237 U.S. 180, at 185 (1915).

48. McDonald v. Massachusetts, 180 U.S. 311 (1901).

49. A shift from a twelve- to an eight-man jury for trial of an offense occurring before the change was held to work a substantial disadvantage to the defendant since the prosecution had to convince fewer people: Thompson v. Utah, 170 U.S. 343 (1898). Changes that were found not to work to the defendant's substantial disadvantage included: Hopt v. Utah, 110 U.S. 574 (1884) (change in rules defining competent witnesses); Duncan v. Missouri, 152 U.S. 377 (1894) (change in structure of appellate courts); Gibson v. Mississippi, 162 U.S. 565, at 588–90 (1896) (change in jury selection procedures); Beazell v. Ohio, 269 U.S. 167 (1925) (change in rules governing trials of jointly indicted defendants).

50. United States v. Trans-Missouri Freight Association, 166 U.S. 290, at 342 (1897). See also *re* this continuing-action rule: Chicago and Alton Railroad Co. v. Tranbarger, 238 U.S. 67, at 73-74 (1915), and Samuels v. McCurdy, 267 U.S. 188, at 193 (1925).

51. Robert A. Rutland, *The Birth of the Bill of Rights 1776–1791* (Chapel Hill: University of North Carolina Press, 1955), 198–218.

52. 7 Pet. 243, at 247, 250 (1833). This conclusion was reaffirmed by the Taney and, then, the Chase Courts: Permoli v. New Orleans, 3 How. 589 (1845); Fox v.

Ohio, 5 How. 410 (1847); Smith v. Maryland, 18 How. 71 (1855); Pervear v. Massachusetts, 5 Wall. 475 (1867); Twitchell v. Pennsylvania, 7 Wall. 321 (1869).

53. 14 Stat. 27, at 27 (1866).

54. A handy summary of the debate can be found in Robert J. Kaczorowski, "Searching for the Intent of the Framers of the Fourteenth Amendment," *Connecticut Law Review* 5 (Winter 1972-1973): 368–98. For more recent installments, compare Raoul Berger, *Government by Judiciary: The Transformation of the Fourteenth Amendment* (Cambridge, Mass.: Harvard University Press, 1977), with Michael K. Curtis, *No State Shall Abridge: The Fourteenth Amendment and the Bill of Rights* (Durham, N.C.: Duke University Press, 1986), Daniel A. Farber and John E. Muench, "The Ideological Origins of the Fourteenth Amendment," *Constitutional Commentary* 1 (Summer 1984): 235-79, and Kaczorowski, "To Begin the Nation Anew: Congress, Citizenship, and Civil Rights after the Civil War," *American Historical Review* 92 (February 1987): 45–68.

55. Still useful pioneering reviews of the Supreme Court's decision-making regarding the applicability of the Bill of Rights to the states via the Fourteenth Amendment are John R. Green, "Liberty under the Fourteenth Amendment," *Washington University Law Quarterly* 27 (Summer 1942): 497–562, and Stanley Morrison, "Does the Fourteenth Amendment Incorporate the Bill of Rights? The Judicial Interpretation," *Stanford Law Review* 2 (December 1949): 140-73. Fuller, and probably the definitive account, is Richard C. Cortner, *The Supreme Court and the Second Bill of Rights: The Fourteenth Amendment and the Nationalization of Civil Liberties* (Madison: University of Wisconsin Press, 1981).

56. The tangled course of this litigation is traced in Charles Fairman, *Reconstruction and Reunion 1864–88, Part One* [*Oliver Wendell Holmes Devise History of the Supreme Court of the United States*, Vol. 6] (New York: Macmillan, 1971): 1320–63. For the larger context out of which the controversy arose, see Mitchell Franklin, "The Foundations and Meaning of the Slaughterhouse Cases," *Tulane Law Review* 18 (October 1943): 1–88, and (December 1943): 218–62.

57. 16 Wall. 36, at 60–65, 77–80 (1873). A perceptive analysis of the adherence by the majority of the justices to a "State-centered nationalism" committed to preserving "the basics of the federal system" is found in Michael L. Benedict, "Preserving Federalism: Reconstruction and the Waite Court," in *The Supreme Court Review 1978*, ed. Philip B. Kurland and Gerhard Casper (Chicago: University of Chicago Press, 1979), 39-79.

58. Bartemeyer v. Iowa, 18 Wall. 129, at 133 (1874) (right to sell liquor not a privilege and immunity of national citizenship); Minor v. Happersett, 21 Wall. 162, at 171 (1875) (voting not a privilege and immunity of national citizenship); Walker v. Sauvinet, 92 U.S. 90, at 92–93 (1876)(Seventh Amendment right to a jury trial in civil cases and, by implication, any of the rights protected by the first eight amendments not a privilege and immunity of national citizenship). Only once has the privileges and immunities clause been used to overturn state legislation: Colgate v. Harvey, 296 U.S. 404 (1935) (striking down a Vermont income tax law imposing higher taxes on income from money loaned to persons outside the state than on income from loans to persons residing within the state); and that decision was overruled five years later: Madden v. Kentucky, 309 U.S. 83 (1940).

59. 16 Wall. 36, at 81 (1873).

60. Strauder v. West Virginia, 100 U.S. 303, at 310 (1880).

61. Missouri v. Lewis, 101 U.S. 22, at 31 (1880). This broader position was reaffirmed in Barbier v. Connolly, 113 U.S. 27 (1885) (equal protection clause safeguarded "all persons" against the imposition of "greater burdens...upon one than are laid upon others in the same calling and condition," at 31).

62. 118 U.S. 356, at 369 (1886).

63. The following draws heavily upon Richard S. Kay, "The Equal Protection Clause in the Supreme Court 1873–1903," *Buffalo Law Review* 29 (Fall 1980): 667-725.

64. Gulf, Colorado & Santa Fé Railway Co. v. Ellis, 165 U.S. 150, at 155 (1897).

65. Bell's Gap Railroad Co. v. Pennsylvania, 134 U.S. 232, at 237 (1890).

66. Plessy v. Ferguson, 163 U.S. 537, at 550 (1896).

67. Lindsley v. Natural Carbonic Gas Co., 220 U.S. 61, at 78 (1911).

68. Buck v. Bell, 274 U.S. 200, at 208 (1927).

69. 16 Wall. 36, at 80–81 (1873).

70. 110 U.S. 516, at 535 (1884). Justice Stephen J. Field did not participate.

71. The classic account is Edward S. Corwin, "The Supreme Court and the Fourteenth Amendment," *Michigan Law Review* 7 (June 1909): 643-72.

72. 123 U.S. 623, at 661 (1887).

73. 134 U.S. 418 (1890).

74. 165 U.S. 578, at 589 (1897).

75. John P. Roche, "Entrepreneurial Liberty and the Fourteenth Amendment," *Labor History* 4 (Winter 1963): 3–31.

76. 198 U.S. 45, at 56–57, 59 (1905).

77. Chicago, Burlington and Quincy Railroad Co. v. Chicago, 166 U.S. 226 (1897). Chief Justice Melville W. Fuller did not participate.

78. 176 U.S. 581, at 603, 597 (1900).

79. 211 U.S. 78, at 106, 99–100 (1908).

80. 262 U.S. 390, at 401–03, 399 (1923). The quote from *Twining* is at 110. In Farrington v. Tokushige, 273 U.S. 284 (1927), the Court relied upon *Meyer* to strike down regulations adopted by the Hawaii legislature and board of public instruction aimed at destroying the Japanese-language schools in the territory.

81. Spies v. Illinois, 123 U.S. 131, at 139 (1887).

82. Patterson v. Colorado, 205 U.S. 454, at 462 (1907).

83. 254 U.S. 325, at 331–32 (1920).

84. Prudential Insurance Co. of America v. Cheek, 259 U.S. 530, at 538 (1922).

85. Gitlow v. New York, 268 U.S. 652, at 654–55, 666 (1925). For background, see Julian F. Jaffe, *Crusade against Radicalism: New York during the Red Scare, 1914–1924* (Port Washington, N.Y.: National University Publications, Kennikat Press, 1972), 198–215, and Harold Josephson, "Political Justice during the Red Scare: The Trial of Benjamin Gitlow," in *American Political Trials*, ed. Michal R. Belknap (Westport, Conn.: Greenwood Press, 1981), pp. 153-75. *Re* Pollak's role: Louis H. Pollak, "Advocating Civil Liberties: A Young Lawyer before an Old Court," *Harvard Civil Rights-Civil Liberties Law Review* 17 (Spring 1982): 1–30.

86. This point relies upon Klaus H. Heberle, "From Gitlow to Near: Judicial 'Amendment' by Absent-Minded Incrementalism," *Journal of Politics* 34 (May 1972): 458–83.

87. 274 U.S. 380 (1927).

88. 274 U.S. 357, at 373 (Brandeis), 371 (Sanford) (1927).

89. New York *ex rel.* Bryant v. Zimmerman, 278 U.S. 63, at 72 (1928).

90. Muselin v. Pennsylvania, 280 U.S. 518 (1929).

91. 283 U.S. 359, at 361, 368 (1931).

92. Near v. Minnesota *ex rel.* Olson, 283 U.S. 697, at 701–02, 707 (1931).

93. 299 U.S. 353, at 364 (1937). Justice Harlan F. Stone did not participate.

94. 1 Stat. 73, at 80 (1789). For the Court's refusal to accept as falling within its original jurisdiction actions by a state against one of its own citizens, see Pennsylvania v. Quicksilver Co., 10 Wall. 553, at 556 (1871).

95. The adoption and subsequent interpretation of the Eleventh Amendment is examined in detail in John J. Gibbons, "The Eleventh Amendment and State Sovereign Immunity: A Reinterpretation," *Columbia Law Review* 83 (December 1983): 1889–2005.

96. 1 Cranch 137, at 173-75 (1803).

97. The Court affirmed the authority of Congress do so in Börs v. Preston, 111 U.S. 252 (1884) and Ames v. Kansas, 111 U.S. 449 (1884). The long-term result was that the Supreme Court retained exclusive original jurisdiction in only two areas: (1) actions by the United States against a state; (2) disputes between two states, typically over boundaries and over mineral and water rights.

98. The classic account of the historical development of the Court's jurisdiction is Felix Frankfurter and James M. Landis, *The Business of the Supreme Court: A Study in the Federal Judicial System* (New York: Macmillan, 1928).

99. Accounts of the historical development of the structure and jurisdiction of the lower federal courts include: Felix Frankfurter, "The Distribution of Judicial Power Between United States and State Courts," *Cornell Law Quarterly* 13 (June 1928): 499–530; John P. Frank, "Historical Bases of the Federal Judicial System," *Law and Contemporary Problems* 13 (Winter 1948): 3–28; and Erwin C. Surrency, "A History of the Federal Courts," *Missouri Law Review* 28 (Spring 1963): 214–44.

100. 1 Stat. 73, at 73-75 (1789). The district courts in what became Kentucky and Maine were authorized to sit as circuit courts (at 77-78).

101. 1 Stat. 333, at 333 (1793).

102. 2 Stat. 156, at 158 (1802).

103. 16 Stat. 44, at 44–45 (1869).

104. Charles Warren, "New Light on the History of the Federal Judiciary Act of 1789," *Harvard Law Review* 37 (November 1923): 49–132.

105. 1 Stat. 73, at 76–80 (1789).

106. 2 Stat. 89, at 92 (1801); 2 Stat. 132 (1802). For further details, see Erwin C. Surrency, "The Judiciary Act of 1801," *American Journal of Legal History* 2 (January 1958): 53–65.

107. The only significant addition to the jurisdiction of the lower federal courts before the Civil War came in the so-called Force Bill of 1833 in response to South Carolina's threatened nullification of the tariff. That legislation gave the federal circuit courts jurisdiction over "all cases...arising under the revenue laws of the United States," provided for removal to the federal courts of suits against federal revenue officers, and authorized federal judges to grant the writ of habeas corpus to prisoners confined "by any authority or law, for any act done, or omitted to be done, in pursuance of a law of the United States, or any order...of any judge or court thereof": 4 Stat. 632, at 632–34 (1833).

108. 1 Stat. 73, at 84 (1789).

109. Henry M. Hart, Jr., and Herbert Wechsler, *The Federal Courts and the Federal System* (Brooklyn: Foundation Press, 1953): pp. 44–45, 1313.

110. 1 Stat. 73, at 85–87 (1789).

111. 14 Stat. 385, at 386–87 (1867).

112. 20 Wall. 590, at 619, 634–36 (1875).

113. Fox Film Corp. v. Muller, 296 U.S. 207, at 210 (1935).

114. United States Mortgage Co. v. Matthews, 293 U.S. 232 (1934) (reversing a state court decision upholding a contract obligation and invalidating an alleged impairment thereof because disagreeing as to the existence of the obligation).

115. Davis v. Wechsler, 263 U.S. 22, at 24 (1923).

116. For full details, see John J. Gibbons, "Federal Law and the State Courts 1790–1860," *Rutgers Law Review* 36 (Spring 1984): 399–453.

117. 16 Stat. 140, at 142 (1870); 17 Stat. 13, at 14–15 (1871).

118. 18 Stat. 470, at 470 (1875).

119. 26 Stat. 826, at 826–28 (1891).

120. 43 Stat. 936, at 938–39 (1925).

121. 38 Stat. 790 (1914). The New York case was Ives v. South Buffalo Railway Co., 201 N.Y. 271 (1911).

122. 43 Stat. 936, at 937 (1925).

123. Francis J. Ulman and Frank H. Spears, " 'Dismissed for Want of a Substantial Federal Question': A Study in the Practice of the Supreme Court in Deciding Appeals from State Courts," *Boston University Law Review* 20 (June 1940): 501–32.

124. Corwin, "The Supreme Court and the Fourteenth Amendment," p. 665.

125. 274 U.S. 380, at 385–86 (1927).

126. Norris v. Alabama, 294 U.S. 587, at 589–90 (1935).

127. 1 Stat. 333, at 335 (1793).

128. Rev. Stat., at 114 (1875).

129. 100 U.S. 303 (1880); 100 U.S. 313 (1880). *Re* how *Rives* and follow-up decisions reduced the civil-rights removal provision to a dead letter, see: Martin H. Redish, *Federal Jurisdiction: Tensions in the Allocation of Judicial Power* (Indianapolis: Michie, 1980), pp. 323–30, and Benno C. Schmidt, Jr., "Juries, Jurisdiction, and Race Discrimination: The Lost Promise of *Strauder v. West Virginia*," *Texas Law Review* 61 (May 1983): 1401–99.

130. 24 Stat. 552, at 553 (1887); 25 Stat. 433, at 434 (1888); Tennessee v. Union and Planters' Bank, 152 U.S. 454, at 459 (1894). For fuller details *re* the limits upon removal, see Charles A. Wright, *The Law of the Federal Courts* (4th ed., St. Paul: West Publishing Co., 1983), 209–25.

131. See for a discussion of the general issue, Joseph D. Block, "Suits Against Government Officers and the Sovereign Immunity Doctrine," *Harvard Law Review* 59 (September 1946): 1060–86.

132. 2 Dall. 419, at 478 (1793).

133. 6 Wheat. 264, at 411–412 (1821). The same position was taken by the Taney Court: United States v. McLemore, 4 How. 287 (1846).

134. 2 Dall. 419 (1793).

135. For in-depth treatments, see Gibbons, "Eleventh Amendment and State Sovereign Immunity," and Clyde E. Jacobs, *The Eleventh Amendment and Sovereign Immunity* (Westport, Conn.: Greenwood Press, 1972).

136. The leading case was Kendall v. United States *ex rel.* Stokes, 12 Pet 524

(1838). The basic line of approach was laid down earlier by John Marshall in Marbury v. Madison, 1 Cranch 137, at 168-70 (1803). Later cases involved where to draw the line between ministerial and discretionary; see: Frederic P. Lee, "The Origins of Judicial Control of Federal Executive Action," *Georgetown Law Journal* 36 (March 1948): 287–95. The same distinction was drawn *re* the issuance by the federal courts of writs of mandamus to state officers: Lankford v. Platte Iron Works Co., 235 U.S. 461 (1915) (no mandamus when state law imposed no duty on officer toward plaintiff).

137. Mississippi v. Johnson, 4 Wall. 475 (1867) (Court had no "jurisdiction of a bill to enjoin the President in the performance of his official duties," at 501); Georgia v. Stanton, 6 Wall. 50 (1868) (suit to enjoin Secretary of War dismissed because asked "for the judgment of the court upon political questions," not the "rights of persons or property," at 76-77).

138. 106 U.S. 196, at 219 (1882).

139. Osborn v. Bank of the United States, 9 Wheat. 738, at 847–58 (1824); Davis v. Gray, 16 Wall. 203 (1873); Board of Liquidation v. McComb, 92 U.S. 531 (1876). The following discussion relies heavily upon John V. Orth, "The Interpretation of the Eleventh Amendment, 1798–1908: A Case Study of Judicial Power," *University of Illinois Law Review* 1983, no. 2: 423-55, and William F. Duker, "Mr. Justice Rufus W. Peckham and the Case of *Ex Parte Young*: Lochnerizing *Munn v. Illinois*," *Brigham Young University Law Review* 1980, no. 3: 539–58.

140. 123 U.S. 443 (1887).

141. 134 U.S. 1 (1890).

142. Gelpcke v. Dubuque, 1 Wall. 175 (1864); Cowles v. Mercer County, 7 Wall. 118 (1869); Lincoln County v. Luning, 133 U.S. 529 (1890); Workman v. New York City, 179 U.S. 552 (1900).

143. Pennoyer v. McConnaughy, 140 U.S. 1 (1891); Reagan v. Farmers' Loan and Trust Co., 154 U.S. 362 (1894); Smyth v. Ames, 169 U.S. 466 (1898); Prout v. Starr, 188 U.S. 537 (1903).

144. 209 U.S. 123, at 159–60 (1908).

145. Looney v. Eastern Texas Railroad Co., 247 U.S. 214 (1918).

146. 287 U.S. 378 (1932).

147. Virginia v. West Virginia, 246 U.S. 565, at 595–601, 603–06 (1918).

148. On this issue, see: Note, "Civil and Criminal Contempt in the Federal Courts," *Yale Law Journal* 57 (November 1947): 83–107, and Walter F. Murphy, "The Contempt Power of the Federal Courts," *Federal Bar Journal* 18 (January-March 1958): 34–55.

149. This distinction was officially recognized in Gompers v. Bucks Stove & Range Co., 221 U.S. 418, at 441–43 (1911).

150. "To render a person amenable to an injunction it is neither necessary that he should have been a party to the suit in which the injunction was issued, nor to have been actually served with a copy of it, so long as he appears to have had actual notice": *In re* Lennon, 166 U.S. 548, at 554 (1897).

151. See, for example, *In re* Chiles, 22 Wall. 157 (1875) (party refusing to obey court order "should be fined and imprisoned until he performs the act required of him or shows that it is not in his power to do it," at 168).

152. 4 Stat. 487, at 488 (1831).

153. *Ex parte* Robinson, 19 Wall. 505, at 510 (1874); Eilenbecker v. District Court of Plymouth County, 134 U.S. 31, at 36 (1890). Not surprisingly, the father of the

inherent power theory was John Marshall, in United States v. Hudson and Goodwin, 7 Cranch 32, at 34 (1812).

154. *In re* Debs, 158 U.S. 564, at 570, 594–96 (1895).

155. The leading cases where such contempt convictions for obstruction of justice were upheld were Patterson v. Colorado, 205 U.S. 454 (1907) (state court) and Toledo Newspaper Co. v. United States, 247 U.S. 402 (1918) (federal district court).

156. 38 Stat. 730, at 738–39 (1914). Sections 21–24, at 738–40, of the same legislation provided for a jury trial when the act of contempt was simultaneously a crime under a federal or state law. But this jury trial requirement did not apply when the contempt was committed in the presence of the court or "so near thereby as to obstruct the administration of justice" and when the contempt arose out of an action prosecuted by the United States. And the Court further narrowed its significance by reading the statute as limited to prosecutions for criminal, not civil, contempt: Michaelson v. United States, 266 U.S. 42, at 64–66 (1924).

157. Chase National Bank v. City of Norwalk, 291 U.S. 431, at 436–37 (1934).

158. 47 Stat. 70, Section 11, at 72-73 (1932).

159. Cooke v. United States, 267 U.S. 517, at 534–39 (1925).

160. United States v. Shipp, 203 U.S. 563, at 573 (1906).

161. 36 Stat. 539, at 557 (1910); 37 Stat. 1013 (1913); 43 Stat. 936, at 938 (1925). In 1937, this device was extended to suits for an interlocutory or permanent injunction to restrain enforcement of an allegedly unconstitutional act of Congress: 50 Stat. 751, at 752–53 (1937).

162. 109 U.S. 123, at 162 (1908).

163. Fenner v. Boykin, 271 U.S. 240, at 243 (1926).

164. Edwin Borchard, *Declaratory Judgments* (2d ed., Cleveland: Banks-Baldwin Law Publishing Co., 1941), p. xiii.

165. Muskrat v. United States, 219 U.S. 346, at 362 (1911).

166. Nashville, Chattanooga & St. Louis Railway Co. v. Wallace, 288 U.S. 249, at 264 (1933).

167. 48 Stat. 955, at 955–56 (1934).

168. Aetna Life Insurance Co. v. Haworth, 300 U.S. 227 (1937).

2 The Scope of Constitutionally Protected Rights

1. On this point, see William Anderson, "The Intention of the Framers: A Note on Constitutional Interpretation," *American Political Science Review* 49 (June 1955): 340–52.

2. Charles A. Beard, "The Living Constitution," *Annals of the American Academy of Political and Social Science* 185 (May 1936): 30.

3. Alpheus T. Mason, *The Supreme Court from Taft to Warren* (Baton Rouge: Louisiana State University Press, 1958), p. vii.

4. William Blackstone, *Commentaries on the Laws of England*, ed. William D. Lewis, 4 vols. (Philadelphia: Rees Welsh, 1897), 4: 1551–53.

5. That position was most closely associated with Justice Hugo L. Black. See his *A Constitutional Faith* (New York: Alfred A. Knopf, 1968), pp. 43–63, and Black and Edmond Cahn, "Justice Black and First Amendment 'Absolutes': A Public Interview," *New York University Law Review* 37 (June 1962): 549–63.

6. James Fitzjames Stephen, *A History of the Criminal Law of England*, 3 vols. (London: Macmillan, 1883), 2: 353.

7. Compare Zechariah Chafee, Jr., *Free Speech in the United States* (Cambridge, Mass.: Harvard University Press, 1941) (framers of the First Amendment "intended to wipe out the common law of sedition, and make further prosecutions for criticism of the government, without any incitement to law-breaking, forever impossible," 21) with Leonard W. Levy, *Legacy of Suppression: Freedom of Speech and Press in Early American History* (Cambridge, Mass: Harvard University Press, 1960) (framers "did not intend to give free rein to criticism of the government that might be deemed seditious libel," vii). Levy has reaffirmed his basic position in "The *Legacy* Reexamined," *Stanford Law Review* 37 (February 1985): 767–93, and *Emergence of a Free Press* (New York: Oxford University Press, 1985); the contrary view has been argued by David A. Anderson, "The Origins of the Press Clause," *UCLA Law Review* 30 (February 1983): 455–541; William T. Mayton, "Seditious Libel and the Lost Guarantee of a Freedom of Expression," *Columbia Law Review* 84 (January 1984): 91–142; and David M. Rabban, "The Ahistorical Historian: Leonard Levy on Freedom of Expression in Early American History," *Stanford Law Review* 37 (February 1985): 795–856.

8. Kent Greenawalt, "Speech and Crime," *American Bar Foundation Research Journal* 1980 (Fall): 687–90.

9. On Chafee's role in the development of First Amendment doctrine, see Jerold S. Auerbach, "The Patrician as Libertarian: Zechariah Chafee, Jr. and Freedom of Speech," *New England Quarterly* 42 (December 1969): 511–31, and Donald L. Smith, *Zechariah Chafee, Jr.: Defender of Liberty and Law* (Cambridge, Mass.: Harvard University Press, 1986).

10. People v. Most, 171 N.Y. 423, at 431 (1902). In-depth accounts documenting the consensus among judges and legal commentators in distinguishing between the responsible and irresponsible exercise of freedom of speech and press include: Norman L. Rosenberg, *Protecting the Best Men: An Interpretive History of the Law of Libel* (Chapel Hill: University of North Carolina Press, 1986), esp. 56-129; Alexis J. Anderson, "The Formative Period of First Amendment Theory, 1870–1915," *American Journal of History* 24 (January 1980): 56-75; David M. Rabban, "The First Amendment in Its Forgotten Years," *Yale Law Journal* 90 (January 1981): 514–95; and Margaret A. Blanchard, "Filling in the Void: Speech and Press in State Courts prior to *Gitlow*," in *The First Amendment Reconsidered: New Perspectives on the Meaning of Freedom of Speech and Press*, ed. Bill F. Chamberlin and Charlene J. Brown (New York: Longman, 1982), 14–59. A handy survey of Supreme Court decisions touching upon the First Amendment (including the religion clauses) can be found in Howard O. Hunter, "Problems in Search of Principles: The First Amendment and the Supreme Court from 1791-1930," *Emory Law Journal* 35 (Winter 1986): 59–137.

11. 205 U.S. 454, at 462 (1907).

12. Fox v. Washington, 236 U.S. 273, at 275-77 (1915).

13. The fullest accounts are Thomas A. Lawrence, "Eclipse of Liberty: Civil Liberties in the United States during the First World War," *Wayne Law Review* 21 (November 1974): 33–112, and Paul L. Murphy, *World War I and the Origin of Civil Liberties in the United States* (New York: W. W. Norton, 1979). *Re* state sedition laws, see Carol E. Jenson, *The Network of Control: State Supreme Courts and State Security Statutes, 1920–1970* (Westport, Conn.: Greenwood Press, 1982), 3–15.

14. 40 Stat. 217, at 219 (1917).

15. 249 U.S. 47, at 51–52 (1919).

16. The sources and development of the clear-and-present-danger rule are examined in: Chester J. Antieau, "The Rule of Clear and Present Danger—Its Origin and Application," *University of Detroit Law Journal* 13 (May 1950): 198–213; Wallace Mendelson, "Clear and Present Danger—From Schenck to Dennis," *Columbia Law Review* 52 (March 1952): 313–33; and Edward S. Corwin, "Bowing Out 'Clear and Present Danger,' " *Notre Dame Lawyer* 27 (Spring 1952): 325–59. The most exhaustive analysis is David M. Rabban, "The Emergence of Modern First Amendment Doctrine," *University of Chicago Law Review* 50 (Fall 1983): 1205–1355.

17. Commonwealth v. Peaslee, 177 Mass. 267, at 272 (1901).

18. 249 U.S. 47, at 51–52 (1919).

19. 249 U.S. 204, at 207, 209 (1919).

20. Debs v. United States, 249 U.S. 211, at 216 (1919). *Re* defense arguments: Rabban, "Emergence of Modern First Amendment Doctrine," 1248-52, and David L. Sterling, "In Defense of Debs: The Lawyers and the Espionage Act Case," *Indiana Magazine of History* 83 (March 1987): 17–42.

21. "Ernst Freund and the First Amendment Tradition," *University of Chicago Law Review* 40 (Winter 1973): 240.

22. Oliver Wendell Holmes, Jr., to Herbert Croly, 12 May 1919, in Mark D. Howe, Jr., ed., *Holmes-Laski Letters: The Correspondence of Mr. Justice Holmes and Harold J. Laski 1916–1935*, 2 vols. (Cambridge, Mass.: Harvard University Press, 1953), 1: 203. Holmes was quoting (with a slight mistake in wording) from his opinion in Nash v. United States, 229 U.S. 373, at 377 (1913) (upholding criminal conviction under the Sherman Antitrust Act).

23. 250 U.S. 616, at 627, 629 (Holmes), 621 (Clarke) (1919). David Bogen, "The Free Speech Metamorphosis of Mr. Justice Holmes," *Hofstra Law Review* 11 (Fall 1982): 97–189, denies that Holmes shifted his position in *Abrams*. More persuasive that he did are Fred D. Ragan, "Justice Oliver Wendell Holmes, Jr., Zechariah Chafee, Jr., and the Clear and Present Danger Test for Free Speech: The First Year, 1919," *Journal of American History* 58 (June 1971): 24–45, and Rabban, "Emergence of Modern First Amendment Doctrine," 1303–17.

24. Schaefer v. United States, 251 U.S. 466, at 479 (1920); Pierce v. United States, 252 U.S. 239, at 250 (1920).

25. Gitlow v. New York, 268 U.S. 652, at 668-71 (1925).

26. 268 U.S. 652, at 673 (1925).

27. 274 U.S. 357, at 375 (1927).

28. 274 U.S. 357, at 366–67 (Brandeis), 359–60 (text of law), 371-72 (Sanford). For Hand's opinion, see Masses Pub. Co. v. Patten, 244 F 535, at 540–41 (S.D.N.Y. 1917).

29. Fiske v. Kansas, 274 U.S. 380, at 386–87 (1927). For details, see Richard C. Cortner, "The Wobblies and Fiske *v.* Kansas: Victory amid Disintegration," *Kansas History* 4 (Spring 1981): 30–38.

30. Stromberg v. California, 283 U.S. 359, at 369-70 (1931).

31. 299 U.S. 353, at 364–65 (1937).

32. 301 U.S. 242, at 246, 260–61, 258 (1937). For background and fuller details, see Charles H. Martin, *The Angelo Herndon Case and Southern Justice* (Baton Rouge: Louisiana State University Press, 1976).

33. Robert M. Cover, "The Left, the Right and the First Amendment: 1918-1928," *Maryland Law Review* 40, no. 3 (1981): 349–88.

34. Learned Hand to Zechariah Chafee, Jr., January 2, 1921, reprinted in Gerald Gunther, "Learned Hand and the Origins of Modern First Amendment Doctrine: Some Fragments of History," *Stanford Law Review* 27 (February 1975): 770.

35. *Re Near* as "a turning point in American law and public policy," Paul L. Murphy, *"Near v. Minnesota* in the Context of Historical Developments," *Minnesota Law Review* 66 (November 1981): 153; its "landmark status": Fred W. Friendly, *Minnesota Rag: The Dramatic Story of the Landmark Supreme Court Case That Gave New Meaning to Freedom of the Press* (New York: Random House, 1981), p. 179.

36. Near v. Minnesota *ex rel.* Olson, 283 U.S. 697, at 716–17, 719-20, 715 (1931).

37. The following—except where otherwise indicated—is based upon: Alfred H. Kelly, "Constitutional Liberty and the Law of Libel: A Historian's View," *American Historical Review* 74 (December 1968): 429–52; Rosenberg, *Protecting the Best Men*, 3–234; Clifton O. Lawhorne, *The Supreme Court and Libel* (Carbondale: Southern Illinois University Press, 1981), xv-xvii, 1–14.

38. The act provided for punishment of "any false, scandalous and malicious writing . . . against the government of the United States, or . . . Congress . . . or the President . . . , with intent . . . to bring them . . . into contempt or disrepute": 1 Stat. 596, at 596 (1798). For the "new libertarianism" embraced by the Jeffersonians in response, see Leonard W. Levy, "Liberty and the First Amendment: 1790–1800," *American Historical Review* 58 (October 1962): 22–37. Walter F. Berns, *The First Amendment and the Future of American Democracy* (New York: Basic Books, 1976), 80–146, argues that the Jeffersonian attack was motivated not so much by libertarian convictions as by a concern to protect state sovereignty and thereby slavery.

39. United States v. Hudson and Goodwin, 7 Cranch 32, at 34 (1812). An attempt by Theodore Roosevelt to revive federal prosecutions for criminal libel was rebuffed by the Supreme Court in United States v. Press Publishing Co., 219 U.S. 1 (1911).

40. Norman L. Rosenberg, "The Law of Political Libel and Freedom of Press in Nineteenth Century America: An Interpretation," *American Journal of Legal History* 17 (October 1973): 336–52. John D. Stevens et al., "Criminal Libel as Seditious Libel, 1916–1965," *Journalism Quarterly* 43 (Spring 1966): 112, found 148 criminal libel prosecutions from 1916 to 1965 with only 31 involving criticisms of public officials.

41. A number of states even modified the rule making truth a complete defense in civil libel suits by requiring in addition proof of good motives and/or justifiable ends: Roy R. Ray, "Truth: A Defense to Libel," *Minnesota Law Review* 16 (December 1931): 49–54.

42. The classic statement of this position was made by Justice Holmes while on the Massachusetts Supreme Judicial Court in Burt v. Advertiser Newspaper Co., 154 Mass. 238 (1891). Drawing a sharp distinction between "fair criticism upon matters of public interest" and "facts [that] are not true," he held that the first was "privileged" but that strict liability applied to the second (at 242–44).

43. White v. Nicholls, 3 How. 266, at 291 (1845). In Peck v. Tribune Co., 214 U.S. 185, at 189–90 (1909), the Court affirmed that the plea of an innocent mistake was no defense. Nor did a libel have to "entail universal hatred to constitute a cause of action." Liability existed if the falsehood "hurt the plaintiff in the estimation of an important and respectable part of the community."

44. 3 How. 266, at 291 (1845).

45. In contrast with his position in *Burt*, Holmes here held that both "comment" and "statement" about public officials were privileged "in the absence of express malice": 222 U.S. 452, at 457 (1912).

46. 283 U.S. 697, at 720 (1931).

47. Zechariah Chafee, Jr., *Government and Mass Communications: A Report from the Commission on Freedom of the Press*, 2 vols. (Chicago: University of Chicago Press, 1947), 1: 97.

48. Robertson v. Baldwin, 165 U.S. 275, at 281 (1897).

49. Patterson v. Colorado, 205 U.S. 454 (1907) (state court); Toledo Newspaper Co. v. United States, 247 U.S. 402 (1918) (federal district court).

50. Gompers v. Bucks Stove & Range Co., 221 U.S. 418, at 439 (1911).

51. *Ex parte* Jackson, 96 U.S. 727 (1878) (upholding federal statute prohibiting the mailing of lottery advertisements); *In re* Rapier, 143 U.S. 110 (1892) (upholding exclusion of newspapers containing lottery advertisements); Public Clearing House v. Coyne, 194 U.S. 497 (1904) (upholding statutory authority of Postmaster General to refuse to deliver mail to a business he considered a lottery or a fraud); Lewis Publishing Co. v. Morgan, 229 U.S. 288 (1913) (upholding federal statute requiring newspapers and magazines enjoying second-class [reduced rate] mailing privileges to label paid advertisements and provide information about ownership, management and editorial personnel, and circulation); United States *ex rel.* Milwaukee Social Democratic Publishing Co. v. Burleson, 255 U.S. 407 (1921) (upholding withdrawal of second-class privileges from a publication some of whose past issues were found to contain seditious matter). The only exception, American School of Magnetic Healing v. McAnnulty, 187 U.S. 94 (1902), holding illegal the nondelivery of mail to a business selling Christian Science healing treatments, rested upon lack of proof of fraud.

52. Davis v. Massachusetts, 167 U.S. 43, at 47–48 (1897).

53. Grosjean v. American Press Co., 297 U.S. 233, at 249–50 (1936).

54. These would be the same rationales adopted by the post-1937 Court when upholding federal licensing and regulation of radio and television broadcasting: National Broadcasting Co. v. United States, 319 U.S. 190 (1943); Red Lion Broadcasting Co. v. Federal Communications Commission, 395 U.S. 367 (1969); Federal Communications Commission v. Pacifica Foundation, 438 U.S. 726 (1978). The institution of federal licensing is traced in Philip T. Rosen, *The Modern Stentors: Radio Broadcasters and the Federal Government, 1920–1934* (Westport, Conn.: Greenwood Press, 1980). Critical analyses challenging the differential treatment of broadcast and print communication are Matthew L. Spitzer, *Seven Dirty Words and Six Other Stories* (New Haven, Conn.: Yale University Press, 1986), and Lucas A. Powe, Jr., *American Broadcasting and the First Amendment* (Berkeley: University of California Press, 1987).

55. Mutual Films Corp. v. Industrial Commission of Ohio, 236 U.S. 230, at 244, 242, 245–47 (1915); Richard S. Randall, *Censorship of the Movies: The Social and Political Control of a Mass Medium* (Madison: University of Wisconsin Press, 1968), 9–25.

56. On the difficulty of ascertaining the framers' intent, see Leonard W. Levy, "No Establishment of Religion: The Original Understanding," in his *Judgments: Essays on American Constitutional History* (Chicago: Quadrangle Books, 1972), 169–224.

57. For the first position, see Leo Pfeffer, *Church, State and Freedom*, (rev. ed.,

Boston: Beacon Press, 1967), and Leonard W. Levy, *The Establishment Clause: Religion and the First Amendment* (New York: Macmillan, 1986); the second, Michael J. Malbin, *Religion and Politics: The Intentions of the Authors of the First Amendment* (Washington, D.C.: American Enterprise Institute for Public Policy Research, 1978), and Robert L. Cord, *Separation of Church and State: Historical Fact and Current Fiction* (New York: Lambeth Press, 1982), and Rodney K. Smith, *Public Prayer and the Constitution: A Case Study in Constitutional Interpretation* (Wilmington, Del.: Scholarly Resources, 1987, 1–120.

58. Thomas J. Curry, *The First Freedoms: Church and State in America to the Passage of the First Amendment* (New York: Oxford University Press, 1986), 193–222.

59. Judicial interpretation of the religion clauses of the First Amendment up through the 1930s is surveyed in Richard E. Morgan, *The Supreme Court and Religion* (New York: Free Press, 1972), pp. 4–58, 76–81, 123–26.

60. Hamilton v. Regents of the University of California, 293 U.S. 245, at 262 (1934); Palko v. Connecticut, 302 U.S. 319, at 324 (1937).

61. For background, see Ray J. Davis, "The Polygamous Prelude," *American Journal of Legal History* 6 (January 1962): 1–27, and James L. Clayton, "The Supreme Court, Polygamy and the Enforcement of Morals in Nineteenth Century America: An Analysis of Reynolds v. United States," *Dialogue: A Journal of Mormon Thought* 12 (Winter 1979): 46–61. The quotation is from *Congressional Globe*, 36th Cong., 1st Sess., p. 1514 (April 3, 1860).

62. 98 U.S. 145, at 164, 166–67 (1879). A full analysis is in C. Peter Magrath, "Chief Justice Waite and the 'Twin Relic': *Reynolds v. United States*," *Vanderbilt Law Review* 18 (March 1965): 507–43. For an examination of the continued viability of the *Reynolds* principle that the courts must balance the individual's right to free exercise against the societal interests involved when dealing with restrictions upon religious-based practices, see Ray J. Davis, "Plural Marriage and Religious Freedom: The Impact of Reynolds v. United States," *Arizona Law Review* 15, no. 2 (1973): 287–306.

63. Miles v. United States, 103 U.S. 304, at 310–11 (1887); Davis v. Beason, 133 U.S. 333, at 333, 342, 345 (1890).

64. The Late Corporation of the Church of Jesus Christ of Latter-Day Saints v. United States and Romney v. United States, 136 U.S. 1 (1890).

65. Selective Draft Law Cases, 245 U.S. 366, at 389–90 (1918).

66. United States v. Schwimmer, 279 U.S. 644 (1929); United States v. Macintosh, 283 U.S. 605 (1931).

67. Hamilton v. Regents of the University of California, 293 U.S. 245 (1934).

68. 268 U.S. 510, at 534–35 (1925). Fuller details are in David B. Tyack, "The Perils of Pluralism: The Background of the Pierce Case," *American Historical Review* 76 (October 1968): 74–98. For the Court's subsequent reading of *Pierce* as a First Amendment case, see Stephen Arons, "The Separation of School and State: *Pierce* Reconsidered," *Harvard Educational Review* 46 (February 1976): 76–104.

69. Saul K. Padover, ed., *The Complete Jefferson* (New York: Duell, Sloan & Pearce, 1943), pp. 518–19.

70. Terrett v. Taylor, 9 Cranch 43, at 49 (1815); Joseph Story, *Commentaries on the Constitution of the United States*, 2 vols. (5th ed., Boston: Little, Brown, 1891), 2: 630–31.

71. Reynolds v. United States, 98 U.S. 145, at 164 (1879); Davis v. Beason, 133 U.S. 333, at 342 (1890).

72. Church of the Holy Trinity v. United States, 143 U.S. 457, at 465, 470-71 (1892).

73. 13 Wall. 679, at 727–29 (1872). Chief Justice Salmon P. Chase did not participate; two justices dissented on the ground that the Court lacked jurisdiction. The following term, the Court in another church property dispute case, Bouldin v. Alexander, 15 Wall. 131 (1872), did affirm the power of the federal courts to inquire into whether a church had acted in accordance with its own rules. But the principle that "[i]n the absence of fraud, collusion, or arbitrariness, the decisions of the proper church tribunals on matters purely ecclesiastical...are accepted in litigation before the secular courts as conclusive" was reaffirmed in Gonzalez v. Roman Catholic Archbishop of Manila, 280 U.S. 1, at 16 (1929) (affirming decision by the Philippine Supreme Court dismissing a challenge to the refusal by the Roman Catholic Archbishop of Manila to appoint as a chaplain a person whom he deemed unqualified under canon law). For the later conversion of this rule into a constitutional requirement under the First Amendment: Kedroff v. St. Nicholas Cathedral, 344 U.S. 94 (1952); Keshick v. St. Nicholas Cathedral, 363 U.S. 190 (1960); and Presbyterian Church in the United States v. Mary Elizabeth Blue Hill Memorial Presbyterian Church, 393 U.S. 658 (1969). An in-depth treatment is Paul G. Kauper, "Church Autonomy and the First Amendment: The Presbyterian Church Case," *The Supreme Court Review 1969*, ed. Philip B. Kurland (Chicago: University of Chicago Press, 1969), pp. 347-78.

74. The following discussion of judicial interpretation of the establishment clause and analogous state constitutional provisions is indebted to David Fellman, "Separation of Church and State in the United States: A Summary View," *Wisconsin Law Review* 1950 (May): 427-78.

75. 175 U.S. 291, at 298–99 (1899).

76. Reuben Quick Bear v. Leupp, 210 U.S. 50, at 81 (1908).

77. 245 U.S. 366, at 390 (1918).

78. The term is from Frank J. Sorauf, *The Wall of Separation: The Constitutional Politics of Church and State* (Princeton, N.J.: Princeton University Press, 1976), p. 10.

79. 262 U.S. 447, at 487–89 (1923). Justice Sutherland's opinion failed to make explicit whether the bar against federal taxpayer suits was based upon the case-or-controversy requirement of Article III or was a prudential rule to prevent the "attendant inconveniences."

80. Elliott v. White, 23 F2d 997 (D.C. Cir. 1928).

81. Otto T. Hamilton, *The Courts and the Curriculum* (New York: Teachers College, Columbia University, 1927), pp. 73–117; Ward W. Keesecker, *Legal Status of Bible Reading and Religious Instruction in Public Schools* [*U.S. Office of Education Bulletin 1930*, no. 14] (Washington, D.C.: Government Printing Office, 1930); Alvin W. Johnson and Frank H. Yost, *Separation of Church and State in the United States* (Minneapolis: University of Minnesota Press, 1948), pp. 33-73; Donald E. Boles, *The Two Swords: Commentaries and Cases in Religion and Education* (Ames: Iowa State University Press, 1967), pp. 83–87; David Tyack and Aaron Benavot, "Courts and Public Schools: Educational Litigation in Historical Perspective," *Law & Society Review* 19, no. 3 (1985): 339–80; and Tyack and Thomas James, "Moral Majorities and the

School Curriculum: Historical Perspectives on the Legalization of Virtue," *Teachers College Record* 86 (Summer 1985): 513–37.

82. Pierce v. Society of Sisters, 268 U.S. 510, at 534 (1925).

83. Alfred W. Meyer, "The Blaine Amendment and the Bill of Rights," *Harvard Law Review* 64 (April 1951): 939–45; Jonathan Lurie, "The Fourteenth Amendment: Use and Application in Selected State Court Civil Liberties Cases, 1870–1890—A Preliminary Assessment," *American Journal of Legal History* 28 (October 1984): 299–304.

84. 281 U.S. 370, at 374-75 (1930).

85. Crandall v. Nevada, 6 Wall. 35 (1868) (striking down state exit tax on departing travellers).

86. Burns Baking Co. v. Bryan, 264 U.S. 504, at 513 (1924).

87. Jay M. Feinman, "The Development of the Employment at Will Rule," *American Journal of Legal History* 20 (April 1976): 118–35, and Sanford M. Jacoby, "The Duration of Indefinite Employment Contracts in the United States and England: An Historical Analysis," *Comparative Labor Law* 5 (Winter 1982): 85–128. The Court constitutionalized the criminal law tradition opposing criminalization of breaches of labor contracts under the Thirteenth Amendment in Bailey v. Alabama, 219 U.S. 219 (1911). For fuller details, see Benno C. Schmidt, Jr., "Principle and Prejudice: The Supreme Court and Race in the Progressive Era. Part 2: The *Peonage Cases*," *Columbia Law Review* 82 (May 1982): 646-718.

88. Janet S. Lindgren, "Beyond Cases: Reconsidering Judicial Review," *Wisconsin Law Review* 1983, no. 3 (1983): 583–638; Melvin I. Urofsky, "Myth and Reality: The Supreme Court and Protective Legislation in the Progressive Era," *Supreme Court Historical Society Yearbook 1983* (Washington, D.C.: Supreme Court Historical Society, 1983), pp. 53-72; Urofsky, "State Courts and Protective Legislation during the Progressive Era: A Reevaluation," *Journal of American History* 72 (June 1985): 63–91; Charles W. McCurdy, "The Roots of 'Liberty of Contract' Reconsidered: Major Premises in the Law of Employment, 1867–1937," *Supreme Court Historical Society Yearbook 1984* (Washington, D.C.: Supreme Court Historical Society, 1984), pp. 20–33.

89. Cummings v. Missouri, 4 Wall. 277, at 319–20 (1867).

90. On this topic generally, see Walter Gellhorn, *Individual Liberty and Governmental Restraints* (Baton Rouge: Louisiana State University Press, 1956), pp. 105–51, and Lawrence M. Friedman, "Freedom of Contract and Occupational Licensing 1890–1910: A Legal and Social Study," *California Law Review* 53 (May 1965): 487–534. Relevant Supreme Court decisions include: Dent v. West Virginia, 129 U.S. 114 (1889) (upholding state law requiring physicians to be a graduate of a reputable medical college, pass a qualifying examination, or have practiced continuously in state for ten years previously as applied to a person who had practiced for six years previously); Reetz v. Michigan, 188 U.S. 505 (1903) (upholding state law establishing a board of registration for licensing physicians); Douglas v. Noble, 261 U.S. 165 (1923) (upholding state law vesting power to license dentists in an examining board of practicing dentists); Semler v. Oregon Board of Dental Examiners, 294 U.S. 608 (1935) (upholding state law authorizing revocation of license to practice dentistry for certain advertising practices). Although the Test Oath Cases had appeared to deny that past behavior could be made a test for practicing a profession, the Court backtracked from this position by upholding a statute excluding from the practice of

medicine anybody convicted of a felony even as applied to a person who had been convicted before the new regulation. The rationale was that the legislation was not an additional punishment for a past offense, but imposed a qualification (i.e., good moral character) reasonably related to professional competence: Hawker v. New York, 170 U.S. 189, at 194, 196–97 (1898).

91. Randall v. Brigham, 7 Wall. 523, at 540 (1869). See also: Bradley v. Fisher, 13 Wall. 335 (1872); *Ex parte* Wall, 107 U.S. 265 (1883); Semling v. Radford, 243 U.S. 46 (1917); Missouri *ex rel.* Hurwitz v. North, 271 U.S. 40 (1926).

92. *In re* Sawyer, 124 U.S. 200, at 202, 210 (1888); Taylor and Marshall v. Beckham (No. 1), 178 U.S. 548, at 576 (1900).

93. The prevailing rule was set forth by the New York Court of Appeals in Conner v. Mayor of New York, 5 N.Y. 285, at 295 (1851): "Public offices . . . are created for the benefit of the public, and not granted for the benefit of the incumbent. Their terms are fixed with a view to public utility and convenience." For the Supreme Court's acceptance of the public employment-as-privilege doctrine: *Ex parte* Hennen, 13 Pet. 230 (1839) (tenure of federal officers not fixed by Constitution or statute is "at the will and discretion of some department of the government, and subject to removal at pleasure," at 259–60); Atkin v. Kansas, 191 U.S. 207 (1903) (upholding statute prescribing eight hours work for those employed by or on behalf of the state and its municipalities); Heim v. McCall, 239 U.S. 175 (1915) (upholding statute prohibiting employment of aliens on public works constructed by the state or any of its municipalities or by any person contracting with the state or any of its munici- palities). For fuller details, see Arch Dotson, "The Emerging Doctrine of Privilege in Public Employment," *Public Administration Review* 15 (Spring 1955): 77-79.

94. McAuliffe v. Mayor and Board of Aldermen of New Bedford, 155 Mass. 216, at 220 (1892). Ten years before, the Supreme Court in *Ex parte* Curtis, 106 U.S. 371 (1882) had upheld a congressional statute forbidding one government employee from requesting, giving to, or receiving a political contribution from another govern- ment employee. While Justice Joseph P. Bradley in dissent argued that denying "to a man the privilege of associating and making joint contributions with such other citizens as he may choose, is an unjust restraint of his right to propagate and promote his views on public affairs" (at 376-77), Chief Justice Morrison Waite for the rest of the Court upheld the law as necessary and proper "to promote efficiency in the discharge of official duties" without even raising the First Amendment issue (at 373, 375).

95. Loan Association v. Topeka, 20 Wall. 655, at 664 (1875). See also: Parkers- burg v. Brown, 106 U.S. 487 (1883) (barring "taxation which takes the private property of one person for the private use of another person," at 501); Cole v. City of La Grange, 113 U.S. 1 (1885) (taxation statute void for taking private property for a private party); Fallbrook Irrigation District v. Bradley, 164 U.S. 112 (1896) ("[t]he use for which private property is to be taken must be a public one, whether the taking be by the exercise of the right of eminent domain or by that of taxation," at 161).

96. Commonwealth v. Davis, 162 Mass. 510, at 511 (1895); Davis v. Massachu- setts, 167 U.S. 43, at 46–47 (1897).

97. *Re* the election of the House of Representatives, Article I, Section 2 provided that "the Electors in each State shall have the Qualifications requisite for Electors of the most numerous Branch of the State Legislature"; the same provision was

included in the Seventeenth Amendment for the popular election of United States Senators. As for the election of the president, Article II, Section 1 simply stipulated that "Each State shall appoint, in such Manner as the Legislature thereof may direct, a Number of Electors." The constitutional status of voting rights is surveyed in Richard Claude, *The Supreme Court and the Electoral Process* (Baltimore: Johns Hopkins Press, 1970), and Ward E. Y. Elliott, *The Rise of Guardian Democracy: The Supreme Court's Role in Voting Rights Disputes, 1845–1969* (Cambridge, Mass.: Harvard University Press, 1974).

98. 21 Wall. 162, at 178, 171 (1875).

99. *Ex parte* Siebold, 100 U.S. 371 (1880); *Ex parte* Clarke, 100 U.S. 399 (1880); United States v. Gale, 109 U.S. 65 (1883); *In re* Coy, 127 U.S. 731 (1888); United States v. Mosley, 238 U.S. 383 (1915).

100. *Ex parte* Yarbrough, 110 U.S. 651 (1884).

101. *In re* Green, 134 U.S. 377 (1890); McPherson v. Blacker, 146 U.S. 1 (1892).

102. Burroughs and Cannon v. United States, 290 U.S. 534 (1934).

103. *Dicta* in United States v. Cruikshank, 92 U.S. 542, at 555–56 (1876) and United States v. Reese, 92 U.S. 214, at 218 (1876), had affirmed the power of Congress under the Fifteenth Amendment to punish racially motivated violations of voting rights in state and local elections whether done by private individuals or public officials. But James v. Bowman, 190 U.S. 217, at 136, 139 (1903) read into the Fifteenth Amendment a state-action requirement, i.e., that Congress could punish under the Fifteenth Amendment only racially motivated action by a state or someone "acting under its authority."

104. Williams v. Mississippi, 170 U.S. 213 (1898) (upholding literacy test; *dicta* upholding poll tax); Mason v. Missouri, 179 U.S. 328 (1900) (upholding special registration law for city of St. Louis); Giles v. Harris, 189 U.S. 475 (1903) (Court lacked authority to compel board of registrars to enroll Negro under a state constitution allegedly in violation of the United States Constitution); Pope v. Williams, 193 U.S. 621 (1904) (upholding residency requirement for voting).

105. 256 U.S. 232 (1921). The fifth, and decisive, justice agreed that the 1911 law was invalid because adopted before the ratification of the Seventeenth Amendment for the popular election of United States Senators, but suggested that the new amendment might make a difference (at 258).

106. Wood v. Broom, 287 U.S. 1, at 6–8 (1932).

107. Robert G. Dixon, Jr., *Democratic Representation: Reapportionment in Law and Politics* (New York: Oxford University Press, 1968), pp. 58–59, 102-07.

108. 7 How. 1 (1849).

109. Pacific States Telephone & Telegraph Co. v. Oregon, 223 U.S. 118, at 141–42 (1912). Since that decision, the Court has consistently refused to entertain on the merits all suits to enforce the guarantee clause on the ground of nonjusticiability. For fuller details, see Arthur E. Bonfield, "The Guarantee Clause of Article IV, Section 4: A Study in Constitutional Desuetude," *Minnesota Law Review* 46 (January 1962): 513-72.

110. Michael Wallace, "Changing Concepts of Party in the United States: New York, 1815–1828," *American Historical Review* 74 (December 1968): 453–91, and Richard Hofstadter, *The Idea of a Party System: The Rise of Legitimate Opposition in the United States, 1780–1840* (Berkeley: University of California Press, 1969).

111. *Re* the right of association generally, see David Fellman, "Constitutional

Rights of Association," in *The Supreme Court Review 1961*, ed. Philip B. Kurland (Chicago: University of Chicago Press, 1961), pp. 74-134, and Fellman, *The Constitutional Right of Association* (Chicago: University of Chicago Press, 1963); the legal status of parties: Joseph R. Starr, "The Legal Status of American Political Parties," Parts I and II, *American Political Science Review* 34 (June 1940): 439–55, and (August 1940): 685–99.

112. See, for example, a lower federal charge to a grand jury, 30 F. ed. Cas. 999, at 1000, #18,258 (CC W.D. N.C. 1875): "Every man has a natural and inherent right of selecting his own associates, and this natural right cannot be properly regulated by legislative action, but must always be under the control of individual taste and inclination."

113. Britton v. Board of Election Commissioners of San Francisco, 129 Cal. 337, at 344 (1900).

114. "It must now be considered as well settled that persons have a right to enter into...associations, and to bind themselves as to their membership and rights in such societies...by the constitution and by-laws of the association which they adopt, or subscribe to after adoption": Brown v. Stoerkel and Gregory, 74 Mich. 269, at 276 (1889). The same principle (i.e., that churches were voluntary associations that should be governed by their own regulations) underlay the rule of federal court noninvolvement in intramural church disputes laid down by the Supreme Court in Watson v. Jones, 13 Wall. 679, at 728–29 (1872).

115. For the spread of such regulations and the courts' response, see John W. Epperson, *The Changing Legal Status of Political Parties in the United States* (New York: Garland Publishing, 1986), pp. 46–151. The classic rationale for judicial approval was given in the first court text of state regulation of party nominating procedures, Leonard v. Commonwealth, 112 Pa. 607 (1886): "Under our frame of government a vast system of political machinery has grown up by which elections have been for many years practically controlled....The influence which these primary elections have for good or evil upon the politics of the country is overshadowing" (at 625).

116. In Nixon v. Condon, 286 U.S. 73 (1932), a five-to-four majority held that the exclusion of blacks from the Texas Democratic primary by the party's state executive committee acting under authority of a statute authorizing the executive committees of the parties to prescribe the qualifications for party membership constituted discriminatory state action in violation of the Fourteenth Amendment. The rationale was that whatever inherent power a party had as a voluntary association to control its membership lay in the state convention as the supreme governing body of the party. But the majority opinion explicitly reserved decision upon the questions: (1) "[w]hether a political party in Texas has inherent power...to determine its own membership." and (2) "[w]hether the effect of Texas legislation" regulating primary elections "has been to work...a transformation of the concept of a political party as a voluntary association" (at 83–84).

117. 295 U.S. 45 (1935).

118. Waugh v. Board of Trustees of the University of Mississippi, 237 U.S. 589 (1915).

119. New York *ex rel*. Bryant v. Zimmerman, 278 U.S. 63, at 73, 75, 72 (1928). Justice McReynolds thought the Court should have refused to hear the case because of the absence of any substantial federal question.

120. Walter Nelles, "Commonwealth v. Hunt," *Columbia Law Review* 32 (November 1932): 1128–69.

121. This summary draws heavily upon Charles O. Gregory and Harold A. Katz, *Labor and the Law* (3rd ed., New York: W.W. Norton, 1979), pp. 13–222; Christopher L. Tomlins, *The State and the Unions: Labor Relations, Law, and the Organized Labor Movement in America, 1880–1960* (Cambridge, Eng., 1985), pp. 32–95, and B.W. Poulson, "Criminal Conspiracy, Injunctions and Damage Suits in Labor Law," *Journal of Legal History* 7 (September 1986): 212–27.

122. Hitchman Coal & Coke Co. v. Mitchell, 245 U.S. 229 (1917).

123. Adair v. United States, 208 U.S. 161 (1908); Coppage v. Kansas, 236 U.S. 1 (1915).

124. Duplex Printing Press Co. v. Deering, 254 U.S. 443, at 468–69 (1921); American Steel Foundries v. Tri-City Central Trades Council, 257 U.S. 184, at 208–09 (1921).

125. United Mine Workers of America v. Coronado Coal Co., 259 U.S. 344, at 407–09 (1922), and Coronado Coal Co. v. United Mine Workers of America, 268 U.S. 295, at 310 (strikes as such minus evidence of clear intent to restrain interstate commerce not in violation of the Sherman Antitrust Act). See for fuller details: Stanley I. Kutler, "Chief Justice Taft, Judicial Unanimity, and Labor: The Coronado Case," *Historian* 24 (November 1961): 68–83.

126. Loewe v. Lawlor, 208 U.S. 274 (1908) (union-organized consumer boycott a restraint of trade in violation of the Sherman Antitrust Act); Duplex Printing Press Co. v. Deering, 254 U.S. 443 (1921), and Bedford Cut Stone Co. v. Journeymen Stone Cutters' Association of North America, 274 U.S. 37 (1927) (secondary labor boycott violation of Sherman and Clayton Antitrust laws); American Steel Foundries v. Tri-City Central Trades Council, 257 U.S. 184 (1921) (provision in Clayton Act barring issuance by federal courts of injunctions in labor disputes does not apply to a dispute "between an employer and persons who are neither ex-employees nor seeking employment" (at 202). For fuller details, see Stanley I. Kutler, "Labor, the Clayton Act, and the Supreme Court," *Labor History* 3 (Winter 1962): 19–38.

127. 47 Stat. 70, at 70, 73 (1932).

128. The fullest treatment is in two articles by Joseph Tanenhaus in the *University of Pittsburgh Law Review*: "Picketing as a Tort: The Development of the Law of Picketing from 1880 to 1940," 14 (Winter 1953): 170–98, and "Picketing as Free Speech: Early Stages in the Growth of the New Law of Picketing," 14 (Spring 1953): 397–418.

129. See, for example, Chief Justice William Howard Taft's holding in American Steel Foundries v. Tri-City Central Trades Council that picket lines composed of four to twelve men "constituted intimidation." He would limit picketing in that case to one "representative" at each entrance to the plant. While allowing judges leeway on the exact number depending upon the circumstances in each instance, he made clear what should be the guiding principle: "The purpose should be to prevent the inevitable intimidation of the presence of groups of pickets, but to allow missionaries." 257 U.S. 184, at 204–07 (1921). And in a follow-up decision, the Court struck down as in violation of the due process clause an Arizona law construed by that state's supreme court as forbidding the issuance of injunctions against tortious or illegal picketing: Truax v. Corrigan, 257 U.S. 312 (1921).

130. In dealing with an analogous issue, the Court had previously in Gompers v.

Bucks Stove & Range Co., 221 U.S. 418 (1911) upheld a federal court injunction against American Federation of Labor leaders publicizing a consumer boycott against a challenge that the injunction violated the constitutional guarantee of free speech with the curt statement that the guarantee did not apply in "an unlawful conspiracy" (at 439). For full details, see Barry F. Helphand, "Labor and the Courts: The Common-Law Doctrine of Criminal Conspiracy and Its Application in the Buck's Stove Case," *Labor History* 18 (Winter 1977): 91–114.

131. Senn v. Tile Layers Protective Union, 301 U.S. 468, at 478 (1937). The decision was read as implicitly upholding the constitutionality of the federal Norris-LaGuardia Act. The Court's formal ruling doing so came the following year in Lauf v. E.G. Shinner & Co., 303 U.S. 323 (1938), and New Negro Alliance v. Sanitary Grocery Co., 303 U.S. 552, 304 U.S. 542 (1938).

132. Patricia Lucie, "On Being a Free Person and a Citizen by Constitutional Amendment," *Journal of American Studies* 12 (December 1978): 343–58. Surveys of the Court's treatment of women's rights include: W. William Hodes, "Women and the Constitution: Some Legal History and a New Approach to the Nineteenth Amendment," *Rutgers Law Review* 25 (Fall 1970): 26–53; John D. Johnston, Jr., and Charles L. Knapp, "Sex Discrimination by Law: A Study in Judicial Perspective," *New York University Law Review* 46 (October 1971): 675-747; and Albie Sachs and Joan Hoff Wilson, *Sexism and the Law: Male Beliefs and Legal Bias* (New York: Free Press, 1978), pp. 67-125.

133. Bradwell v. State, 16 Wall. 130, at 139 (Miller), 140–42 (Bradley) (1873). Fuller details are given in: Charles E. Corker, "*Bradwell v. State*: Some Reflections Prompted by Myra Bradwell's Hard Case That Made 'Bad' Law," *Washington Law Review* 53 (February 1978): 215–29; Robert M. Spector, "Woman against the Law: Myra Bradwell's Struggle for Admission to the Illinois Bar," *Journal of the Illinois State Historical Society* 68 (June 1975): 228-42; and Nancy T. Gilliam, "A Professional Pioneer: Myra Bradwell's Fight to Practice Law," *Law and History Review* 5 (Spring 1987): 105–33.

134. 21 Wall. 162, at 169, 174 (1875).

135. 100 U.S. 303, at 310 (1880).

136. *In re* Lockwood, 154 U.S. 116, at 118 (1894).

137. David P. Bryden, "Brandeis's Facts," *Constitutional Commentary* 1 (Summer 1984): 293–97.

138. 208 U.S. 412, at 421–23 (1908).

139. 261 U.S. 525, at 553 (Sutherland), 569-70 (Holmes) (1923).

140. 300 U.S. 379 (1937).

141. Fay v. New York, 332 U.S. 261, at 289–90 (1947).

142. The following relies heavily upon Milton R. Konvitz, *The Alien and Asiatic in American Law* (Ithaca, N.Y.: Cornell University Press, 1946), and E.P. Hutchinson, *Legislative History of American Immigration Policy 1798-1965* (Philadelphia: University of Pennsylvania Press, 1981). A brief survey of relevant Supreme Court decisions is in Leonard Dinnerstein, "The Supreme Court and the Rights of Aliens," *this Constitution: A Bicentennial Chronicle*, No. 8 (Fall 1985): 25–35.

143. 118 U.S. 356, at 369 (1886).

144. Wing Wong v. United States, 163 U.S. 228 (1896) (Constitution precludes punishment of alien for being illegally in the United States except by trial in accordance with the Fifth and Sixth Amendments).

145. Henderson v. Mayor of the City of New York, 92 U.S. 259 (1876) (striking down a state regulation requiring ship owners to post a bond to indemnify the state in the event an immigrant passenger became a public charge or alternatively to pay a fee for each passenger as an infringement upon the power of Congress to regulate foreign commerce); Head Money Cases, 112 U.S. 580 (1884) (upholding, on the basis of the commerce power, a tax by Congress upon ship owners for alien passengers brought into the country).

146. 130 U.S. 581 (1889). In 1933, the Court reaffirmed that "[t]he power of Congress to prescribe the terms and conditions upon which aliens may enter or remain in the United States is no longer open to serious question": United States *ex rel.* Volpe v. Smith, 289 U.S. 422, at 425. For a highly critical appraisal of the decision and its results, see Louis Henkin, "The Constitution and United States Sovereignty: A Century of *Chinese Exclusion* and Its Progeny," *Harvard Law Review* 100 (February 1987): 853–86.

147. United States v. Ju Toy, 198 U.S. 253 (1904).

148. 32 Stat. 1213, at 1214 (1903).

149. United States *ex rel.* Turner v. Williams, 194 U.S. 279, at 292 (1904). Thus given the green light, Congress proceeded to extend the scope of this ban. The Immigration Act of 1917 excluded persons "who advocate or teach the unlawful destruction of property; persons who are members of or affiliated with any organization entertaining and teaching disbelief in or opposition to organized government, or who advocate or teach the duty, necessity, or propriety of the unlawful assaulting or killing of any officer": 39 Stat. 874, at 876 (1917). Another statute adopted the following year, as amended in 1920, provided for exclusion of "[a]liens who believe in, advise, advocate, or teach, or who are members of or affiliated with any organization, association, society, or group that believes in, advises, advocates, or teaches...the overthrow by force or violence of the Government of the United States": 40 Stat. 1012 (1918); 41 Stat. 1008, at 1009 (1920).

150. United States v. Wong Kim Ark, 169 U.S. 649 (1898).

151. Terrace v. Thompson, 263 U.S. 197, at 220 (1923).

152. 1 Stat. 103, at 103 (1790).

153. 16 Stat. 254, at 256 (1870).

154. 22 Stat. 58, at 61 (1882).

155. The relevant Supreme Court decisions were: Ozawa v. United States, 260 U.S. 178 (1922) (Japanese); United States v. Thind, 261 U.S. 209 (1922) (Hindus); Toyota v. United States, 268 U.S. 402, at 410–12 (1924) (Filipinos, except for those who had served in the United States armed forces). The other ineligibility rulings were lower court decisions.

156. Morrison v. California, 291 U.S. 82, at 86 (1934).

157. 34 Stat. 596, at 597 (1906).

158. United States v. Schwimmer, 279 U.S. 644 (1929); United States v. Macintosh, 283 U.S. 605 (1931).

159. Fong Yue Ting v. United States, 149 U.S. 698, at 707 (1893). As Justice Holmes reaffirmed in Bugajewitz v. Adams, 228 U.S. 585, at 591 (1913): "It is thoroughly established that Congress has power to order the deportation of aliens whose presence in the country it deems hurtful."

160. 32 Stat. 1213, at 1218 (1903); 39 Stat. 874, at 887–88 (1917); 40 Stat. 1012 (1918); 41 Stat. 593 (1920).

161. Ng Fung Ho v. White, 259 U.S. 276 (1922).

162. United States *ex rel.* Bilokumsky v. Tod, 263 U.S. 149, at 152–55 (1923).

163. Low Wah Suey v. Backus, 225 U.S. 460, at 468 (1911).

164. Fong Yue Ting v. United States, 149 U.S. 698 (1893); Li Sing v. United States, 180 U.S. 486 (1901); Bugajewitz v. Adams, 228 U.S. 585 (1913); United States *ex rel.* Bilokumsky v. Tod, 263 U.S. 149 (1923); Mahler v. Eby, 264 U.S. 32 (1924).

165. 34 Stat. 596, at 601 (1906); Johannessen v. United States, 225 U.S. 227 (1912); Luria v. United States, 231 U.S. 9 (1913). As the Court summed up the rule in United States v. Ginsberg, 243 U.S. 472, at 474-75 (1917):

An alien who seeks political rights as a member of this Nation can rightfully obtain these only upon terms and conditions specified by Congress.... No alien has the slightest right to naturalization unless all statutory requirements are complied with; and every certificate of citizenship must be treated as granted upon condition the Government may challenge it... and demand its cancellation unless issued in accordance with such requirements. If procured when prescribed qualifications have no existence in fact it is illegally procured.

166. The first case was United States v. Swelgin, 254 F 884 (DC Or. 1918); the second, Rowan v. United States, 18 F2d 246 (CCA 9th Cir. 1927).

167. 7 Cranch 603 (1813); Orr v. Hodgson, 4 Wheat. 453 (1819); Hauenstein v. Lynham, 100 U.S. 483 (1880); Sullivan v. Burnett, 105 U.S. 334 (1882). In Mager v. Grima, 8 How. 490 (1850), Chief Justice Roger B. Taney went so far as to apply the same principle to "either real or personal property" (at 493). The Court similarly upheld exclusion of aliens from sharing on an equal basis with citizens natural resources that were public property: McCready v. Virginia, 94 U.S. 391 (1877); Patsone v. Pennsylvania, 232 U.S. 138 (1914).

168. Terrace v. Thompson, 263 U.S. 197 (1923); Porterfield v. Webb, 263 U.S. 225 (1923); Webb v. O'Brien, 263 U.S. 313 (1923); Frick v. Webb, 263 U.S. 326 (1923). And in Cockrill v. California, 268 U.S. 258 (1925), the Court upheld the provision in the California Alien Land Law of 1920—designed to prevent Japanese from circumventing the ban against farm land purchases by placing ownership in their American-born children or a white friend—establishing a *prima facie* presumption of illegality if a person eligible to hold such land took title to it after an ineligible person had provided the funds. All the laws applied exclusively to farm land because the 1911 treaty between the United States and Japan allowed the citizens of each country in the territories of the other to own, lease, or occupy houses, manufactories, warehouses and shops, and to lease land for residential and commercial purposes upon the same basis as citizens. For fuller details, see M. Browning Carrot, "Prejudice Goes to Court: The Japanese & the Supreme Court in the 1920s," *California History* 62 (Summer 1983): 122–38.

169. 118 U.S. 356 (1886).

170. Truax v. Raich, 239 U.S. 33, at 43 (1915).

171. Ohio *ex rel.* Clarke v. Deckebach, 274 U.S. 392, at 396–97 (upholding city ordinance prohibiting aliens from conducting pool and billiard rooms).

172. Heim v. McCall, 239 U.S. 175 (1915).

3 The Dilemma of Race

1. John Higham, *Strangers in the Land: Patterns of American Nativism, 1860–1925* (New Brunswick, N.J.: Rutgers University Press, 1955); Barbara M. Solomon, *Ancestors and Immigrants: A Changing New England Tradition* (Cambridge, Mass.: Harvard University Press, 1956).

2. Stuart C. Miller, *The Unwelcome Immigrant: The American Image of the Chinese, 1785–1882* (Berkeley: University of California Press, 1969); Robert McClellan, *The Heathen Chinese: A Study of American Attitudes toward China, 1890–1905* (Columbus: Ohio State University Press, 1971).

3. Stephen J. Field to John Norton Pomeroy, April 14, 1882, in Howard J. Graham, *Everyman's Constitution: Historical Essays on the Fourteenth Amendment, the "Conspiracy Theory", and American Constitutionalism* (Madison: State Historical Society of Wisconsin, 1968), 105.

4. 16 Wall. 36, at 71 (1873).

5. The texts are reprinted in Robert K. Carr, *Federal Protection of Civil Rights: Quest for a Sword* (Ithaca, N.Y.: Cornell University Press, 1947), 211–49.

6. For examples, see: Eugene Gressman, "The Unhappy History of Civil Rights Legislation," *Michigan Law Review* 50 (June 1952): 1323–58; Robert J. Harris, *The Quest for Equality: The Constitution, Congress and the Supreme Court* (Baton Rouge: Louisiana State University Press, 1960); and Loren Miller, *The Petitioners: The Story of the Supreme Court of the United States and the Negro* (New York: Pantheon Books, 1966). A handy, brief factual survey of the Court's decision-making in this area is Edward F. Waite, "The Negro in the Supreme Court," *Minnesota Law Review* 30 (March 1946): 219–304.

7. 106 U.S. 583, at 585 (1883).

8. Even Field—a War Democrat—had been a Lincoln appointee. The only other Democrat, Nathan Clifford, was a Buchanan appointee who served until his death in 1881. Republicans Noah H. Swayne, Samuel F. Miller, and David Davis were Lincoln appointees; Joseph P. Bradley, William Strong, Ward Hunt, and Waite himself were Grant appointees. After Davis resigned in 1877, Hayes filled his place with the Kentucky Republican John Marshall Harlan. Hayes's second appointee was William B. Woods, and ex-Ohioan who had moved to Georgia after the Civil War, to replace Strong. The Senate Judiciary Committee balked at Hayes's selection of Stanley Matthews to take Swayne's place, but when his successor, James Garfield, resubmitted Matthews's name, the Senate narrowly confirmed him. Chester Arthur was responsible for naming Horace Gray to succeed Clifford and Samuel Blatchford to fill Hunt's seat. Not until 1888 would another Democrat be elevated to the Court. For details, see Henry J. Abraham, *Justices and Presidents: A Political History of Appointments to the Supreme Court* (New York: Oxford University Press, 1974), pp. 106–32.

9. On the tension between the Republicans' wish to protect black rights and their commitment to preserving the federal system, see: Michael L. Benedict, "Preserving the Constitution: The Conservative Basis of Radical Reconstruction," *Journal of American History* 61 (June 1974): 65–90; Benedict, "Preserving Federalism: Reconstruction and the Waite Court," in *The Supreme Court Review 1978*, ed. Philip B. Kurland and Gerhard Casper (Chicago: University of Chicago Press, 1979), pp. 39–

79; Phillip S. Paludan, *A Covenant with Death: The Constitution, Law, and Equality in the Civil War Era* (Urbana: University of Illinois Press, 1975); Herman Belz, *A New Birth of Freedom: The Republican Party and Freedmen's Rights, 1861 to 1866* (Westport, Conn.: Greenwood Press, 1976); and Harold M. Hyman and William M. Wiecek, *Equal Justice Under Law: Constitutional Development 1835–1875* (New York: Harper & Row, 1982), 232–515.

10. Samuel F. Miller to William P. Ballinger, February 6, 1867, in Charles Fairman, *Reconstruction and Reunion 1864–88, Part One [Oliver Wendell Holmes Devise History of the Supreme Court of the United States,* Volume VI] (New York: Macmillan, 1971), 281–85.

11. 14 Stat. 27, at 27 (1866).

12. Robert J. Kaczorowski, *The Politics of Judicial Interpretation: The Federal Courts, Department of Justice and Civil Rights, 1866–1876* (New York: Oceana Publications, 1985), 1–25, 71-72, 117–34.

13. 17 Stat. 13, at 14–15 (1871).

14. James E. Sefton, *The United States Army and Reconstruction 1865–1877* (Baton Rouge: Louisiana State University Press, 1967), 222–25.

15. *Ex parte* Milligan, 4 Wall. 2 (1866).

16. *Re* the reliance by Congress on the federal courts for protecting Negro rights: Harold M. Hyman, *A More Perfect Union: The Impact of the Civil War and Reconstruction on the Constitution* (New York: Alfred A. Knopf, 1973), 481–542; the difficulties in the way of such enforcement: William W. Davis, "The Federal Enforcement Acts," in *Studies in Southern History and Politics Inscribed to William Archibald Dunning* (New York: Columbia University Press, 1914), 203–28; Everette Swinney, "Enforcing the Fifteenth Amendment, 1870–1877," *Journal of Southern History* 28 (May 1962): 202–18, and Swinney, *Suppressing the Ku Klux Klan: The Enforcement of the Reconstruction Amendments 1870–1877* (New York: Garland Publishing, 1987); Kaczorowski, *Politics of Judicial Interpretation*, pp. 27-78, 225; Stephen Cresswell, "Enforcing the Enforcement Acts: The Department of Justice in Northern Mississippi, 1870–1890," *Journal of Southern History* 53 (August 1987): 421–40.

17. The Grant administration's retreat from activist enforcement of Negro rights is traced in William B. Hesseltine, *Ulysses S. Grant: Politician* (New York: Dodd, Mead, 1935); Kenneth Stampp, *The Era of Reconstruction 1865–1877* (New York: Alfred A. Knopf, 1965); William Gillette, *Retreat from Reconstruction 1869–1879* (Baton Rouge: Louisiana State University Press, 1979); Kaczorowski, *Politics of Judicial Interpretation*, 79–134.

18. 13 Wall. 251 (1872).

19. United States v. Rhodes, 27 Fed. Cas. 785, #16,151 (CC Ky. 1866).

20. 13 Wall. 581, at 588–95 (1872). Bradley and Swayne dissented; Chase did not participate. The precedent was United States v. Ortega, 11 Wheat. 467 (1826).

21. John V. Orth, "The Interpretation of the Eleventh Amendment, 1798-1908: A Case Study of Judicial Power," *University of Illinois Law Review* 1983, no. 2: 423–55.

22. 16 Wall. 36, at 68–69, 76–80 (1873). For Miller's attitude in favor of allowing wide latitude to state regulatory power, see Charles Fairman, *Mr. Justice Miller and the Supreme Court 1862–1890* (Cambridge, Mass.: Harvard University Press, 1939), 179–206; on the role of the police power issue in *Slaughter-House*, see Kaczorowski,

Politics of Judicial Interpretation, 143–59, 222–23; Loren P. Beth, "The Slaughter-House Cases—Revisited," *Louisiana Law Review* 23 (April 1963): 487–505.

23. The Thirteenth Amendment did not have such a restriction. And the Civil Rights Act of 1866 had been adopted under its authority. But Congress, when readopting its provisions in the Civil Rights Act of May 31, 1870, did so under the authority of the Fourteenth and Fifteenth Amendments: 16 Stat. 140, Section 18, at 144 (1870).

24. Laurent B. Frantz, "Congressional Power to Enforce the Fourteenth Amendment Against Private Acts," *Yale Law Journal* 73 (July 1964): 1353–84. This position was challenged by Alfred Avins, "The Ku Klux Klan Act of 1871: Some Reflected Light on State Action and the Fourteenth Amendment," *Saint Louis University Law Journal* 11 (Spring 1967): 331–81. For a rebuttal reaffirming the state inaction argument, see Michael P. Zuckert, "Congressional Power Under the Fourteenth Amendment—The Original Understanding of Section Five," *Constitutional Commentary* 3 (Winter 1986): 123–56.

25. 11 Wall. 113, at 125 (1871). And Justice Samuel Nelson even anticipated *Slaughter-House*'s dual-citizenship holding by explaining in justification that the national and state governments were "separate and distinct sovereignties, acting separately and independently of each other, within their respective spheres" (124).

26. State Tax on Railway Gross Receipts, 15 Wall. 284, at 293 (1873).

27. A more critical assessment than is given here is C. Peter Magrath, *Morrison R. Waite: The Triumph of Character* (New York: Macmillan, 1963), 111-71.

28. Strauder v. West Virginia, 100 U.S. 303, at 305 (1880).

29. *Ex parte* Virginia, 100 U.S. 339, at 347 (1880).

30. 118 U.S. 356, at 373-74 (1886).

31. 100 U.S. 313, at 321–22 (1880); 103 U.S. 370 (1881). For the implications, see Benno C. Schmidt, Jr., "Juries, Jurisdiction, and Race Discrimination: The Lost Promise of *Strauder v. West Virginia*," *Texas Law Review* 61 (May 1983): 1401–99.

32. The fullest over-all treatment is Charles Fairman, "What Makes a Great Justice? Mr. Justice Bradley and the Supreme Court, 1870–1892," *Boston University Law Review* 30 (January 1950): 49–102. *Re* Bradley's role in the state debt default cases, see John V. Orth, "The Fair Fame and Name of Louisiana," *Tulane Lawyer* 2 (Fall 1980): 2–15. John A. Scott, "Justice Bradley's Evolving Concept of the Fourteenth Amendment from the Slaughterhouse Cases to the Civil Rights Cases," *Rutgers Law Review* 25 (Summer 1971): 552–69, mistakenly dates Bradley's shift as coming after the 1876 disputed election.

33. Joseph Bradley to William Woods, March 12, 1871, quoted in John F. Roche, "Civil Liberty in the Age of Enterprise," *University of Chicago Law Review* 31 (Autumn 1963): 109.

34. 13 Wall. 581, at 597 (1872).

35. 16 Wall. 36, at 111-24 (1873).

36. United States v. Cruikshank, 25 Fed. Cas. 707, at 711–13, 710, #14,897 (CC La. 1874).

37. Texas v. Gaines, 23 Fed. Cas. 869, at 870-71, #13,847 (CC W.D. Texas 1874).

38. 16 Stat. 140, at 141 (1870).

39. 92 U.S. 542, at 552–54, 556 (1876). The justices were unanimous in over-

turning the convictions. But only eight joined in Waite's opinion; the ninth concurred on the ground of technical defects in the indictment.

40. 92 U.S. 542, at 555–56 (1876).

41. 92 U.S. 214 (1876). Only one justice dissented; another concurred in reversing the convictions on technical grounds.

42. *Ex parte* Siebold, 100 U.S. 371 (1880); *Ex parte* Clarke, 100 U.S. 399 (1880); *Ex parte* Yarbrough, 110 U.S. 651 (1884). The basis was Article I, Section 4: "The Times, Places and Manner of holding Elections for Senators and Representatives, shall be prescribed in each State by the Legislature thereof; but the Congress may at any time by Law make or alter such Regulations, except as to the Places of chusing Senators."

43. 17 Stat. 13, at 13 (1871).

44. 106 U.S. 629, at 641, 639 (1883). Harlan dissented on the question of jurisdiction, but expressed no opinion on the merits.

45. 18 Stat. 335, at 335–36 (1875). For the adoption of this legislation, see: James M. McPherson, "Abolitionists and the Civil Rights Act of 1875," *Journal of American History* 52 (December 1965): 493–510; Bertram Wyatt-Brown, "The Civil Rights Act of 1875," *Western Political Quarterly* 18 (December 1965): 763-75; and S. G. F. Spackman, "American Federalism and the Civil Rights Act of 1875," *Journal of American Studies* 10 (December 1976): 313–28.

46. 109 U.S. 3, at 11, 13, 17, 20–25 (Bradley), 58–59, 34, 26 (Harlan). In-depth analyses include: Michael J. Horan, "Political Economy and Sociological Theory as Influences Upon Judicial Decision-Making: The *Civil Rights Cases* of 1883," *American Journal of Legal History* 16 (July 1972): 71-86; Spackman, "American Federalism"; Alan F. Westin, "The Case of the Prejudiced Doorkeeper," in *Quarrels That Have Shaped the Constitution*, ed. John A. Garraty (New York: Harper & Row, 1964), 128–44; and Ira Nerken, "A New Deal for the Protection of Fourteenth Amendment Rights: Challenging the Doctrinal Bases of the *Civil Rights Cases* and State Action Theory," *Harvard Civil Rights–Civil Liberties Law Review* 12 (Spring 1977): 297–366.

47. John Hope Franklin, "The Enforcement of the Civil Rights Act of 1875," *Prologue* 6 (Winter 1974): 225–35.

48. John S. Ezell, "The Civil Rights Act of 1875," *Mid-America* 50 (October 1968): 268-70; Emma Lou Thornbrough, *T. Thomas Fortune: Militant Journalist* (Chicago: University of Chicago Press, 1972), 47–48. *Reconstruction, the Negro, and the New South*, ed. LaWanda Cox and John H. Cox (Columbia: University of South Carolina Press, 1973), 147, 149.

49. The fullest account of the Court's personnel and rulings from 1890 to 1920 is John E. Semonche, *Charting the Future: The Supreme Court Responds to a Changing Society, 1890–1920* (Westport, Conn.: Greenwood Press, 1978). The standard account of developments within the South is C. Vann Woodward, *Origins of the New South 1877–1913* (Baton Rouge: Louisiana State University Press, 1951). *Re* northern attitudes, see: Paul H. Buck, *The Road to Reunion 1865–1900* (Boston: Little, Brown, 1937), and George M. Frederickson, *The Black Image in the White Mind: The Debate on Afro-American Character and Destiny, 1817–1914* (New York: Harper & Row, 1971). *Re* the Republican party's post–1877 abandonment of the southern Negro: Stanley P. Hirshon, *Farewell to the Bloody Shirt: Northern Republicans & the Southern Negro, 1877–1893* (Bloomington: Indiana University Press, 1962).

50. 92 U.S. 542, at 555–56 (1876); 92 U.S. 214, at 218 (1876).

51. James v. Bowman, 190 U.S. 217 (1903). The defendants had been indicted for bribing black voters in a congressional election under Section 5507 of the Revised Statutes of 1875 (based upon Section 5 of the Civil Rights Act of 1870) punishing "[e]very person who prevents, hinders, controls, or intimidates another from exercising, or in exercising the right of suffrage, to whom that right is guaranteed by the fifteenth amendment . . . by means of bribery or threats" (at 1073). The provision was held unconstitutional under the Fifteenth Amendment because not limited to state action. And though applied to a congressional election in this case, the provision was held unconstitutional under Article I, Section 4 because not limited in so many words exclusively to federal elections. *Re* the application of a state action restriction to the Fifteenth Amendment, see Note, "The Strange Career of 'State Action' under the Fifteenth Amendment," *Yale Law Journal* 78 (July 1965): 1448–61.

52. 100 U.S. 313, at 321 (1880).

53. Barney v. City of New York, 193 U.S. 430 (1904).

54. 109 U.S. 3, at 22 (1883).

55. 203 U.S. 1, at 16–19 (1906). Justices Harlan and William R. Day dissented; Justice Henry B. Brown concurred in the judgment but disassociated himself from the opinion.

56. Examples include: Smith v. Mississippi, 162 U.S. 592 (1896); Murray v. Louisiana, 163 U.S. 101 (1896); Thomas v. Texas, 212 U.S. 278 (1909).

57. Carter v. Texas, 177 U.S. 442 (1900); Rogers v. Alabama, 192 U.S. 226 (1904).

58. Hall v. DeCuir, 95 U.S. 485 (1878).

59. Louisville, New Orleans and Texas Railway Co. v. Mississippi, 133 U.S. 587 at 589–91 (1890).

60. Solomon Wolff, comp., *Constitution and Statutes of Louisiana*, 3 vols. (Indianapolis: Bobbs-Merrill, 1920), 3:1884–85.

61. The account of *Plessy* that follows relies heavily upon the in-depth analysis in Charles A. Lofgren, *The Plessy Case: A Legal-Historical Interpretation* (New York: Oxford University Press, 1987). Other treatments that have proved helpful include: Otto H. Olsen, ed. *The Thin Disguise: Turning Point in Negro History. Plessy v. Ferguson, A DocumentaryPresentation (1864–1896)* (New York: Humanities Press, 1967); Paul Oberst, "The Strange Career of Plessy v. Ferguson," *Arizona Law Review* 15, no. 2 (1973): 389–418; and Richard Maidment, *"Plessy v. Ferguson* Re-examined," *Journal of American Studies* 7 (August 1973): 125–32.

62. 163 U.S. 537, at 543–44, 550–51 (1896). Justice Brewer did not participate.

63. Examples include: Barton J. Bernstein, "Plessy v. Ferguson: Conservative Sociological Jurisprudence," *Journal of Negro History* 48 (July 1963): 196–205; Loren P. Beth, *The Development of the American Constitution 1877–1917* (New York: Harper & Row, 1971), 196–98; C. Vann Woodward, "The Case of the Louisiana Traveler," in *Quarrels That Have Shaped the Constitution*

64. Alfred H. Kelly, "The Fourteenth Amendment Reconsidered: The Segregation Question," *Michigan Law Review* 54 (June 1956): 1049–86.

65. Alexander M. Bickel, "The Original Understanding and the Segregation Decision," *Harvard Law Review* 69 (November 1955): 1–65. Alfred H. Kelly—who was responsible for much of the research for the National Association for the Advancement of Colored People's historical brief against school segregation for Brown v. Board of Education of Topeka, 347 U.S. 294 (1954)—acknowledges that Bickel's

article was "entirely correct in its conclusion with respect to specific immediate intent": "Clio and the Court: An Illicit Love Affair," in *The Supreme Court Review 1965*, ed. Philip B. Kurland (Chicago: University of Chicago Press, 1965), 145, ft. 101. And even John P. Frank and Robert F. Munro, "The Original Understanding of 'Equal Protection of the Laws,' " *Washington University Law Quarterly* 1972 (Summer)—the most inclined of the studies on the question to find an anti-segregation purpose behind the amendment—admits that "there is room for substantial difference of opinion concerning the dominant intent . . . as to mixed schools" (p. 458).

66. When asked if his proposal would require "that each and every school shall be open to children of both races," Sumner replied that such was his personal desire "but the proposition is necessarily general in its character; it does not go into details." Even so, the proposal lost on a 20-to-40 tie vote: David Tyack, Thomas James, and Aaron Benavot, *Law and the Shaping of Public Education, 1785–1954* (Madison: University of Wisconsin Press, 1987), 140–42.

67. Alfred H. Kelly, "The Congressional Controversy over School Segregation, 1867–1875," *American Historical Review* 64 (April 1959): 537–63; William P. Vaughn, "Separate and Unequal: The Civil Rights Act of 1875 and Defeat of the School Segregation Clause," *Southwestern Social Science Quarterly* 48 (September 1967): 146–54.

68. Frank and Munro, "Original Understanding," 467.

69. Lofgren, *Plessy Case*, 65–66.

70. On the basis of those votes, Frank and Munro, "Original Understanding," flatly concludes that the intention of the equal protection clause was to bar "segregation of individuals on the basis of race or color in the use of utilities, such as transportation or hotels" (452–56, 477). But *re* the support of the separate-but-equal approach by Amendment supporters in the debate preceding adoption of the Civil Rights Act of 1875, see Alfred Avins, "Racial Segregation in Public Accommodations: Some Reflected Light on the Fourteenth Amendment From the Civil Rights Act of 1875," *Western Reserve Law Review* 18 (May 1967): 1251–83.

71. 163 U.S. 537, at 544–45 (1896).

72. For Brown's twisting the precedents to suit his purposes, see Barton J. Bernstein, "Case Law in Plessy v. Ferguson," *Journal of Negro History* 47 (July 1962): 192–98; *re* the substantive correctness of his reading of the case law: David W. Bishop, "Plessy v. Ferguson: A Reinterpretation," *ibid.* 62 (April 1977): 125–33.

73. 5 Cushing 198, at 206, 209–10 (1849). For fuller details—including the long-term influence of the decision—see Leonard W. Levy and Harlan B. Phillips, "The *Roberts* Case: Source of the 'Separate but Equal' Doctrine," *American Historical Review* 56 (April 1951): 510–18.

74. For illuminating brief surveys, see: Stephen J. Riegel, "The Persistent Career of Jim Crow: Lower Federal Courts and the 'Separate but Equal' Doctrine," *American Journal of Legal History* 28 (January 1984): 17-40, and Jonathan Lurie, "The Fourteenth Amendment: Use and Application in Selected State Court Civil Liberties Cases, 1870–1890—A Preliminary Assessment," *ibid.* 28 (October 1984): 295–313.

75. Lofgren, *Plessy Case*, 116–47. That position was implicitly accepted by Chief Justice Waite in Hall v. DeCuir, 95 U.S. 485, at 490 (1878).

76. 24 Stat. 379, at 380 (1887); Councill v. Western Atlantic R.R., 1 ICC 638, at 641 (1887). See also: Heard v. Georgia R.R., 1 ICC 719 (1888) and Heard v. Georgia Railroad Co., 3 ICC 111 (1889). The Supreme Court affirmed that a railroad's

practice of separating interstate passengers by race did not violate any federal law in Chiles v. Chesapeake and Ohio Railway Co., 218 U.S. 71 (1910). Fuller details can be found in Catherine A. Barnes, *Journey from Jim Crow: The Desegregation of Southern Transit* (New York: Columbia University Press, 1983), 1–19.

77. Examples include: Charge to the Grand Jury—The Civil Rights Act, 30 Fed. Cas. 999, #18,258 (CC W.D. N.C. 1875); United States v. Dodge, 25 Fed. Cas. 882, #14,976 (W.D. Texas 1877); Green v. City of Bridgeton, 10 Fed. Cas. 1090, #5,754 (S.D. Ga. 1879).

78. J. Morgan Kousser, *Dead End: The Development of Nineteenth-Century Litigation on Racial Discrimination in Schools* (Oxford: Clarendon Press, 1986), 5, 9, 18–25, 58, 61. The one case holding that racial separation as such violated the Fourteenth Amendment was Commonwealth *ex rel.* v. Davis, 10 WNC 156 (1881). Opinions holding the separate-but-equal facilities did not violate the Fourteenth Amendment include: Ward v. Flood, 48 Cal. 36 (1874); State *ex rel.* Garnes v. McCann, 21 Oh. State 198 (1871); State *ex rel.* Stoutmeyer v. Duffy, 7 Nev. 342, at 346, 348 (1872); Cory v. Carter, 48 Ind. 327 (1874); Bertonneau v. Board of Directors of City Schools, 3 Fed. Cas. 294, #1,361 (CC La. 1878). Although finding for the Negro plaintiff, United States v. Buntin, 10 F 730 (CC S.D. Ohio 1882), did so upon separate-but-equal grounds.

79. Thomas M. Cooley, *The Elements of Torts* (Chicago: Callaghan, 1895), pp. 104–05.

80. Pace v. Alabama, 106 U.S. 583 (1883).

81. 113 U.S. 27, at 31 (1885).

82. Ray A. Brown, "Due Process, Police Power, and the Supreme Court," *Harvard Law Review* 40 (May 1927): 943–68; Janet S. Lindgren, "Beyond Cases: Reconsidering Judicial Review," *Wisconsin Law Review* 1983, no. 3: 583–638; Melvin I. Urofsky, "Myth and Reality: The Supreme Court and Protective Legislation in the Progressive Era," *Supreme Court Historical Society Yearbook 1983* (Washington, D.C.: Supreme Court Historical Society, 1983), 53–72; Urofsky, "State Courts and Protective Legislation in the Progressive Era: A Reevaluation," *Journal of American History* 72 (June 1985): 63–91.

83. Louisville & Nashville Railroad Co. v. Kentucky, 161 U.S. 677, at 701 (1896). For more on Brown, see Robert J. Glennon, Jr., "Justice Henry Billings Brown: Values in Tension," *University of Colorado Law Review* 44 (May 1973): 553–604.

84. 163 U.S. 537, at 550–51 (1896).

85. *Re* the dominance of racist assumptions in not only popular attitudes but in the scientific thought of the time: Frederickson, *Black Image in the White Mind*; John S. Haller, Jr., *Outcasts from Evolution: Scientific Attitudes of Racial Inferiority, 1859–1900*; James W. Vander Zanden, "The Ideology of White Supremacy," *Journal of History of Ideas* 20 (June-September 1959): 385–402.

86. The leading example is C. Vann Woodward, *The Career of Jim Crow* (New York: Oxford University Press, 1955).

87. The situation in the North is treated in Leon Litwack, *North of Slavery: The Negro in the Free States, 1790–1860* (Chicago: University of Chicago Press, 1961), and James C. Mohr, ed., *Radical Republicans in the North: State Politics during Reconstruction* (Baltimore: Johns Hopkins University Press, 1976).

88. John A. Scott, "Segregation: A Fundamental Aspect of Southern Race Relations, 1800–1860," *Journal of the Early Republic* 4 (Winter 1984): 421-41.

89. The entrenchment of segregation in the post-Civil War South is documented in Howard N. Rabinowitz, "From Exclusion to Segregation: Southern Race Relations, 1865–1890," *Journal of American History* 63 (September 1976): 325–50. Examples of segregation provisions in the Johnson government "Black Codes" can be found in Walter L. Fleming, *Documentary History of Reconstruction: Political, Military, Social, Religious, Educational & Industrial, 1865 to the Present Time*, 2 vols. (Cleveland: Arthur H. Clark, 1906), 1: 273–312. Fuller details on individual states are given in Vernon L. Wharton, *The Negro in Mississippi, 1865–1890* (Chapel Hill: University of North Carolina Press, 1947); Joel Williamson, *After Slavery: The Negro in South Carolina During Reconstruction, 1861–1877* (Chapel Hill: University of North Carolina Press, 1965); and Roger A. Fischer, *The Segregation Struggle in Louisiana 1862-77* (Urbana: University of Illinois Press, 1974). The New Orleans experiment in desegregated public education is examined in Louis Harlan, "Desegregation in New Orleans Public Schools during Reconstruction," *American Historical Review* 67 (April 1962): 663-75. *Re* the imposition of legally required school segregation after the restoration of white rule: John Hope Franklin, "Jim Crow Goes to School: The Genesis of Legal Segregation in Southern Schools," *South Atlantic Quarterly* 58 (Spring 1959): 225–35; the first wave of separate railroad car laws and post-*Plessy* developments: Lofgren, *Plessy Case*, 7–27, 200–04.

90. Robert A. Margo, "Race Differences in Public School Expenditures: Disenfranchisement and School Finance in Louisiana, 1890–1910," *Social Science History* 6 (Winter 1982): 9–12.

91. 175 U.S. 528, at 543–45 (1899). In argument before the Supreme Court, an attempt was made to broaden the issue and attack the county's practice of segregated education. But since not raised below, the Court refused to consider that question. On the background and significance of the case, see J. Morgan Kousser, "Separate but *not* Equal: The Supreme Court's First Decision on Racial Discrimination in Schools," *Journal of Southern History* 46 (February 1980): 17–44.

92. Berea College v. Kentucky, 123 Ky. 209, at 213–14, 224–26, 228; Berea College v. Kentucky, 211 U.S. 45, at 54–57 (Brewer), 69 (Harlan) (1908). Justice William R. Day also dissented, but without opinion. For background, see Paul D. Nelson, "Experiment in Interracial Education at Berea College, 1858–1908," *Journal of Negro History* 59 (January 1974): 13-27.

93. John A. Garraty, *Henry Cabot Lodge: A Biography* (New York: Alfred A. Knopf, 1953), pp. 117–21.

94. The details are given in W. Roy Smith, "Negro Suffrage in the South," *Studies in Southern History and Politics*, pp. 229–56, and, more fully, J. Morgan Kousser, *The Shaping of Southern Politics: Suffrage Restriction and the Establishment of the One-Party South, 1880–1910* (New Haven, Conn.: Yale University Press, 1974).

95. *Re* the link between disenfranchisement and the widening disparity in school expenditures for whites and blacks that followed: Margo, "Race Differences in Public School Expenditures," pp. 9–33, and J. Morgan Kousser, "Progressivism—For Middle-Class Whites Only: North Carolina Education, 1880–1910," *Journal of Southern History* 46 (May 1980): 169–94.

96. Williams v. Mississippi, 170 U.S. 213, at 222 (1898).

97. 189 U.S. 475, at 486–88 (1903). The same plaintiff then brought actions in the state courts asking for damages because of the local board's refusal to register him and for a writ of mandamus ordering the board to register him. The Alabama

Supreme Court resorted to much the same rationale as Holmes had in ruling against him. When appeal was brought to the United States Supreme Court, the justices—with only Harlan in an unexplained dissent and McKenna concurring separately without opinion—dismissed on the ground that the Alabama court had decided the case on an adequate independent state ground: Giles v. Teasley, 193 U.S. 146 (1904).

98. Jack T. Kirby, *Darkness at the Dawning: Race and Reform in the Progressive South* (Philadelphia: J. B. Lippincott, 1972).

99. David W. Southern, *The Malignant Heritage: Yankee Progressives and the Negro Question 1900–1914* (Chicago: Loyola University Press, 1968).

100. Charles F. Kellogg, *NAACP: A History of The National Association for the Advancement of Colored People, Volume I 1909–1920* (Baltimore: Johns Hopkins Press, 1967).

101. The White Court's treatment of civil rights is exhaustively examined in a series of three articles by Benno C. Schmidt, Jr., in the *Columbia Law Review* under the over-all title "Principle and Prejudice: The Supreme Court and Race in the Progressive Era": "Part 1: The Heyday of Jim Crow," 82 (April 1982): 444–524; "Part 2: The *Peonage Cases*," 82 (May 1982): 646–718; and "Part 3: Black Disenfranchisement from the KKK to the Grandfather Clause," 82 (June 1982): 835–905. This material has been incorporated into Alexander M. Bickel and Schmidt, *The Judiciary and Responsible Government 1910–21* [*Oliver Wendell Holmes Devise History of the Supreme Court of the United States*, Volume 9] (New York: Macmillan, 1984). A more negative appraisal is given by Randall Kennedy, "Race Relations Law and the Tradition of Celebration: The Case of Professor Schmidt," *Columbia Law Review* 86 (December 1986): 1622–61.

102. 193 U.S. 430, at 437 (1904).

103. 227 U.S. 278, at 287 (1913). That position was reaffirmed in Iowa-Des Moines National Bank v. Bennett, 284 U.S. 239 (1931): "When a state official, acting under color of state authority, invades, in the course of his duties, a private right secured by the federal Constitution, that right is violated, even if the state officer not only exceeded his authority but disregarded special commands of the state law" (at 246).

104. Carr, *Federal Protection of Civil Rights*, pp. 70-73, 105–15; Woodford Howard and Cornelius Bushoven, "The *Screws* Case Revisited," *Journal of Politics* 29 (August 1967): 617–36.

105. 14 Stat. 546, at 546 (1867).

106. For a full treatment, see Pete Daniel, *The Shadow of Slavery: Peonage in the South 1901–1969* (Urbana: University of Illinois Press, 1972).

107. Clyatt v. United States, 197 U.S. 207, at 215 (1905).

108. 219 U.S. 219, at 227–28, 245 (1911). The case is examined in detail in Pete Daniel, "Up from Slavery and Down to Peonage: The Alonzo Bailey Case," *Journal of American History* 57 (December 1970): 654-70.

109. 235 U.S. 133, at 146–47 (1914).

110. McCabe v. Atchison, Topeka & Santa Fe Railway Co., 235 U.S. 151, at 160–62 (1914). And because of procedural shortcomings in the suit, the majority refused to issue the requested injunction against compliance by the railroad with even the offending provision (at 162–64).

111. South Covington & Cincinnati Street Railway Co. v. Kentucky, 252 U.S. 399, at 404 (1920).

112. "If two or more persons conspire to injure, oppress, threaten, or intimidate

any citizen in the free exercise or enjoyment of any right or privilege secured to him by the Constitution or laws of the United States, or because of his having so exercised the same": 35 Stat. 1088, at 1092 (1909).

113. 238 U.S. 383 (1915). Justice Joseph R. Lamar dissented; Justice James C. McReynolds did not participate.

114. United States v. Gradwell, 243 U.S. 476, at 487 (1917).

115. United States v. Bathgate, 246 U.S. 220, at 226 (1918).

116. Guinn and Beal v. United States, 238 U.S. 347, at 363–64, 366–67 (1915). Justice McReynolds did not participate.

117. 238 U.S. 368 (1915). And as in *Guinn*, White threw out the statute's property qualification for voting for those not exempted by the grandfather clause.

118. Garrett Power, "Apartheid Baltimore Style: The Residential Segregation Ordinances of 1910–1913," *Maryland Law Review* 42, no. 2 (1983): 289–328.

119. Harris v. City of Louisville, 165 Ky. 559, at 572 (1917). For fuller details, see Roger L. Rice, "Residential Segregation by Law, 1900–1917," *Journal of Southern History* 34 (May 1968): 179–99.

120. State v. Gurry, 121 Md. 534, at 550–51 (1913). Similar rulings were handed down in State v. Darnell, 166 N.C. 300 (1914) and Carey v. City of Atlanta, 143 Ga. 192 (1915). But such ordinances were upheld in Hopkins v. City of Richmond, 117 Va. 692 (1915) and Harden v. City of Atlanta, 147 Ga. 248 (1917).

121. *Re* the background of zoning laws, see Marc A. Weiss, *The Rise of the Community Builders: The American Real Estate Industry and Urban Land Planning* (New York: Columbia University Press, 1987), pp. 1–12, 53–72, 79–86; support for geographical restriction of the urban black population, Herbert Hovenkamp, "Social Science and Segregation before *Brown*," *Duke Law Journal* 1985 (June-September): 657–64.

122. Hadacheck v. Sebastian, 239 U.S. 394 (1915).

123. Buchanan v. Warley, 245 U.S. 60, at 72–82 (1917). In brief *per curiam* decisions, the Court in later years struck down two ordinances thinly disguised to circumvent *Buchanan*: Harmon v. Tyler, 273 U.S. 668 (1927); City of Richmond v. Deans, 281 U.S. 704 (1930). Further evidence of the decisive role in *Buchanan* of the racially discriminatory aspect can be found in the fact that seven years later—in the heyday of substantive due process—a six-to-three majority upheld a comprehensive local zoning law aimed protecting residential neighborhoods from the encroachment of industry, business, and even apartment houses in Village of Euclid v. Ambler Realty Co., 272 U.S. 365 (1926). For a survey showing the generally permissive attitute taken by the courts toward municipal land-use regulations, see W. L. Pollard, "Outline of the Law of Zoning in the United States," *Annals of the American Academy of Political and Social Science* 155 (May 1931): 15–33.

124. *Re* Taft as Chief Justice and his Court, see Alpheus T. Mason, *William Howard Taft: Chief Justice* (New York: Simon and Schuster, 1965). A strongly negative appraisal of the Taft Court's record on civil liberties/civil rights issues—too much so at least regarding criminal procedure questions—is given by Russell W. Galloway, Jr., "The Taft Court (1921–29)," *Santa Clara Law Review* 25 (Winter 1985): 1–64.

125. 271 U.S. 323, at 331–32 (1926). The spread of, and resulting litigation over, restrictive covenants is thoroughly traced in Clement E. Vose, *Caucasians Only: The Supreme Court, the NAACP, and the Restrictive Covenant Cases* (Berkeley: University of California Press, 1967).

126. Gong Lum v. Rice, 275 U.S. 78, at 85–86 (1927).

127. 256 U.S. 232 (1921). At issue was the conviction of Senator Truman Newberry for violating the Federal Corrupt Practices Act of 1911 by excessive spending in the 1918 Michigan Republican senatorial primary. Although all the justices were agreed upon overturning the conviction, only four, in fact, did so on the basis of a lack of power in Congress to regulate primaries. A fifth agreed that the act was beyond the power of Congress when adopted, but suggested that the ratification of the Seventeenth Amendment for the popular election of United States Senators might make a difference (at 258).

128. Darlene C. Hine, *Black Victory: The Rise and and Fall of the White Primary in Texas* (Millwood, N.Y.: KTO Press, 1979), is a thorough examination. See also Conrey Bryson, *Dr. Lawrence A. Nixon and the White Primary* [*Southwestern Studies*, Monograph No. 42] (El Paso, 1974).

129. 273 U.S. 536, at 541 (1927).

130. A federal district court ruled that Virginia's primary law empowering the Democratic Party to establish voting qualifications for primary voting violated the Fourteenth and Fifteenth Amendments: West v. Bliley, 33 F2d 177 (E.D. Va. 1929). When the Circuit Court of Appeals affirmed that decision (Bliley v. West, 42 F2d 101 [CCA 4th Cir. 1930]), Virginia Democratic party leaders decided not to appeal to the Supreme Court. The Arkansas Supreme Court upheld the power of the state Democratic party as a private voluntary association to prescribe qualifications for party membership and thus primary voting: Robinson v. Holman, 26 SW2d 66 (1930). But the United States Supreme Court refused to grant certiorari—apparently on technical grounds: Robinson v. Holman, 282 U.S. 804 (1930). The Negro complainants were successful in the Florida Supreme Court, but that decision was not handed down until October 1932: Hine, *Black Victory*, pp. 99–101.

131. Nixon v. Condon, 286 U.S. 73, at 82–85, 88–89 (1932).

132. 295 U.S. 45, at 47, 54–55, 50–53 (1935).

133. Breedlove v. Suttles, 302 U.S. 277 (1937).

134. Frank v. Magnum, 237 U.S. 309, at 335–36. A full account of the affair is given by Leonard Dinnerstein, *The Leo Frank Case* (New York: Columbia University Press, 1968).

135. Moore v. Dempsey, 261 U.S. 86, at 91–92 (1923). *Re* Taft's role and the decision's importance, see Robert M. Cover, "The Left, the Right and the First Amendment: 1918–1928," *Maryland Law Review* 40, no. 3 (1981): 355–57.

136. Powell v. Alabama, 287 U.S. 45 (1932). The fullest account is Dan T. Carter, *Scottsboro: A Tragedy of the American South* (rev. ed., Baton Rouge: Louisiana State University Press, 1979).

137. Brown v. Mississippi, 297 U.S. 278, at 285–86 (1936). Full details are given in Richard C. Cortner, *A "Scottsboro" Case in Mississippi: The Supreme Court and Brown v. Mississippi* (Jackson: University Press of Mississippi, 1986).

138. Norris v. Alabama, 294 U.S. 587, at 590–99; Schmidt, "Juries, Jurisdiction, and Race Discrimination," 1476–82. Justice McReynolds did not participate.

139. Thurgood Marshall, "The Rise and Collapse of the 'White Democratic Primary,'" in *The Making of Black America: Essays in Negro Life & History*, ed. August Meier and Elliott Rudwich, 2 vols. (New York: Atheneum, 1969), 2: 277.

140. Harvard Sitkoff, *A New Deal for Blacks: The Emergence of Civil Rights as a National Issue, Volume I: The Depression Decade* (New York: Oxford University Press, 1978).

141. Richard L. Watson, Jr., "The Defeat of Judge Parker: A Study in Pressure Groups and Politics," *Mississippi Valley Historical Review* 50 (September 1963): 213–34.

142. On Houston's role, see Richard Kluger, *Simple Justice: The History of* Brown v. Board of Education *and Black America's Struggle for Equality* (New York: Alfred A. Knopf, 1976), and Genna R. McNeil, *Groundwork: Charles Hamilton Houston and the Struggle for Civil Rights* (Philadelphia: University of Pennsylvania Press, 1983).

4 The Criminal Defendant

1. Francis A. Allen, "The Supreme Court and State Criminal Justice," *Wayne Law Review* 4 (Summer 1958): 191–95.

2. District of Columbia: Callan v. Wilson, 127 U.S. 540, at 550 (1888); Capital Traction Co. v. Hof, 174 U.S. 1, at 5 (1899). Territories: Reynolds v. United States, 98 U.S. 145, at 162 (1879); Lovato v. New Mexico, 242 U.S. 199, at 201 (1916). Alaska: Rassmussen v. United States, 197 U.S. 516 (1905). In the so-called unincorporated territories (i.e., Hawaii, the islands acquired as a result of the Spanish–American War, and the Virgin Islands) only what the Court deemed fundamental provisions of the Constitution applied. The basic rule was laid down in the so-called Insular Cases: De Lima v. Bidwell, 182 U.S. 1 (1901); Dooley v. United States, 182 U.S. 222 (1901); Downes v. Bidwell, 182 U.S. 244 (1901). Follow-up cases involving the criminal procedure guarantees include: Hawaii v. Mankichi, 190 U.S. 197 (1903); Dorr v. United States, 195 U.S. 138 (1904); Balzac v. Porto Rico, 258 U.S. 298 (1922); Francis v. Virgin Islands, 11 F2d 860 (CCA 3rd Cir. 1926), cert. denied, *sub nomine* Francis v. Williams, 273 U.S. 693 (1926).

3. A still useful overview of the Supreme Court's decision-making in the criminal law area is David Fellman, *The Rights of the Defendant* (New York: Rinehart, 1958).

4. Murray's Lessee v. Hoboken Land and Improvement Co., 18 How. 272, at 277 (1856).

5. Holden v. Hardy, 169 U.S. 366, at 387 (1898).

6. Twining v. New Jersey, 211 U.S. 78, at 101 (1908).

7. Hurtado v. California, 110 U.S. 516, at 535 (1884); Holden v. Hardy, 169 U.S. 366, at 389 (1898); Twining v. New Jersey, 211 U.S. 78, at 113 (1908).

8. Hagar v. Reclamation District No. 108, 111 U.S. 701, at 708 (1884).

9. Rosen v. United States, 161 U.S. 29, at 40 (1896).

10. Connally v. General Construction Co., 269 U.S. 385, at 391 (1926). The most famous application of the void-for-vagueness rule came in United States v. L. Cohen Grocery Co., 255 U.S. 81, at 86–91 (1921), when the Court struck down a World War I statute making it a crime for anyone to make "any unjust or unreasonable rate or charge in handling or dealing in or with any necessaries."

11. McBoyle v. United States, 283 U.S. 25, at 27 (1931).

12. Nash v. United States, 229 U.S. 373, at 376-77 (1913).

13. United States v. Cruikshank, 92 U.S. 542, at 557–59 (1876).

14. Hagner v. United States, 285 U.S. 427, at 431 (1932).

15. The citations are listed in *In re* Winship, 397 U.S. 358, at 361–64 (1970).

16. Shelvin-Carpenter Co. v. Minnesota, 218 U.S. 57, at 70 (1910); reaffirmed, United States v. Balint, 258 U.S. 250, at 251–52 (1922). On this issue, see Herbert L. Packer, "Mens Rea and the Supreme Court," in *The Supreme Court Review 1962*,

ed. Philip B. Kurland (Chicago: University of Chicago Press, 1962), pp. 107–52. Related to the guilty intent issue was the question of the entrapment defense—the plea as a defense against conviction that the criminal action had been induced by law enforcement authorities. The entrapment defense was first accepted at the federal court level by the Ninth Circuit Court of Appeals in Woo Wai v. United States, 223 F 412, at 415 (CCA 9th Cir. 1915). By the 1920s, the entrapment defense was widely accepted in the federal courts. But the Supreme Court did not deal with the question until 1932 in a prohibition law violation case, Sorrells v. United States, 287 U.S. 435 (1932). Then eight justices agreed that entrapment was a defense under federal law, but five of those rested the decision upon a narrow construction of the national prohibition law (at 448–49) and only three on the broader equitable ground of protecting against "prostitution of the criminal law" (at 457). For fuller details, see Kenneth M. Murchison, "The Entrapment Defense in Federal Courts: Emergence of a Legal Doctrine," *Mississippi Law Journal* 47 (April 1976): 211–36.

17. Schlesinger v. Wisconsin, 270 U.S. 230 (1926) (a Wisconsin statute providing that every gift of a material part of a decedent's estate made by him within six years of his death should be construed as having been made in contemplation of death for tax purposes held invalid as a "conclusive presumption" that "cannot be overcome by evidence" (at 239); Heiner v. Donnan, 285 U.S. 312 (1932) and Handy v. Delaware Trust Co., 285 U.S. 352 (1932) (holding similarly invalid a federal tax statute providing that gifts made within two years of the death of the donor shall be treated as having been made in contemplation of death on the ground that "a statute creating a presumption which operates to deny a fair opportunity to rebut it violates the due process clause" (at 329).

18. Mobile, Jackson & Kansas City Railroad Co. v. Turnipseed, 219 U.S. 35, at 43 (1910). The Court, for example, struck down as arbitrary and thus denying due process, a law establishing a presumption of fraud by a bank's officers whenever a bank failed: Manley v. Georgia, 279 U.S. 1 (1929). By contrast, the Court upheld as a reasonable presumption the provision in the 1914 Anti-Narcotics Act making possession of narcotic drugs without the required stamps *prima facie* evidence of the act's violation: Casey v. United States, 276 U.S. 413 (1928). For a fuller discussion, see Edward M. Watson, "Use of Statutory Presumptions in Criminal Cases," *Michigan Law Review* 38 (January 1940): 366–81.

19. The exception was Bram v. United States, 168 U.S. 532 (1897). The following draws heavily upon Otis H. Stephens, Jr., *The Supreme Court and Confessions of Guilt* (Knoxville: University of Tennessee Press, 1973).

20. See the citations in Warszower v. United States, 312 U.S. 342, at 347 (1941).

21. Hopt v. Utah, 110 U.S. 574, at 583–87 (1884); Sparf and Hansen v. United States, 156 U.S. 51, at 54–56 (1895); Wilson v. United States, 162 U.S. 613, at 621–24 (1896). For fuller details on common-law treatment of involuntary confessions, see Albert R. Beisel, Jr., *Control over Illegal Enforcement of the Criminal Law: Role of the Supreme Court* (Boston: Boston University Press, 1955), 44–48.

22. Ziang Sung Wan v. United States, 266 U.S. 1, at 14–17 (1924).

23. 297 U.S. 278 (1936).

24. United States v. Hudson and Goodwin, 7 Cranch 32, at 34 (1812). See also United States v. Coolidge, 1 Wheat. 415 (1816). For the debate over the extent to which federal judges prior to that decision accepted the existence of a federal common law of crimes, see Stewart Jay, "Origins of the Federal Common Law: Part I," and

"Part II," *University of Pennsylvania Law Review* 133 (June 1985): 1003–1116, and (July 1985): 1231–1333 along with the articles by Kathryn Preyer ("Jurisdiction to Punish: Federal Authority, Federalism and the Common Law of Crimes in the Early Republic"), Robert C. Palmer ("The Federal Common Law of Crime"), and Stephen B. Presser ("The Supra-Constitution, the Courts, and the Federal Common Law of Crimes: Some Comments on Palmer and Preyer") in "Symposium: Federal Common Law of Crime," *Law and History Review* 4 (Fall 1986): 223–335.

25. Henry M. Hart, Jr., and Herbert Wechsler, *The Federal Courts and the Federal System* (Brooklyn: Foundation Press, 1953), p. 1313.

26. For fuller documentation, see Kenneth M. Murchison, "Prohibition and the Fourteenth Amendment: A New Look at Some Old Cases," *Journal of Criminal Law and Criminology* 73 (Summer 1982): 471–532; and Murchison, "Property Forfeiture in the Era of National Prohibition: A Study of Judicial Response to Legislative Reform," *Buffalo Law Review* 32 (Spring 1983): 417–63.

27. The fullest treatment is Jacob W. Landynski, *Search and Seizure and the Supreme Court: A Study in Constitutional Interpretation* (Baltimore: Johns Hopkins Press, 1966). But see also the excellent introductions to the rules for the guidance of law enforcement officers by Ernest W. Machen, Jr.: *The Law of Arrest* (Chapel Hill: Institute of Government, University of North Carolina, 1950) and *The Law of Search and Seizure* (Chapel Hill: Institute of Government, University of North Carolina, 1950).

28. *Ex parte* Burford, 3 Cranch 448 (1806).

29. Marron v. United States, 275 U.S. 192 (1927). But the degree of particularity would depend to some extent on the nature of the goods. In the case of contraband liquor, for example, the Court held that the description "cases of whiskey" sufficed: Steele v. United States, No. 1, 267 U.S. 498, at 504 (1925).

30. West v. Cabell, 153 U.S. 78, at 85 (1894).

31. Dumbra v. United States, 268 U.S. 435, at 441 (1925).

32. Locke v. United States, 7 Cranch 339, at 348 (1813).

33. Nathanson v. United States, 290 U.S. 41, at 46–47 (1933).

34. Byars v. United States, 273 U.S. 28, at 29 (1927).

35. *Re* the law of arrest: Francis H. Bohlen and Harry Shulman, "Arrest with and without a Warrant," *University of Pennsylvania Law Review* 75 (April 1927): 485–504, and Lester B. Orfield, *Criminal Procedure From Arrest to Appeal* (New York: New York University Press, 1947), 3–48.

36. For the Supreme Court's approval of warrantless arrests for felonies upon probable cause, see the citations in Draper v. United States, 358 U.S. 307, at 310–13 (1959).

37. Carroll v. United States, 267 U.S. 132, at 156–59 (1925).

38. Hale v. Henkel, 201 U.S. 43, at 76-77 (1906); Silverthorne Lumber Co. v. United States, 251 U.S. 385, at 392 (1920).

39. Agnello v. United States, 209 U.S. 20, at 30–33 (1925).

40. Hester v. United States, 265 U.S. 57, at 59 (1924).

41. 267 U.S. 132 (1925). The same reasoning, and thus the same rule, was applied to boats: United States v. Lee, 274 U.S. 559 (1927). See Gary C. Robb, "The *Carroll* Case: The Expansion of the Automobile Exception in Warrantless Search and Seizure Cases," *Willamette Law Review* 15 (Winter 1978): 39–59.

42. Husty v. United States, 282 U.S. 694 (1931).

43. 232 U.S. 383, at 392 (1914).

44. Agnello v. United States, 269 U.S. 20, at 28–30, 35 (1925).

45. Marron v. United States, 275 U.S. 192, at 198–99 (1927).

46. Go-Bart Importing Co. v. United States, 282 U.S. 344, at 357–58 (1931); United States v. Lefkowitz, 285 U.S. 452 (1932).

47. Murray's Lessee v. Hoboken Land and Improvement Co., 18 How. 272 (1856).

48. 116 U.S. 616, at 622–24, 630, 633–35 (1886). The other two justices concurred in overturning the forfeiture judgment, but exclusively on the ground that the required production of the records violated the guarantee against self-incrimination.

49. Adams v. New York, 192 U.S. 585, at 597–98 (1904).

50. 255 U.S. 298, at 312, 309–10 (1921).

51. Contrast Marron v. United States, 275 U.S. 192, at 198–99 (1927) with United States v. Lefkowitz, 285 U.S. 452, at 455, 465 (1932).

52. Adams v. New York, 192 U.S. 585, at 594–98 (1904).

53. 232 U.S. 383, at 393 (1914).

54. Silverthorne Lumber Co. v. United States, 251 U.S. 385, at 392 (1920). On like reasoning, the Court went on to hold that a witness could not testify about what he saw during an illegal search: Amos v. United States, 255 U.S. 313 (1921). The term "fruit of the poisonous tree" was coined by Justice Felix Frankfurter in Nardone v. United States, 308 U.S. 338, at 341 (1939).

55. 256 U.S. 465 (1921).

56. 232 U.S. 383, at 398 (1914).

57. National Safe Deposit Co. v. Stead, 232 U.S. 58, at 71 (1914).

58. Byars v. United States, 273 U.S. 28, at 33–34 (1927); Gambino v. United States, 275 U.S. 310, at 316 (1927).

59. For a fuller discussion, see William M. Beaney, "The Constitutional Right to Privacy in the Supreme Court," in *The Supreme Court Review 1962*, ed. Philip B. Kurland (Chicago: University of Chicago Press, 1962), pp. 218-29.

60. 277 U.S. 438, at 464, 467–68 (1928).

61. 277 U.S. 438, at 469-70 (Holmes), 485, 478, 473, 476, 478-79 (Brandeis) (1928).

62. 277 U.S. 438, at 465–66 (Taft), 481 (Brandeis) (1928); 44 Stat. 1162, at 1172 (1927).

63. 48 Stat. 1064, at 1103 (1934): "no person . . . shall intercept any communication and divulge or publish the existence, contents, substance, purport, effect, or meaning of such intercepted communication to any person."

64. Nardone v. United States, 302 U.S. 379, at 382–83 (1937). Two years later— in an appeal from the same defendant reconvicted upon retrial after the reversal of his first conviction—the Court followed the "fruit of the poisonous tree" doctrine to bar the admission in federal courts of not simply the intercepted conversation but any use of any information obtained as a result of a wiretap: Nardone v. United States, 308 U.S. 338 (1939).

65. A lucid and thorough analysis of Supreme Court rulings in the self-incrimination area is given in Edward S. Corwin, "The Supreme Court's Construction of the Self-Incrimination Clause," *Michigan Law Review* 29 (November 1930): 1–27 and (December 1930): 191–207.

66. For the argument that the Fifth Amendment provision was limited to giving

a right to silence to defendants in criminal trials, see Lewis Mayers, "The Federal Witness' Privilege Against Self-Incrimination: Constitutional or Common-Law?" *American Journal of Legal History* 4 (April 1960): 107–41.

67. It should be noted, however, that suspects could be, and were, questioned at their preliminary examination when not under oath; that English law did not require until 1848 that the suspect be informed of his legal right not to answer; and that incriminating statements made at the preliminary examination could be, and were used, against the defendant at his trial. These findings are summarized in Leonard W. Levy and Lawrence H. Leder, " 'Exotic Fruit': The Right Against Compulsory Self-Incrimination in Colonial New York," *William and Mary Quarterly* 3rd Ser., 20 (January 1963): 3–32, and Levy, "The Right Against Self-Incrimination: History and Judicial History," *Political Science Quarterly* 84 (March 1969): 1–29. Fuller elaboration and supporting evidence are provided in Levy, *Origins of the Fifth Amendment: The Right Against Self-Incrimination* (New York: Oxford University Press, 1968).

68. As Moody admitted in *Twining*, the "meager records of the early colonial time, so far as they have come to our attention," supplied "light too uncertain for guidance" on the intended meaning of the self-incrimination clause: 211 U.S. 78, at 108 (1908).

69. J.A.C. Grant, *Our Common Law Constitution* (Boston: Boston University Press, 1960), pp. 37–41. A related question was if a codefendant who was being tried separately was competent to testify at the trial of his alleged partner in crime. The Supreme Court answered yes in Benson v. United States, 146 U.S. 325 (1892). The situation regarding the spouse of a defendant was more complicated. In 1893, the Court ruled that a "wife was not a competent witness either in behalf of, or against her husband": Graves v. United States, 150 U.S. 118, at 121 (1893). The Court reaffirmed this position in Hendrix v. United States, 219 U.S. 79, at 91 (1911), and Jin Fuey Moy v. United States, 254 U.S. 189, at 195 (1920). In Funk v. United States, 290 U.S. 371 (1933), however, the Court reversed itself and held that a wife could testify in behalf of her husband (at 380–82). On the other hand, the Court has continued to hew to the longstanding common-law rule that a wife could not testify against her husband without his consent: Hawkins v. United States, 358 U.S. 74 (1958).

70. 20 Stat. 30, at 31 (1878).

71. Wilson v. United States, 149 U.S. 60 (1893).

72. Twining v. New Jersey, 211 U.S. 78, at 114 (1908).

73. 142 U.S. 547, at 562 (1892). As Justice Louis D. Brandeis reaffirmed in McCarthy v. Arndstein, 266 U.S. 34 (1924): "The privilege is not ordinarily dependent upon the nature of the proceeding in which the testimony is sought or is to be used. It applies alike to civil and criminal proceedings, wherever the answer might tend to subject to criminal responsibility him who gives it. The privilege protects a mere witness as fully as it does one who is a party defendant" (at 40).

74. 201 U.S. 43, at 74-77 (1906). See also: Grant and Burlingame v. United States, 227 U.S. 74 (1913) and Johnson v. United States, 228 U.S. 457 (1913).

75. Wilson v. United States, 221 U.S. 361, at 377–82 (1911); Wheeler v. United States, 226 U.S. 478 (1913); Essgee Co. v. United States, 262 U.S. 151, at 158 (1923).

76. 249 U.S. 47, at 50 (1919).

77. Rev. Stat., Section 860, at 162 (1875).

78. 142 U.S. 547, at 585–86 (1892).
79. 27 Stat. 443, at 444 (1893).
80. 161 U.S. 591, at 597, 605–08 (1896).
81. Hale v. Henkel, 201 U.S. 43, at 68–69 (1906); Nelson v. United States, 201 U.S. 92, at 116 (1906). Conversely, an immunity granted to a witness under a state statute would not prevent a prosecution of such a witness for violation of a federal statute: Jack v. Kansas, 199 U.S. 372, at 380 (1905). The rationale—as spelled out in United States v. Murdock, 284 U.S. 141, at 149 (1931)—was that nation and state constituted two distinct sovereignties, and therefore, testimony compelled by one sovereign pursuant to a grant of immunity from that sovereign could be used in a criminal prosecution by another sovereign.
82. Blair v. United States, 250 U.S. 273 (1919); Blackmer v. United States, 284 U.S. 421, at 438, 442 (1932).
83. Brown v. United States, 276 U.S. 134, at 144 (1932). Even a grant of immunity did not automatically bar any prosecution whatever, but simply provided a defense to be raised against successful prosecution: Heike v. United States, 217 U.S. 423, at 429–32 (1910).
84. Brown v. Walker, 161 U.S. 591, at 597 (1896); McCarthy v. Arndstein, 262 U.S. 355 (1923).
85. Brown v. Walker, 161 U.S. 591, at 597–98 (1896); Raffel v. United States, 271 U.S. 494 (1926).
86. 218 U.S. 245, at 252–53 (1910).
87. Holt v. United States, 218 U.S. 245, at 247–48 (1910).
88. *Ex parte* Wilson, 114 U.S. 417, at 427–29 (1885).
89. 35 Stat. 1088, at 1152 (1909); 46 Stat. 1029, at 1030–31 (1930).
90. Duke v. United States, 301 U.S. 492, at 494–95 (1937).
91. Margaret Jones, "What Constitutes Double Jeopardy?" *Journal of Criminal Law and Criminology* 38 (November-December 1947): 379–90, is a useful brief survey. The fullest treatment is Jay A. Sigler, *Double Jeopardy: The Development of a Legal and Social Policy* (Ithaca, N.Y.: Cornell University Press, 1969).
92. 18 Wall. 163, at 168–69, 172-76, 178 (1874). Lange had been convicted of an offense that carried a maximum penalty of either one year imprisonment or a $200 fine, but was mistakenly sentenced both to pay a fine of $200 and to serve one year in prison. When the mistake was brought to the trial judge's attention, he set aside the first sentence and imposed a new sentence of one year in prison without taking into account that the defendant had already paid the fine. Overturning the prison sentence, the Supreme Court held that even though the fine had been paid under an illegal sentence, to punish the defendant further would be to violate the double jeopardy clause. "If there is anything settled in the jurisprudence of England and America, it is that no man can be twice lawfully punished for the same offence" (at 168). *Re* the Court's second rationale—that the sentence was invalid because exceeding the maximum that the legislature had intended and thus amounted to double punishing: "We are of opinion that when the prisoner, as in this case, . . . had fully served one of the alternative punishments to which alone the law subjected to him, the power of the court to punish further was gone" (at 176).
93. Kepner v. United States, 195 U.S. 100, at 128 (1904).
94. Bassing v. Cady, 208 U.S. 386 (1908); Collins v. Loisel, 262 U.S. 426 (1923); United States *ex rel.* Rutz v. Levy, 268 U.S. 390 (1925).

95. United States v. Thompson, 251 U.S. 407, at 413 (1920).

96. Taylor v. United States, 207 U.S. 120, at 127 (1907) and United States v. Bitty, 208 U.S. 393, at 399–400 (1908) (upholding constitutionality of Criminal Appeals Act of 1907–34 Stat. 1246 [1907]—giving the federal government the right of appeal to the Supreme Court when a trial court judge quashed or dismissed an indictment on grounds of the construction or constitutional validity of a federal statute before the defendant was put in jeopardy).

97. Murphy v. Massachusetts, 177 U.S. 155 (1900).

98. United States v. Perez, 9 Wheat. 579, at 580 (1824). See also: Thompson v. United States, 155 U.S. 271, at 273-74 (1894) (a juror found to have served on the grand jury that had brought in the indictment); Simmons v. United States, 142 U.S. 148 (1891) (juror discovered prejudiced against defendant); Lovato v. New Mexico, 242 U.S. 199 (1916) (defective indictment); Logan v. United States, 144 U.S. 263, at 298 (1892) and Dreyer v. Illinois, 187 U.S. 71, at 84–86 (1902) (hung juries).

99. United States v. Ball, 163 U.S. 662, at 669-71 (1896); Kepner v. United States, 195 U.S. 100, at 130–33 (1904).

100. For examples, see: Trono v. United States, 199 U.S. 521 (1905) (person tried for murder in the first degree but acquitted and convicted instead of assault could after a successful appeal be retried for homicide [in substance, second-degree murder]); Brantley v. Georgia, 217 U.S. 284 (1910) (person tried for murder but convicted of manslaughter could after a successful appeal be retried for murder); and Stroud v. United States, 251 U.S. 15 (1919) (permitting imposition of the death penalty after a successful appeal when the jury in the first trial had recommended life imprisonment).

101. Stone v. United States, 167 U.S. 178, at 184–89 (1897).

102. Compare Coffey v. United States, 116 U.S. 436 (1886) (forfeiture of distillery apparatus used to defraud the government of tax on distilled spirits a "punishment" [at 444–45]) with Various Items of Personal Property v. United States, 282 U.S. 577 (1931) (forfeiture of distillery used to defraud the government of tax on distilled spirits "no part of the punishment for the criminal offense" [at 581]).

103. Carter v. McClaughry, 183 U.S. 365, at 394–95 (1902) (conspiracy to defraud the United States and causing false and fraudulent claims to be made were two offenses).

104. Albrecht v. United States, 273 U.S. 1, at 11 (1927).

105. Nielsen, Petitioner, 131 U.S. 176, at 186–91 (1889).

106. United States v. Furlong, 5 Wheat. 184, at 197 (1820).

107. Nielsen v. Oregon, 212 U.S. 315, at 320 (1909).

108. 14 How. 13, at 19–20 (1852).

109. Fox v. Ohio, 5 How. 410, at 434 (1847); United States v. Marigold, 9 How. 560, at 569-70 (1850); Cross v. North Carolina, 132 U.S. 131, at 139–40 (1889); Crossley v. California, 168 U.S. 640, at 641 (1898).

110. 260 U.S. 377, at 382 (1922); 272 U.S. 312 (1926). The background of and influences shaping the *Lanza* doctrine are illuminated by Kenneth M. Murchison, "The Dual Sovereignty Exception to Double Jeopardy," *New York University Review of Law & Social Change* 14, no. 2 (1986): 383–407.

111. The fullest over-all survey is Francis H. Heller, *The Sixth Amendment to the Constitution of the United States: A Study in Constitutional Development* (Lawrence: University of Kansas Press, 1951).

112. Counselman v. Hitchcock, 142 U.S. 547, at 563 (1892).

113. Zucker v. United States, 161 U.S. 475, at 480–81 (1896) was the leading case. See also: Hepner v. United States, 213 U.S. 103 (1909) and Oceanic Steam Navigation Co. v. Stranahan, 214 U.S. 320 (1909).

114. 1 Stat. 112, at 118 (1790).

115. United States v. Van Duzee, 140 U.S. 169, at 173 (1891).

116. 1 Stat. 112, at 118–19 (1790).

117. Thus, for example, the Court held that a judge could not communicate with the jury in the absence of the defendant: Shields v. United States, 273 U.S. 583 (1927).

118. Kirby v. United States, 174 U.S. 47, at 48, 53–61 (1899). See also: Motes v. United States, 178 U.S. 458 (1900) (Sixth Amendment prohibits reading of testimony given by an absent witness at a preliminary hearing, even though the accused had been then present). *Re* the right of cross-examination, see: Alford v. United States, 282 U.S. 687 (1931); District of Columbia v. Clawans, 300 U.S. 617, at 630–32 (1937).

119. Mattox v. United States, 156 U.S. 237 (1895); Reynolds v. United States, 98 U.S. 145, at 158 (1879); Kirby v. United States, 174 U.S. 47, at 61 (1899).

120. An excellent treatment is provided by William M. Beaney, *The Right to Counsel in American Courts* (Ann Arbor: University of Michigan Press, 1955).

121. 1 Stat. 112, at 118 (1790).

122. See, for example, United States v. Van Duzee, 140 U.S. 169, at 173 (1891). What appears to have been the only case where a conviction was reversed because of lack of counsel was Cooke v. United States, 267 U.S. 517, at 537–38 (1925), reversing a summary conviction for out-of-court contempt because of the failure to give the defendant an opportunity to retain counsel.

123. Powell v. Alabama, 287 U.S. 45, at 71 (1932).

124. Callan v. Wilson, 127 U.S. 540, at 549–50 (1888); Patton v. United States, 281 U.S. 276 (1930).

125. 4 Wall. 2 (1866); reaffirmed United States v. L. Cohen Grocery Company, 255 U.S. 81, at 88 (1921).

126. Schick v. United States, 195 U.S. 65, at 68 (1904) (buying unstamped margarine for sale punishable by a $50 fine was a petty offense not requiring a jury trial); Callan v. Wilson, 127 U.S. 540, at 555–57 (1888)(conspiracy to interfere with a man's calling, even though a misdemeanor liable to only a $25 fine or thirty days in jail, required a jury trial); District of Columbia v. Colts, 282 U.S. 63 (1930) (reckless driving and speeding a serious offense requiring a jury trial); District of Columbia v. Clawans, 300 U.S. 617 (1937) (selling second-hand goods without a license punishable by not more than a $300 fine or a 90-day jail sentence a petty offense). *Re* the Court's "moral judgment" about the "gravity of danger to the community from the misconduct" as the determining factor in its distinguishing petty from serious offenses, see Felix Frankfurter and Thomas C. Corcoran, "Petty Offenses and the Constitutional Guaranty of Trial by Jury," *Harvard Law Review* 39 (June 1926): 917–1019 (at 980).

127. 281 U.S. 276, at 298, 312, 288 (1930).

128. Justice Hugo L. Black observed that he could find no record of a single criminal trial conducted in secret in a federal, state, or municipal court: *In re* Oliver, 333 U.S. 257, at 266 (1948).

129. Beavers v. Haubert, 198 U.S. 77, at 87 (1905).

130. Worthington v. United States, 1 F2d 154 (CCA 7th Cir. 1924), cert. denied 266 U.S. 626 (1924); Daniels v. United States, 17 F2d 339 (CCA 9th Cir. 1927), cert. denied 274 U.S. 744 (1927).

131. 1 Stat. 73, at 88 (1789).

132. Strauder v. West Virginia, 100 U.S. 303, at 310 (1880).

133. Franklin v. South Carolina, 218 U.S. 161, at 167–68 (1910).

134. The Court's harder line *re* exclusion of blacks from juries was signalled by Norris v. Alabama, 294 U.S. 587 (1935).

135. Ruthenberg v. United States, 245 U.S. 480 (1918).

136. Lewis v. United States, 146 U.S. 370, at 375-76 (1892). See also Aldridge v. United States, 283 U.S. 308 (1931) (affirming right of black defendant to question on *voir dire* about racial bias).

137. Stilson v. United States, 250 U.S. 583, at 586–87 (1919).

138. Hopt v. Utah, 120 U.S. 430, at 433 (1887).

139. United States v. Burr, 25 Fed. Cas. 49, at 51, #14,692g (CC Va. 1807).

140. Reynolds v. United States, 98 U.S. 145, at 155–56 (1879). *Re* the broad discretion left to the trial judge: his decision could be reversed only if "made clearly to appear that upon the evidence the court ought to have found the juror has formed such an opinion that he could not in law be deemed impartial. The case must be one in which it is manifest that the law left nothing to the 'conscience or discretion' of the court" (at 156).

141. Crawford v. United States, 212 U.S. 183 (1909).

142. 49 Stat. 682 (1935); 299 U.S. 123, at 145–46 (1936).

143. On this point, see William E. Nelson, "The Restraint of Power in Pre-Revolutionary America: Massachusetts As a Case Study, 1760–1775," *American Journal of Legal History* 18 (January 1974): 1–32.

144. 156 U.S. 51, at 101–02 (1895). The process is detailed in Mark D. Howe, "Juries as Judges of Criminal Law," *Harvard Law Review* 52 (February 1939): 582–616.

145. Quercia v. United States, 289 U.S. 466 (1933).

146. Sparf and Hansen v. United States, 156 U.S. 51, at 105–06 (1895).

147. Caleb Foote, "The Coming Constitutional Crisis in Bail: I," *University of Pennsylvania Law Review* 113 (May 1965): 965–89, argues the first position. But William F. Duker, "The Right to Bail: A Historical Inquiry," *Albany Law Review* 42 (Fall 1977): 33–120, adduces convincing evidence that bail was never historically regarded as an absolute right.

148. 1 Stat. 73, at 91 (1789). For retention of this distinction between capital and noncapital offenses, see Rev. Stat., at 189 (1875).

149. 156 U.S. 277 (1895) (upholding Supreme Court Rule 36, 139 U.S. 706 [1891], making bail during appeals from a trial court conviction a matter of judicial discretion). And on the basis of *Hudson*, a lower federal court held that a defendant was not entitled as a matter of right to bail during trial: United States v. Rice, 192 F 721 (CC S.D. N.Y. 1911). When the Court did finally deal squarely with the question in Carlson v. Landon, 342 U.S. 524 (1952), a five-to-four majority concluded that the Eighth Amendment "has never been thought to accord a right to bail in all cases, but merely to provide that bail shall not be excessive in those cases where it is proper

to grant bail" (at 544–46). And the bail clause remains one of the few Bill of Rights provisions that has been applied to the states via the Fourteenth Amendment.

150. *Ex parte* Taylor, 14 How. 3, at 12–13 (1852) (mandamus does not extend to a case where a judge has set an amount of bail in his discretion).

151. Waters-Pierce Oil Company v. Texas (No. 1), 212 U.S. 86, at 111 (1909).

152. A brief survey of the historical roots and judicial exegesis can be found in David Fellman, "Cruel and Unusual Punishments," *Journal of Politics* 19 (February 1957): 34–45.

153. Wilkerson v. Utah, 99 U.S. 130, at 136 (1879).

154. 217 U.S. 349, at 362–69, 372-78, 380–82 (1910).

155. See, for example, Howard v. Fleming, 191 U.S. 126 (1903) (upholding a ten-year prison sentence for a "gold brick" swindle); Badders v. United States, 240 U.S. 391 (1916) (upholding a five-year prison sentence and $7,000 fine for mail fraud).

156. Howard v. Fleming, 191 U.S. 126, at 136 (1903).

157. Moore v. Missouri, 159 U.S. 673 (1895); Graham v. West Virginia, 224 U.S. 616 (1912).

158. McElvaine v. Brush, 142 U.S. 155 (1891).

159. *In re* Kemmler, 136 U.S. 436, at 447 (1890) (upholding execution by electrocution). See also: Wilkerson v. Utah, 99 U.S. 130 (1879) (upholding execution by shooting). And the prosecution could challenge for cause jurors who had conscientious scruples against the death penalty in trials for crimes punishable by death: Logan v. United States, 144 U.S. 263, at 298 (1892).

160. 20 How. 65, at 81 (1858).

161. 4 Wall. 2, at 123 (1866).

162. *In re* Grimley, 137 U.S. 147, at 150 (1890).

163. William T. Generous, Jr., *Swords and Scales: The Development of the Uniform Code of Military Justice* (Port Washington, N.Y.: National University Publications, Kennikat Press, 1973), pp. 165–68.

164. Full details with accompanying citations can be found in John R. Green, "Liberty under the Fourteenth Amendment," *Washington University Law Quarterly* 32 (Summer 1942): 497–562.

165. Hurtado v. California, 110 U.S. 516 (1884); reaffirmed in Gaines v. Washington, 277 U.S. 81, at 86–87 (1928).

166. 176 U.S. 581, at 603 (1900).

167. Although the denial that the requirement of a unanimous jury verdict applied to the states in Minneapolis and St. Louis Railroad Co. v. Bombolis, 241 U.S. 211 (1916) dealt with the Seventh Amendment's requirement of jury trial in civil cases, the decision was widely read as permitting nonunanimous verdicts in state criminal cases.

168. West v. Louisiana, 194 U.S. 258 (1904). For the prohibition of this practice in the federal courts: Motes v. United States, 178 U.S. 458 (1900).

169. Twining v. New Jersey, 211 U.S. 78 (1908).

170. Missouri *ex rel.* Hurwitz v. North, 271 U.S. 40, at 42 (1926).

171. McKane v. Durston, 153 U.S. 684, at 687–88 (1894).

172. Moore v. Dempsey, 261 U.S. 86, at 90–91 (1923).

173. Tumey v. Ohio, 273 U.S. 510, at 532 (1927). At issue was a provision in the Ohio prohibition law allowing trial of offenses under the law by mayors of rural villages without a jury. The mayor received payment in the form of court costs only

if he convicted and thus had "a direct, personal, substantial, pecuniary interest . . . in convicting the defendant" (at 523).

174. 287 U.S. 45, at 71, 68–69 (1932).

175. 287 U.S. 45, at 65–68 (1932).

176. 291 U.S. 97, at 106, 116, 122 (Cardozo), 130–31 (Justice Owen J. Roberts for the dissenters) (1934).

177. 302 U.S. 319, at 324–28 (1937). Butler alone dissented without opinion.

178. 39 Stat. 726, at 726–27 (1916).

179. 25 Stat. 655, at 656 (1889); 28 Stat. 826, at 827 (1891); In re Claasen, 140 U.S. 200, at 205 (1891); 29 Stat. 492 (1897); 36 Stat. 1087, at 1133–34 (1911).

180. The historical development of the writ in England and the United States is traced in William F. Duker, *A Constitutional History of Habeas Corpus* (Westport, Conn.: Greenwood Press, 1980).

181. 1 Stat. 73, at 81–82 (1789).

182. 4 Cranch 75, at 101 (1807).

183. *Ex parte* Watkins, 7 Pet. 568, at 572-73 (1833); *Ex parte* Yerger, 8 Wall. 85, at 102–03 (1869). For fuller details, see Dallin H. Oaks, "The 'Original' Writ of Habeas Corpus in the Supreme Court," in *The Supreme Court Review 1962*, ed. Philip B. Kurland (Chicago: University of Chicago Press, 1962), pp. 159–65, 173-79.

184. Dallin H. Oaks, "Legal History in the High Court—Habeas Corpus," *Michigan Law Review* 64 (January 1966): 451-72.

185. *Ex parte* Watkins, 3 Pet. 193, at 202–03 (1830).

186. 1 Stat. 73, at 82 (1789).

187. 4 Cranch 75, at 93–94 (1807). An excellent brief survey of congressional legislation *re* the habeas corpus powers of the federal courts is given in Stephen A. Saltzburg, "Habeas Corpus: The Supreme Court and the Congress," *Ohio State Law Journal* 44, no. 2 (1983): 367–91.

188. *Ex parte* Dorr, 3 How. 103, at 105 (1845).

189. 14 Stat. 385, at 385–86 (1867). For the narrow interpretation of the intent of Congress, see Lewis Mayers, "The Habeas Corpus Act of 1867: The Supreme Court as Legal Historian," *University of Chicago Law Review* 33 (Autumn 1965): 31–59; for the broader interpretation that Congress intended to give the federal courts the power to issue the writ to state prisoners, see the two articles by William M. Wiecek, "The Reconstruction of Federal Judicial Power, 1863–1875," *American Journal of Legal History* 13 (October 1969): 333–59, and "The Great Writ and Reconstruction: The Habeas Corpus Act of 1867," *Journal of Southern History* 36 (November 1970): 530–48.

190. For fuller details, see Stanley I. Kutler, "*Ex parte McCardle*: Judicial Impotency? The Supreme Court and Reconstruction Reconsidered," *American Historical Review* 72 (April 1967): 833–51.

191. 117 U.S. 241, at 245–50 (1886). As even Mayers has acknowledged, "Congress, by its inaction, may be said to have ratified the Supreme Court's expansion of the federal courts' powers in this field": "Habeas Corpus Act of 1867," p. 32.

192. Harlan v. McGourin, 218 U.S. 442, at 448 (1910).

193. Examples include: *Ex parte* Siebold, 100 U.S. 371 (1880) ("An unconstitutional law is void and is as no law. . . . A conviction under it is not merely erroneous, but is illegal and void, and cannot be a legal cause of imprisonment," at 376-77); *Ex parte* Yarbrough, 110 U.S. 651 (1884) (if persons were convicted under an unconsti-

tutional law, "the court was without jurisdiction and the prisoners must be released," at 654); Yick Wo v. Hopkins, 118 U.S. 356 (1886) (discharge of a prisoner from state custody because of the discriminatory enforcement of the ordinance under which he was convicted in violation of the Fourteenth Amendment); *Ex parte* Medley, 134 U.S. 160 (1890) (discharge of a state prisoner convicted in violation of the ban against ex post facto laws).

194. Examples include: *Ex parte* Lange, 18 Wall. 163 (1874) (release of a prisoner sentenced to both parts of alternative sentence of fine or imprisonment on the ground that once the defendant had paid the fine, "the authority of the court to punish the prisoner was gone," at 176); *Ex parte* Wilson, 114 U.S. 417, at 429 (1885) (release of a prisoner sentenced to hard labor for an "infamous" crime within the meaning of the Fifth Amendment without indictment by grand jury); *In re* Snow, 120 U.S. 274 (1887) (Fifth Amendment prohibits imposition of more than one sentence for what the Court held was a single continuing offense rather than three separate offenses).

195. Note, "Developments in the Law—Federal Habeas Corpus," *Harvard Law Review* 83 (March 1970): 1045–50.

196. *In re* Chapman, 156 U.S. 211, at 216–17 (1895).

197. *In re* Lincoln, 202 U.S. 178, at 182 (1906); Glasgow v. Moyer, 225 U.S. 420, at 428–30 (1912); Henry v. Henkel, 235 U.S. 219, at 229 (1914).

198. 140 U.S. 278, at 286–87 (1891). Justice Horace Gray did not participate. See also: *In re* Jugiro, 140 U.S. 291 (1891); Andrews v. Swartz, 156 U.S. 272 (1895); and Bergemann v. Backer, 157 U.S. 655 (1895).

199. "[W]e hold that such a determination of the facts as was thus made by the court of last resort of Georgia respecting the alleged interference with the trial through disorder and manifestations of hostile sentiment cannot in this collateral hearing be treated as a nullity, but must be taken as setting forth the truth of the matter, certainly until some reasonable ground is shown for an inference that the court which rendered it . . . erred . . . [T]he mere assertion by the prisoner that the facts of the matter are other than the state court upon full examination determined them to be will not be deemed sufficient to raise an issue respecting the correctness of that determination.": Frank v. Magnum, 237 U.S. 309, at 335–36 (1915).

200. Thus, Justice Mahlon Pitney acknowledged that under the 1867 statute the federal courts had the responsibility when dealing with an application for a writ of habeas corpus from a state prisoner "to look beyond forms and inquire into the very substance of the matter, to the extent of deciding whether the prisoner had been deprived of his liberty without due process," i.e., whether he had been given an adequate hearing upon his constitutional claim by the state courts "having regard to the entire course of the proceedings, in the appellate as well as in the trial court": 237 U.S. 309, at 330–33 (1915).

201. 261 U.S. 86, at 91–92 (1923). For the narrower interpretation of the decision's import, see Paul M. Bator, "Finality in Criminal Law and Federal Habeas Corpus for State Prisoners," *Harvard Law Review* 76 (January 1963): 483–93; for the broader interpretation: Curtis R. Reitz, "Federal Habeas Corpus: Impact of an Abortive State Proceeding," *Harvard Law Review* 74 (May 1961): 1324–30. The Supreme Court did not definitively settle the question until Fay v. Noia, 372 U.S. 391 (1963), when the broader interpretation was adopted (at 421) by a seven-to-two bench.

202. The genesis of the exhaustion doctrine was *Ex parte* Royall, 117 U.S. 241 (1886), where the Court informed the lower federal courts that they had "discretion"

(at 251) not to issue the writ to a state prisoner in advance of his trial. Later that same year, the rule was applied to the case of a convicted state prisoner who had state appellate processes available: *Ex parte* Fonda, 117 U.S. 516 (1886). Although first phrased as a matter of "discretion," the rule became that the federal courts should refuse to issue the writ until the prisoner had exhausted all the available state remedies. See, for examples, Minnesota v. Brundage, 180 U.S. 499 (1901), and Reid v. Jones, 187 U.S. 153 (1902).

203. Mooney v. Holohan, 294 U.S. 103 (1935). The Court remanded the case, without prejudice, to the state courts. The California Supreme Court appointed a referee to investigate; the referee decided against Mooney; that decision was accepted by that tribunal; and the United States Supreme Court refused to grant review. Full details on the case are found in Richard H. Frost, *The Mooney Case* (Stanford: Stanford University Press, 1968).

5 The Old Court and Individual Rights Reappraised

1. David M. Gold, "State-Court Protection of Individual Rights: The Historians' Neglect," *Constitutional Commentary* 2 (Summer 1985): 419–24.

2. The classic account of the Supreme Court's adoption of substantive due process is Edward S. Corwin, "The Supreme Court and the Fourteenth Amendment," *Michigan Law Review* 7 (June 1909): 643-72.

3. J. A. C. Grant, "The Natural Law Background of Due Process," *Columbia Law Review* 31 (January 1931): 56–81.

4. Edward S. Corwin, "The 'Higher Law' Background of American Constitutional Law" (1928-1929) and "The Debt of American Constitutional Law to Natural Law Concepts" (1950), reprinted in Richard Loss, ed., *Corwin on the Constitution: Volume One, The Foundations of American Constitutional and Political Thought, the Powers of Congress, and the President's Power of Removal* (Ithaca, N.Y.: Cornell University Press, 1981), pp. 79–139, 195–212.

5. Charles C. Tansill, ed., *Documents Illustrative of the Formation of the Union of the American States* (Washington, D.C.: Government Printing Office, 1927), 22.

6. Examples include: Justice Samuel Chase in Calder v. Bull, 3 Dall. 386 (1798) ("An act of the Legislature...contrary to the great first principles of the social compact, cannot be considered a rightful exercise of legislative authority," at 388); Chief Justice John Marshall in Fletcher v. Peck, 6 Cranch 87 (1810) (Georgia's revocation of a land grant invalid "by general principles, which are common to our free institutions," at 139); Justice Joseph Story in Terrett v. Taylor, 9 Cranch 43 (1815) (appropriation of church-owned property "utterly inconsistent with...the principles of natural justice," at 50–52).

7. Henry v. Dubuque & Pacific Railroad Co., 10 Ia. 540, at 543–44 (1860).

8. For fuller development, see: Eric Foner, *Free Soil, Free Labor, Free Men: The Ideology of the Republican Party Before the Civil War* (New York: Oxford University Press, 1970); William E. Nelson, "The Impact of the Antislavery Movement upon Styles of Judicial Reasoning in Nineteenth Century America," *Harvard Law Review* 87 (January 1974): 513–66; Charles W. McCurdy, "The Roots of 'Liberty of Contract' Reconsidered: Major Premises in the Law of Employment, 1867–1937," *Supreme Court Historical Society Yearbook 1984* (Washington, D.C.: Supreme Court Historical

Society, 1984), pp. 20–33; and Bernard H. Siegan, "Rehabilitating *Lochner*," *San Diego Law Review* 22 (May-June 1985): 453–97.

9. 14 Stat. 27, at 27 (1866).

10. Herbert Spencer, *Social Statics; or, The Conditions Essential to Human Happiness Specified, and the First of Them Developed* (New York: D. Appleton, 1888), pp. 121. This point is more fully elaborated in Michael L. Benedict, "Laissez-Faire and Liberty: A Re-Evaluation of the Meaning and Origins of Laissez-Faire Constitutionalism," *Law and History Review* 3 (Fall 1985): 293–331.

11. Boyd v. United States, 116 U.S. 616, at 630 (1886).

12. Charles Warren, "The New 'Liberty' under the Fourteenth Amendment," *Harvard Law Review* 39 (February 1926): 431–65.

13. Griswold v. Connecticut, 381 U.S. 479, at 481–83 (1965) (striking down that state's anti-contraceptive law). For further details on how the Modern Court has drawn upon the substantive due process decisions of the Old Court as precedents in support of noneconomic libertarian values, see Rogers M. Smith, "The Constitution and Autonomy," *Texas Law Review* 60 (February 1982): 184–85.

14. As a lower court federal judge pointedly put the issue: shall unions be allowed "to issue orders that free men are bound to obey": *In re* Higgins, 27 F 443, at 445 (CC N.D. Tex. 1886).

15. Pierce v. Society of Sisters, 268 U.S. 510 (1925). As just as *Meyer* was cited in *Griswold*, *Pierce* was cited in Yoder v. Wisconsin, 406 U.S. 205, at 213–14 (1972) (upholding a challenge by Amish parents to that state's compulsory education law as violating the First Amendment's guarantee of the free exercise of religion).

16. Susan M. Okin, *Women in Western Political Thought* (Princeton, N.J.: Princeton University Press, 1979), especially pp. 233–64.

17. Frances Olsen, "From False Paternalism to False Equality: Judicial Assaults on Feminist Community, Illinois 1869–1895," *Michigan Law Review* 84 (June 1986): 1518–41.

18. Elmer E. Smead, "*Sic Utere Tuo Ut Alienum Non Laedas*: A Basis of the State Police Power," *Cornell Law Quarterly* 21 (February 1936): 276–92.

19. 7 Cushing 53, at 84–85 (1851).

20. Thorpe v. Rutland and Burlington Railroad Co., 27 Vermont 140, at 150 (1854).

21. 94 U.S. 113, at 124–25 (1877).

22. Scott M. Reznick, "Empiricism and the Principle of Conditions in the Evolution of the Police Power: A Model for Definitional Scrutiny," *Washington University Law Quarterly* 1978 (Winter): 1–58.

23. Ray A. Brown, "Due Process of Law, Police Power, and the Supreme Court," *Harvard Law Review* 40 (May 1927): 943–45, finds that between 1868 and 1920 the Court had held economic or social legislation unconstitutional under the due process clauses of the Fifth and Fourteenth Amendments in only thirteen out of one hundred and ninety-five such cases—or in less than seven percent of such cases. For fuller documentation regarding judicial permissiveness toward economic regulations, see: Janet S. Lindgren, "Beyond Cases: Reconsidering Judicial Review," *Wisconsin Law Review* 1983, no. 3 (1983): 583–638; Melvin I. Urofsky, "Myth and Reality: The Supreme Court and Protective Legislation in the Progressive Era," *Supreme Court Historical Society Yearbook 1983* (Washington, D.C.: Supreme Court Historical Society, 1983), pp. 53-72; Urofsky, "State Courts and Protective Legislation during the Pro-

gressive Era: A Reevaluation," *Journal of American History* 72 (June 1985): 63–91; and Harry Scheiber, "Public Rights and the Rule of Law in American Legal History," *California Law Review* 72 (March 1984): 217–51.

24. As John Locke emphasized in the second of his *Two Treatises of Government*, edited by Thomas I. Cook (New York: Hafner Publishing Co., 1947), pp. 123–29, the "state of liberty" must be distinguished from a "state of licence." Even in the state of nature, men's reason taught that there were certain moral duties sanctioned by God; those who misunderstood liberty as freedom to invade "others' rights" were "beasts of prey" who had fallen below the level of humanity.

25. Sir Edward Coke, *The Second Part of the Institutes of the Laws of England*, 2 vols. (London: W. Clarke and Sons, 1809), 1:182.

26. A fuller analysis is in Kent Greenawalt, "Speech and Crime," *American Bar Foundation Research Journal* 1980 (Fall): 645-706.

27. Robert E. Cushman, " 'Clear and Present Danger' in Free Speech Cases: A Study in Judicial Semantics," in *Essays in Political Theory Presented to George H. Sabine*, ed. Milton R. Konvitz and Arthur E. Murphy (Ithaca, N.Y.: Cornell University Press, 1948), pp. 311–18; Howard O. Hunter, "Problems in Search of Principles: The First Amendment in the Supreme Court from 1791-1930," *Emory Law Journal* 35 (Winter 1986): 129–37.

28. The most influential examination of the classical republican ideology has been J. G. A. Pocock, *The Machiavellian Moment: Florentine Political Thought and the Atlantic Republican Tradition* (Princeton, N.J.: Princeton University Press, 1975). The pioneering exposition of its influence upon the American revolutionary generation— although the term "republicanism" did not feature prominently in his text—was Bernard Bailyn, *Ideological Origins of the American Revolution* (Cambridge, Mass.: Harvard University Press, 1967). Further elaborations have been added by Joyce Appleby, *Capitalism and a New Social Order: The Republican Vision of the 1790s* (New York: New York University Press, 1984), and Gordon S. Woods, *The Creation of the American Republic, 1776–1787* (Chapel Hill: University of North Carolina Press, 1969).

29. The analysis here is indebted to the suggestive observation in Rogers M. Smith, "The Meaning of American Citizenship," *this Constitution: A Bicentennial Chronicle*, no. 8 (Fall 1985): 12-18.

30. Michael L. Benedict, "Preserving Federalism: Reconstruction and the Waite Court," in *The Supreme Court Review 1978*, ed. Philip B. Kurland and Gerhard Casper (Chicago: University of Chicago Press, 1979), 39-79.

31. Michael J. Horan, "Political Economy and Sociological Theory as Influences Upon Judicial Policy-Making: The *Civil Rights Cases* of 1883," *American Journal of Legal History* 16 (January 1972): 71–86; Ira Nerken, "A New Deal for the Protection of Fourteenth Amendment Rights: Challenging the Doctrinal Bases of the *Civil Rights Cases* and State Action Theory," *Harvard Civil Rights-Civil Liberties Law Review* 12 (Spring 1977): 297–366.

32. The racist assumptions dominating American social science during this period are dissected in Hamilton Cravens, *The Triumph of Evolution: American Scientists and the Heredity-Environment Controversy 1900-1941* (Philadelphia: University of Pennsylvania Press, 1978), and Stephen J. Gould, *The Mismeasure of Man* (New York: W. W. Norton, 1981); their influence on the law by Herbert Hovenkamp, "Social Science and Segregation Before *Brown*," *Duke Law Journal* 1985 (June-September): 624-72.

33. Oliver Wendell Holmes, Jr., to Harold J. Laski, August 24, 1927, in Mark

D. Howe, ed., *Holmes-Laski Letters: The Correspondence of Mr. Justice Holmes and Harold J. Laski 1916–1935*, 2 vols. (Cambridge, Mass: Harvard University Press, 1953), 2: 974-75.

34. Warden v. Hayden, 387 U.S. 294 (1967).

35. J. A. C. Grant, *Our Common Law Constitution* (Boston: Boston University Press, 1960).

36. Powell v. Alabama, 287 U.S. 45, at 73 (1932).

37. Funk v. United States, 290 U.S. 371, at 382 (1933).

38. Richard M. Brown, "Legal and Behavioral Perspectives on American Vigilantism," *Perspectives in American History* 5 (1971): 135–44.

39. M. Browning Carrott, "The Supreme Court and Law and Order in the 1920s," *Maryland Historian* 16 (Fall/Winter 1985): 12–26.

40. Carroll v. United States, 267 U.S. 132, at 149 (1925).

41. William Howard Taft to Horace Taft, June 12, 1928, quoted in Carrott, "Supreme Court and Law and Order," p. 15.

42. Robert M. Cover, "The Left, the Right and the First Amendment: 1918-1928," *Maryland Law Review* 40, no. 3 (1981): 354–57; Carrott, "Supreme Court and Law and Order," pp. 19–20.

43. Pierce Butler, "Some Opportunities and Duties of Lawyers," *American Bar Association Journal* 9 (September 1923): 585.

44. United States v. Motlow, 10 F2d 657, at 662 (CCA 7th Cir. 1926).

45. See the perceptive comments on this point by William F. Duker, "The Fuller Court and State Criminal Process: Threshold of Modern Limitations on Government," *Brigham Young University Law Review* 1980, no. 2: 275–93.

46. Leeper v. Texas, 139 U.S. 462, at 468 (1891).

47. Norris v. Alabama, 294 U.S. 587, at 590 (1935).

48. Henry P. Weihofen, "Supreme Court Review of State Criminal Procedure," *American Journal of Legal History* 10 (July 1966): 189–200.

49. Kenneth M. Murchison, "Prohibition and the Fourth Amendment: A New Look at Some Old Cases," *Journal of Criminal Law and Criminology* 73 (Summer 1982): 471–532, and Murchison, "Property Forfeiture in the Era of National Prohibition: A Study of Judicial Response to Legislative Reform," *Buffalo Law Review* 32 (Spring 1983): 417–63.

50. National Commission on Law Observance and Enforcement: *Report on Criminal Procedure* (Washington, D.C.: Government Printing Office, 1931); *Report on Police* (Washington, D.C.: Government Printing Office, 1931); *Report on Lawlessness in Law Enforcement* (Washington, D.C.: Government Printing Office, 1931).

51. Robert M. Cover, "The Origins of Judicial Activism in the Protection of Minorities," *Yale Law Journal* 91 (June 1982): 1305–06.

52. *Re* the importance of shifting the question from whether "a civilized system could be imagined that would not accord the particular protection" to whether "a particular procedure is fundamental...to an Anglo-American regime of ordered liberty" as the rationale for incorporation in the Fourteenth Amendment of most of the Bill of Rights criminal law provisions, see footnote 14 to Justice Byron R. White's opinion in Duncan v. Louisiana, 391 U.S. 145, at 149–50 (1968).

53. The expansion of the Court's control over its docket is traced in Felix Frankfurter and James M. Landis, *The Business of the Supreme Court: A Study in the Federal Judicial System* (New York: Macmillan, 1928).

54. See, for example, the classic exposition by Chief Justice Charles Evans Hughes in Aetna Life Insurance Co. v. Haworth, 300 U.S. 227, at 240–41 (1937):

a [justiciable] 'controversy'...must be one that is appropriate for judicial determination. . . . A justiciable controversy is thus distinguished from a difference or dispute of a hypothetical or abstract character; from one that is academic or moot. . . . The controversy must be definite and concrete, touching the legal relations of parties having adverse legal interests. . . . It must be a real and substantial controversy admitting of specific relief through a decree of a conclusive character, as distinguished from an opinion advising what the law would be upon a hypothetical state of facts.

As a federal Court of Appeals judge would acknowledge, "the standards by which cases and controversies are distinguished from claims premature or insufficiently adverse are not susceptible of ready application to a particular case. The considerations, while catholic, are not concrete": McCahill v. Borough of Fox Chapel, 438 F2d 213, at 215 (CA 3rd Cir. 1971).

55. Charles A. Wright, *The Law of Federal Courts* (4th ed., St. Paul: West Publishing Co., 1983), 90-104, surveys the tangled complex of decisions dealing with the meaning of case or controversy "arising under this Constitution, the Laws of the United States, and Treaties made...under their Authority."

56. Creswill v. Grand Lodge Knights of Pythias of Georgia, 225 U.S. 246 (1912); Ward v. Board of County Commissioners of Love County, 253 U.S. 17 (1920); Ancient Egyptian Arabic Order of Nobles of the Mystic Shrine v. Michaux, 279 U.S. 737 (1929).

Select Bibliography

Books

Abraham, Henry J. *Justices and Presidents: A Political History of Appointments to the Supreme Court*. New York: Oxford University Press, 1974.
————. *Freedom and the Court: Civil Rights and Civil Liberties in the United States*. 4th ed. New York: Oxford University Press, 1982.
————. *The Judicial Process: An Introductory Analysis of the Courts of the United States, England, and France*. 4th ed., New York: Oxford University Press, 1984.
Barnes, Catherine A. *Journey from Jim Crow: The Desegregation of Southern Transit*. New York: Columbia University Press, 1983.
Beaney, William M. *The Right to Counsel in American Courts*. Ann Arbor: University of Michigan Press, 1955.
Beisel, Albert R., Jr. *Control over Illegal Enforcement of the Criminal Law*. Boston: Boston University Press, 1955.
Belz, Herman. *A New Birth of Freedom: The Republican Party and Freedmen's Rights, 1861 to 1866*. Westport, Conn.: Greenwood Press, 1976.
Benedict, Michael L. *Civil Rights and Civil Liberties*. Washington, D.C.: American Historical Association, 1987.
Berger, Raoul. *Government by Judiciary: The Transformation of the Fourteenth Amendment*. Cambridge, Mass.: Harvard University Press, 1977.
Berns, Walter F. *The First Amendment and the Future of American Democracy*. New York: Basic Books, 1976.
Beth, Loren P. *The Development of the American Constitution 1877–1917*. New York: Harper & Row, 1971.
Bickel, Alexander M., and Benno C. Schmidt, Jr. *The Judiciary and Responsible Government 1910–21* [*Oliver Wendell Holmes Devise History of the Supreme Court of the Unites States*, Volume 9]. New York: Macmillan, 1984.
Blackstone, William. *Commentaries on the Laws of England*. Edited by William D. Lewis. Philadelphia: Rees Welsh, 1897.
Boles, Donald E. *The Two Swords: Commentaries and Cases in Religion and Education*. Ames: Iowa State University, 1967.

Bryson, Conrey. *Dr. Lawrence A. Nixon and the White Primary.* El Paso: Texas Western Press, 1974.

Buck, Paul H. *The Road to Reunion 1865-1900.* Boston: Little, Brown, 1937.

Carr, Robert K. *Federal Protection of Civil Rights: The Quest for a Sword.* Ithaca, N.Y.: Cornell University Press, 1947.

Carter, Dan T. *Scottsboro: A Tragedy of the American South.* Rev. ed. Baton Rouge: Louisiana State University Press, 1979.

Chafee, Zechariah, Jr. *Free Speech in the United States.* Cambridge, Mass.: Harvard University Press, 1941.

Claude, Richard. *The Supreme Court and the Electoral Process.* Baltimore: Johns Hopkins Press, 1970.

Cord, Robert L. *Separation of Church and State: Historical Fact and Current Fiction.* New York: Lambeth Press, 1982.

Cortner, Richard C. *The Supreme Court and the Second Bill of Rights: The Fourteenth Amendment and the Nationalization of Civil Liberties.* Madison: University of Wisconsin Press, 1981.

————. *A "Scottsboro" Case in Mississippi: The Supreme Court and Brown v. Mississippi.* Jackson: University Press of Mississippi, 1986.

Corwin, Edward S. *Constitutional Revolution, Ltd.* Claremont, Calif.: Claremont Colleges, 1941.

Cox, Archibald. *The Role of the Supreme Court in American Government.* New York: Oxford University Press, 1976.

Currie, David P. *The Constitution in the Supreme Court: The First Hundred Years.* Chicago: University of Chicago Press, 1985.

Curtis, Michael K. *No State Shall Abridge: The Fourteenth Amendment and the Bill of Rights.* Durham, N.C.: Duke University Press, 1986.

Danelski, David J., and Joseph S. Tulchin, eds. *The Autobiographical Notes of Charles Evans Hughes.* Cambridge, Mass.: Harvard University Press, 1973.

Daniel, Pete. *The Shadow of Slavery: Peonage in the South 1901-1969.* Urbana: University of Illinois Press, 1972.

Dinnerstein, Leonard. *The Leo Frank Case.* New York: Columbia University Press, 1968.

Dixon, Robert G., Jr. *Democratic Representation: Reapportionment in Law and Politics.* New York: Oxford University Press, 1968.

Duker, William F. *A Constitutional History of Habeas Corpus.* Westport, Conn.: Greenwood Press, 1980.

Elliott, Ward E.Y. *The Rise of Guardian Democracy: The Supreme Court's Role in Voting Rights Disputes, 1845–1969.* Cambridge, Mass.: Harvard University Press, 1974.

Epperson, John W. *The Changing Legal Status of Political Parties in the United States.* New York: Garland Publishing, 1986.

Fairman, Charles. *Mr. Justice Miller and the Supreme Court 1862–1870.* Cambridge, Mass.: Harvard University Press, 1939.

————. *Reconstruction and Reunion 1864–88, Part One [Oliver Wendell Holmes Devise History of the Supreme Court of the United States, Volume 6].* New York: Macmillan, 1971.

Fehrenbacher, Don E. *The Dred Scott Case: Its Significance in American Law and Politics.* New York: Oxford University Press, 1978.

Fellman, David. *The Rights of the Defendant.* New York: Rinehart, 1958.

————. *The Constitutional Rights of Association*. Chicago: University of Chicago Press, 1963.

Frankfurter, Felix, and James M. Landis. *The Business of the Supreme Court: A Study in the Federal Judicial System*. New York: Macmillan, 1928.

Frederickson, George M. *The Black Image in the White Mind: The Debate on Afro-American Character and Destiny, 1817–1914*. New York: Harper & Row, 1971.

Friendly, Fred W. *Minnesota Rag: The Dramatic Story of the Landmark Supreme Court Case That Gave New Meaning to Freedom of the Press*. New York: Random House, 1981.

Frost, Richard H. *The Mooney Case*. Stanford: Stanford University Press, 1968.

Gellhorn, Walter. *Individual Liberty and Governmental Restraints*. Baton Rouge: Louisiana State University Press, 1956.

Generous, William T., Jr. *Swords and Scales: The Development of the Uniform Code of Military Justice*. Port Washington, N.Y.: National University Publications, Kennikat Press, 1973.

Graham, Howard J. *Everyman's Constitution: Historical Essays on the Fourteenth Amendment, the "Conspiracy Theory", and American Constitutionalism*. Madison: State Historical Society of Wisconsin, 1968.

Grant, J.A.C. *Our Common Law Constitution*. Boston: Boston University Press, 1960.

Gregory, Charles O., and Harold A. Katz, *Labor and the Law*. 3d ed. New York: W. W. Norton, 1979.

Hamilton, Otto T. *The Courts and the Curriculum*. New York: Teachers College, Columbia University, 1927.

Harris, Robert J. *The Quest for Equality: The Constitution, Congress and the Supreme Court*. Baton Rouge: Louisiana University Press, 1960.

Hart, Henry M., Jr., and Herbert Wechsler. *The Federal Courts and the Federal System*. Brooklyn: Foundation Press, 1953.

Heller, Francis H. *The Sixth Amendment to the Constitution of the United States: A Study in Constitutional Development*. Lawrence: University of Kansas Press, 1951.

Hutchinson, E.P. *Legislative History of American Immigration Policy*. Philadelphia: University of Pennsylvania Press, 1981.

Hyman, Harold M. *Era of the Oath: Northern Loyalty Tests during the Civil War and Reconstruction*. Philadelphia: University of Pennsylvania Press, 1954.

————. *A More Perfect Union: The Impact of the Civil War and Reconstruction on the Constitution*. New York: Alfred A. Knopf, 1973.

Hyman, Harold M, and William M. Wiecek. *Equal Justice Under Law: Constitutional Development 1835–1875*. New York: Harper & Row, 1982.

Jackson, Robert H. *The Struggle for Judicial Supremacy. A Study of a Crisis in American Power Politics*. New York: Alfred A. Knopf, 1941.

Jacobs, Clyde E. *The Eleventh Amendment and Sovereign Immunity*. Westport, Conn.: Greenwood Press, 1972.

Jaffe, Julian F. *Crusade against Radicalism: New York during the Red Scare, 1914–1924*. Port Washington, N.Y.: National University Publications, Kennikat Press, 1972.

Jenson, Carol E. *The Network of Control: State Supreme Courts and State Security Statutes, 1920–1970*. Westport, Conn.: Greenwood Press, 1972.

Johnson, Alvin W., and Frank H. Yost. *Separation of Church and State in the United States*. Minneapolis: University of Minnesota Press, 1948.

Kaczorowski, Robert. *The Politics of Judicial Interpretation: The Federal Courts, De-partment of Justice and Civil Rights, 1866–1876*. New York: Oceana Publications, 1985.

Keesecker, Ward W. *Legal Status of Bible Reading and Religious Instruction in Public Schools [U.S. Office of Education Bulletin*, 1930, no. 14]. Washington, D.C.: Government Printing Office, 1930.

Kellogg, Charles F. *NAACP: A History of the National Association for the Advancement of Colored People, Volume One 1909–1920*. Baltimore: Johns Hopkins Press, 1967.

Kirby, Jack T. *Darkness at the Dawning: Race and Reform in the Progressive South*. Philadelphia: J.B. Lippincott, 1972.

Kluger, Richard. *Simple Justice: The History of Brown v. Board of Education and Black America's Struggle for Equality*. New York: Alfred A. Knopf, 1976.

Konvitz, Milton R. *The Alien and Asiatic in American Law*. Ithaca, N.Y.: Cornell University Press, 1946.

———. *Expanding Liberties: Freedom's Gains in Postwar America*. New York: Viking Press, 1966.

Kousser, J. Morgan. *The Shaping of Southern Politics: Suffrage Restriction and the Es-tablishment of the One-Party South, 1880–1910*. New Haven, Conn.: Yale University Press, 1974.

———. *Dead End: The Development of Nineteenth-Century Litigation on Racial Discrim-ination in Schools*. Oxford: Clarendon Press, 1986.

Landynski, Jacob W. *Search and Seizure in the Supreme Court: A Study in Constitutional Interpretation*. Baltimore: Johns Hopkins Press, 1966.

Lawhorne, Clifton O. *The Supreme Court and Libel*. Carbondale: Southern Illinois University Press, 1981.

Levy, Leonard W. *The Law of the Commonwealth and Chief Justice Shaw*. Cambridge, Mass.: Harvard University Press, 1957.

———. *Legacy of Suppression: Freedom of Speech and Press in Early America*. Cambridge, Mass.: Harvard University Press, 1960.

———. *Origins of the Fifth Amendment: The Right Against Self-Incrimination*. New York: Oxford University Press, 1968.

———. *Judgments: Essays on American Constitutional History*. Chicago: Quadrangle Books, 1972.

———. *Emergence of a Free Press*. New York: Oxford University Press, 1985.

———. *The Establishment Clause: Religion and the First Amendment*. New York: Mac-millan, 1986.

Litwack, Leon. *North of Slavery: The Negro in the Free States, 1790–1860*. Chicago: University of Chicago Press, 1961.

Lofgren, Charles A. *The Plessy Case: A Legal-Historical Interpretation*. New York: Oxford University Press, 1987.

Loss, Richard, ed. *Corwin on the Constitution: Volume One, The Foundations of American Constitutional and Political Thought, the Power of Congress, and the President's Power of Removal*. Ithaca, N.Y.: Cornell University Press, 1981.

Machen, Ernest W., Jr. *The Law of Arrest*. Chapel Hill: Institute of Government, University of North Carolina, 1950.

———. *The Law of Search and Seizure*. Chapel Hill: Institute of Government, University of North Carolina, 1950.

Magrath, C. Peter. *Morrison R. Waite: The Triumph of Character*. New York: Macmillan, 1963.

Malbin, Michael J. *Religion and Politics: The Intentions of the Authors of the First Amendment*. Washington, D.C.: American Enterprise Institute for Public Policy Research, 1978.

Martin, Charles H. *The Angelo Herndon Case and Southern Justice*. Baton Rouge: Louisiana University Press, 1976.

Mason, Alpheus T. *The Supreme Court from Taft to Warren*. Baton Rouge: Louisiana State University Press, 1958.

——. *William Howard Taft: Chief Justice*. New York: Simon and Schuster, 1965.

McCloskey, Robert G. *The Modern Supreme Court*. Cambridge, Mass.: Harvard University Press, 1972.

McNeil, Genna R. *Groundwork: Charles Hamilton Houston and the Struggle for Civil Rights*. Philadelphia: University of Pennsylvania Press, 1983.

Miller, Loren. *The Petitioners: The Story of the Supreme Court of the United States and the Negro*. New York: Pantheon, 1972.

Morgan, Donald G. *Congress and the Constitution: A Study of Responsibility*. Cambridge, Mass.: Harvard University Press, 1967.

Morgan, Richard E. *The Supreme Court and Religion*. New York: Free Press, 1972.

Murphy, Paul L. *The Meaning of Freedom of Speech: First Amendment Freedoms from Wilson to FDR*. Westport, Conn.: Greenwood Publishing Co., 1972.

——. *The Constitution in Crisis Times 1918–1969*. New York: Harper & Row, 1972.

——. *World War I and the Origin of Civil Liberties in the United States*. New York: W. W. Norton, 1979.

Mykkeltvedt, Roald Y. *The Nationalization of the Bill of Rights: Fourteenth Amendment Due Process and the Procedural Rights*. Port Washington, N.Y.: National University Publications, Associated Faculty Press, 1983.

Okin, Susan M. *Women in Western Political Thought*. Princeton, N.J.: Princeton University Press, 1979.

Olsen, Otto H., ed. *The Thin Disguise: Turning Point in Negro History*. Plessy v. Ferguson, *A Documentary Presentation (1864–1896)*. New York: Humanities Press, 1967.

Orfield, Lester B. *Criminal Procedure from Arrest to Appeal*. New York: New York University Press, 1947.

Paludan, Phillip S. *A Covenant with Death: The Constitution, Law, and Equality in the Civil War Era*. Urbana: University of Illinois Press, 1975.

Pfeffer, Leo. *Church, State and Freedom*. Boston: Beacon Press, 1967.

Powe, Lucas A., Jr. *American Broadcasting and the First Amendment*. Berkeley: University of California Press, 1987.

Randall, Richard S. *Censorship of the Movies: The Social and Political Control of a Mass Medium*. Madison: University of Wisconsin Press, 1968.

Redish, Martin H. *Federal Jurisdiction: Tensions in the Allocation of Judicial Power*. Indianapolis: Michie, 1980.

Roche, John P. *The Quest for the Dream: The Development of Civil Rights and Human Relations in Modern America*. New York: Macmillan, 1963.

Rosenberg, Norman L. *Protecting the Best Men: An Interpretive History of the Law of Libel*. Chapel Hill: University of North Carolina Press, 1986.

Sachs, Albie, and Joan Hoff Wilson. *Sexism and the Law: Male Beliefs and Legal Bias.* New York: Free Press, 1978.

Sefton, James E. *The United States Army and Reconstruction 1865–1877.* Baton Rouge: Louisiana State University Press, 1967.

Semonche, John E. *Charting the Future: The Supreme Court Responds to a Changing Society, 1890–1920.* Westport, Conn.: Greenwood Press, 1978.

Sigler, Jay A. *Double Jeopardy: The Development of a Legal and Social Policy.* Ithaca, N.Y.: Cornell University Press, 1969.

Silver, David M. *Lincoln's Supreme Court.* Urbana: University of Illinois Press, 1956.

Sitkoff, Harvard. *A New Deal for Blacks: The Emergence of Civil Rights as a National Issue, Volume I: The Depression Decade.* New York: Oxford University Press, 1978.

Smith, Donald L. *Zechariah Chafee, Jr.: Defender of Liberty and Law.* Cambridge, Mass.: Harvard University Press, 1986.

Smith, Rodney K. *Public Prayer and the Constitution: A Case Study in Constitutional Interpretation.* Wilmington, Del.: Scholarly Resources, 1987.

Stephens, Otis H., Jr. *The Supreme Court and Confessions of Guilt.* Knoxville: University of Tennessee Press, 1973.

Story, Joseph. *Commentaries on the Constitution of the United States.* 5th ed. Boston: Little, Brown, 1891.

Swinney, Everette. *Suppressing the Ku Klux Klan: The Enforcement of the Reconstruction Amendments 1870–1877.* New York: Garland Publishing, 1987.

Tomlins, Christopher L. *The State and the Unions: Labor Relations, Law, and the Organized Labor Movement in America.* Cambridge: Cambridge University Press, 1985.

Tyack, David, Thomas James, and Aaron Benavot. *Law and the Shaping of Public Education, 1785–1954.* Madison: University of Wisconsin Press, 1987.

Vose, Clement. *Caucasians Only: The Supreme Court, the NAACP, and the Restrictive Covenant Cases.* Berkeley: University of California Press, 1967.

Woodward, C. Vann. *Origins of the New South 1877–1913.* Baton Rouge: Louisiana State University Press, 1951.

———. *The Strange Career of Jim Crow.* New York: Oxford University Press, 1955.

Wright, Benjamin F. *The Contract Clause of the Constitution.* Cambridge, Mass.: Harvard University Press, 1938.

Wright, Charles A. *The Law of the Federal Courts.* 4th ed. St. Paul: West Publishing Co. 1983.

Articles

Allen, Francis A. "The Supreme Court and State Criminal Justice." *Wayne Law Review* 4 (Summer 1958): 191–204.

Anderson, Alexis J. "The Formative Period of First Amendment Theory, 1870–1915." *American Journal of Legal History* 24 (January 1980): 56-75.

Anderson, David. "The Origins of the Press Clause." *UCLA Law Review* 30 (February 1983): 455–541.

Anderson, William. "The Intention of the Framers: A Note on Constitutional Interpretation." *American Political Science Review* 49 (June 1955): 340-52.

Antieau, Charles J. "The Rule of Clear and Present Danger—Its Origin and Application." *University of Detroit Law Journal* 13 (May 1950): 198–213.

Arons, Stephen. "The Separation of School and State: *Pierce* Reconsidered." *Harvard Educational Review* 46 (February 1976): 76–104.

Auerbach, Jerold S. "The Patrician as Libertarian: Zechariah Chafee, Jr. and Freedom of Speech." *New England Quarterly* 42 (December 1969): 511–31.

Avins, Alfred. "The Ku Klux Klan Act of 1871: Some Reflected Light on State Action and the Fourteenth Amendment." *Saint Louis University Law Journal* 11 (Spring 1967): 331–81.

————. "Racial Segregation in Public Accommodations: Some Reflected Light on the Fourteenth Amendment From the Civil Rights Act of 1875." *Western Reserve Law Review* 18 (May 1967): 1251–83.

Bator, Paul M. "Finality in Criminal Law and Federal Habeas Corpus for State Prisoners." *Harvard Law Review* 76 (January 1963): 441–528.

Beaney, William M. "The Constitutional Right of Privacy in the Supreme Court." In *The Supreme Court Review 1962*, pp. 212–51. Edited by Philip B. Kurland. Chicago: University of Chicago Press, 1962.

Benedict, Michael L. "Preserving the Constitution: The Conservative Basis of Radical Reconstruction." *Journal of American History* 61 (June 1974): 65–90.

————. "Preserving Federalism: Reconstruction and the Waite Court." In *The Supreme Court Review 1978*, pp. 39-79. Edited by Philip B. Kurland and Gerhard Casper. Chicago: University of Chicago Press, 1979.

————. "Laissez-Faire and Liberty: A Re-Evaluation of the Meaning and Origins of Laissez-Faire Constitutionalism." *Law and History Review* 3 (Fall 1985): 293–331.

Berger, Raoul. "Bills of Attainder: A Study of Amendment by the Court." *Cornell Law Review* 63 (March 1978): 355–404.

Bernstein, Barton J. "The Case Law in Plessy *v.* Ferguson." *Journal of Negro History* 47 (July 1962): 192–98.

————. "Plessy v. Ferguson: Conservative Sociological Jurisprudence." *Journal of Negro History* 48 (July 1963): 196–205.

Beth, Loren P. "The Slaughter-House Cases—Revisited." *Louisiana Law Review* 23 (April 1963): 487–505.

Bickel, Alexander M. "The Original Understanding and the Segregation Decision." *Harvard Law Review* 69 (November 1965): 1–65.

Bishop, David W. "Plessy v. Ferguson: A Reinterpretation." *Journal of Negro History* 62 (April 1977): 125–33.

Blanchard, Margaret A. "Filling in the Void: Speech and Press in State Courts prior to *Gitlow*." In *The First Amendment Reconsidered: New Perspectives on the Meaning of Freedom of Speech and Press*, pp. 14–59. Edited by Bill F. Chamberlin and Charlene J. Brown. New York: Longman, 1982.

Block, Joseph D. "Suits Against Government Officers and the Sovereign Immunity Doctrine." *Harvard Law Review* 59 (September 1946): 1060–86.

Bogen, David. "The Free Speech Metamorphosis of Mr. Justice Holmes." *Hofstra Law Review* 11 (Fall 1982): 97–189.

Bohlen, Francis H., and Harry Schulman. "Arrest with and without Warrant," *University of Pennsylvania Law Review* 75 (April 1927): 485–504.

Bonfield, Arthur E. "The Guarantee Clause of Article IV, Section 4: A Study in Constitutional Desuetude." *Minnesota Law Review* 46 (January 1968): 513-72.

Brown, Ray A. "Due Process, Police Power, and the Supreme Court." *Harvard Law Review* 40 (May 1927): 943–68.

Brown, Richard M. "Legal and Behavioral Perspectives on American Vigilantism" *Perspectives in American History* 5 (1971): 93–144.

Carrott, M. Browning. "Prejudice Goes to Court: The Japanese & the Supreme Court in the 1920s." *California History* 62 (Summer 1983): 122–38.

————. "The Supreme Court and Law and Order in the 1920s." *Maryland Historian* 16 (Fall/Winter 1985): 12–26.

Clayton, James L. "The Supreme Court, Polygamy and the Enforcement of Morals in Nineteenth Century America: An Analysis of Reynolds v. United States." *Dialogue: A Journal of Mormon Thought* 12 (Winter 1979): 46–61.

Comment. "The Bounds of Legislative Specification: A Suggested Approach to the Bill of Attainder Clause." *Yale Law Journal* 72 (December 1962): 330–67.

————. "The Supreme Court's Bill of Attainder Doctrine: A Need for Clarification." *California Law Review* 54 (March 1966): 212–50.

Corker, Charles E. "*Bradwell v. State*: Some Reflections Prompted by Myra Bradwell's Hard Case That Made 'Bad Law.' " *Washington Law Review* 53 (February 1978): 215–47.

Cortner, Richard C. "The Wobblies and Fiske *v.* Kansas: Victory amid Disintegration." *Kansas History* 4 (Spring 1981): 30–38.

Corwin, Edward S. "The Supreme Court and Unconstitutional Acts of Congress." *Michigan Law Review* 4 (June 1906): 618–30.

————. "The Supreme Court and the Fourteenth Amendment." *Michigan Law Review* 7 (June 1909): 643-72.

————. "The Supreme Court's Construction of the Self-Incrimination Clause." *Michigan Law Review* 29 (November 1930): 1–27 and (December 1930): 191-207.

————. "Bowing Out 'Clear and Present Danger.' " *Notre Dame Lawyer* 27 (Spring 1952): 325–59.

Cover, Robert M. "The Left, the Right and the First Amendment: 1918–1928." *Maryland Law Review* 40, no. 3 (1981): 349–88.

————. "The Origins of Judicial Activism in the Protection of Minorities," *Yale Law Journal* 91 (June 1982): 1287–1316.

Cresswell, Stephen. "Enforcing the Enforcement Acts: The Department of Justice in Northern Mississippi, 1870–1890." *Journal of Southern History* 53 (August 1987): 421–40.

Cushman, Robert E. " 'Clear and Present Danger' in Free Speech Cases: A Study in Judicial Semantics." In *Essays in Political Theory Presented to George H. Sabine*, pp. 311–24. Edited by Milton R. Konvitz and Arthur E. Murphy. Ithaca, N.Y.: Cornell University Press, 1948.

Daniel, Pete. "Up from Slavery and Down to Peonage: The Alonzo Bailey Case." *Journal of American History* 57 (December 1970): 654-70.

Davis, Ray J. "The Polygamous Prelude." *American Journal of Legal History* 6 (January 1962): 1–27.

————. "Plural Marriage and Religious Freedom: The Impact of Reynolds v. United States." *Arizona Law Review* 15, no. 2 (1973): 287–306.

Davis, William W. "The Federal Enforcement Acts." In *Studies in Southern History and Politics Inscribed to William Archibald Dunning*, pp. 203–28. New York: Columbia University Press, 1914.

Dinnerstein, Leonard. "The Supreme Court and the Rights of Aliens." *this Constitution: A Bicentennial Chronicle*, no. 8 (Fall 1985): 23–35.

Dotson, Arch. "The Emerging Doctrine of Privilege in Public Employment." *Public Administration Review* 15 (Spring 1955): 77–88.

Duker, William F. "The Right to Bail: An Historical Inquiry." *Albany Law Review* 42 (Fall 1977): 3–120.

———. "Mr. Justice Rufus W. Peckham: The Police Power and the Individual in a Changing World," *Brigham Young University Law Review* 1980, no. 1: 47–67.

———. "The Fuller Court and State Criminal Process: Threshold of Modern Limitations on Government," *Brigham Young University Law Review* 1980, no. 2: 275–93.

———. "Mr. Justice Rufus W. Peckham and the Case of *Ex Parte Young*: Lochnerizing *Munn v. Illinois*," *Brigham Young University Law Review* 1980, no. 3: 539–58.

Ezell, John S. "The Civil Rights Act of 1875," *Mid-America* 50 (October 1968): 251–71.

Fairman, Charles. "What Makes a Great Justice? Mr. Justice Bradley and the Supreme Court, 1870–1892," *Boston University Law Review* 30 (June 1950): 49–102.

Farber, Daniel A., and John E. Muench. "The Ideological Origins of the Fourteenth Amendment." *Constitutional Commentary* 1 (Summer 1984): 235-79.

Feinman, Jay M. "The Development of the Employment at Will Rule." *American Journal of Legal History* 20 (April 1976): 118–35.

Fellman, David. "Separation of Church and State in the United States: A Summary View." *Wisconsin Law Review* 1950 (May): 427-78.

———. "Constitutional Right of Association." In *The Supreme Court Review 1961*, pp. 74–134. Edited by Philip B. Kurland. Chicago: University of Chicago Press, 1961.

Foote, Caleb. "The Coming Constitutional Crisis in Bail: I." *University of Pennsylvania Law Review* 113 (May 1965): 959–99.

Frank, John P. "Historical Bases of the Federal Judicial System." *Law and Contemporary Problems* 13 (Winter 1948): 3–28.

Frank, John P. and Robert F. Munro. "The Original Understanding of 'Equal Protection of the Laws.' " *Washington University Law Quarterly* 1972 (Summer): 421-78.

Frankfurter, Felix. "Distribution of Judicial Power Between United States and State Courts." *Cornell Law Quarterly* 13 (June 1928): 499-530.

Frankfurter, Felix, and Thomas C. Cochran. "Petty Offenses and the Constitutional Guaranty of Trial by Jury." *Harvard Law Review* 39 (June 1926): 917–1010.

Franklin, John Hope. "Jim Crow Goes to School: The Genesis of Legal Segregation in Southern Schools." *South Atlantic Quarterly* 58 (Spring 1959): 225–35.

———. "The Enforcement of the Civil Rights Act of 1875." *Prologue* 6 (Winter 1974): 225–35.

Franklin, Mitchell. "The Foundations and Meaning of the Slaughterhouse Cases." *Tulane Law Review* 18 (October 1943): 1–88, and (December 1943): 218–62.

Frantz, Laurent B. "Congressional Power to Enforce the Fourteenth Amendment Against Private Acts." *Yale Law Journal* 73 (July 1964): 1353–84.

Friedman, Lawrence M. "Freedom of Contract and Occupational Licensing 1890–1910: A Legal and Social Study." *California Law Review* 53 (May 1965): 487–534.

Funston, Richard. "The Supreme Court and Critical Elections." *American Political Science Review* 69 (September 1975): 795–811.

Galloway, Russell W., Jr. "The Taft Court (1921–1929)." *Santa Clara Law Review* 25 (Winter 1985): 1–64.

Gibbons, John J. "The Eleventh Amendment and State Sovereign Immunity: A Reinterpretation." *Columbia Law Review* 83 (December 1983): 1889–2005.

———. "Federal Law and the State Courts 1790–1860." *Rutgers Law Review* 36 (Spring 1984): 399–453.

Gilliam, Nancy T. "A Professional Pioneer: Myra Bradwell's Fight to Practice Law." *Law and History Review* 5 (Spring 1987): 105–33.

Glennon, Robert J., Jr. "Justice Henry Billings Brown: Values in Tension." *University of Colorado Law Review* 44 (May 1973): 553–604.

Gold, David M. "State-Court Protection of Individual Rights: The Historians' Neglect." *Constitutional Commentary* 2 (Summer 1985): 419–24.

Goldstein, Leslie F. "Popular Sovereignty, the Origins of Judicial Review, and the Revival of Unwritten Law." *Journal of Politics* 48 (February 1986): 51-71.

Grant, J.A.C. "The Natural Law Background of Due Process." *Columbia Law Review* 31 (January 1931): 56–81.

Green, John R. "Liberty under the Fourteenth Amendment." *Washington University Law Quarterly* 27 (Summer 1942): 497–562.

Greenawalt, Kent. "Speech and Crime." *American Bar Foundation Research Journal* 1980 (Fall): 645-785.

Gressman, Eugene. "The Unhappy History of Civil Rights Legislation." *Michigan Law Review* 50 (June 1952): 1323–58.

Grey, Thomas C. "Origins of the Unwritten Constitution: Fundamental Law in American Revolutionary Thought." *Stanford Law Review* 30 (May 1978): 843-93.

Gunther, Gerald. "Learned Hand and the Origins of Modern First Amendment Doctrine: Some Fragments of History." *Stanford Law Review* 27 (February 1975): 719-73.

Harlan, Louis. "Desegregation in New Orleans Public Schools during Reconstruction." *American Historical Review* 67 (April 1962): 663-75.

Heberle, Klaus H. "From Gitlow to Near: Judicial 'Amendment' by Absent-Minded Incrementalism." *Journal of Politics* 34 (May 1972): 458–83.

Hellman, Arthur D. "The Business of the Supreme Court under the Judiciary Act of 1925: The Plenary Docket in the 1970's." *Harvard Law Review* 91 (June 1978): 1709–1803.

Helphand, Barry F. "Labor and the Courts: The Common-Law Doctrine of Criminal Conspiracy and Its Application in the Buck's Stove Case." *Labor History* 18 (Winter 1977): 91–114.

Henkin, Louis. "The Constitution and United States Sovereignty: A Century of *Chinese Exclusion* and Its Progeny." *Harvard Law Review* 100 (February 1987): 853–86.

Hodes, W. William. "Women and the Constitution: Some Legal History and a New

Approach to the Nineteenth Amendment." *Rutgers Law Review* 25 (Fall 1970): 26–53.

Horan, Michael J. "Political Economy and Sociological Theory as Influences upon Judicial Decision-Making: The *Civil Rights Cases* of 1883." *American Journal of Legal History* 16 (July 1972): 71–86.

Hovenkamp, Herbert. "Social Science and Segregation before *Brown.*" *Duke Law Journal* 1985 (June-September): 624-72.

Howe, Mark D. "Juries as Judges of Criminal Law." *Harvard Law Review* 52 (February 1939): 582–616.

Hunter, Howard O. "Problems in Search of Principles: The First Amendment in the Supreme Court from 1791–1930." *Emory Law Journal* 35 (Winter 1986): 59–137.

Jacoby, Sanford M. "The Duration of Indefinite Employment Contracts in the United States and England: An Historical Analysis." *Comparative Labor Law* 5 (Winter 1982): 85–128.

Johnston, John D., Jr., and Charles L. Knapp. "Sex Discrimination by Law: A Study in Judicial Perspective." *New York University Law Review* 46 (October 1971): 675-747.

Jones, Margaret. "What Constitutes Double Jeopardy?" *Journal of Criminal Law and Criminology* 38 (November-December 1947): 379–90.

Josephson, Harold. "Political Justice during the Red Scare: The Trial of Benjamin Gitlow." In *American Political Trials*, pp. 153-75. Edited by Michal R. Belknap. Westport, Conn.: Greenwood Press, 1981.

Kaczorowski, Robert J. "Searching for the Intent of the Framers of the Fourteenth Amendment." *Connecticut Law Review* 5 (Winter 1972–1973): 368–98.

———. "To Begin the Nation Anew: Congress, Citizenship, and Civil Rights after the Civil War." *American Historical Review* 92 (February 1987): 45–68.

Kauper, Paul G. "Church Autonomy and the First Amendment: The Presbyterian Church Case." In *The Supreme Court Review 1969*, 347-78. Edited by Philip B. Kurland. Chicago: University of Chicago Press, 1969.

Kay, Richard S. "The Equal Protection Clause in the Supreme Court 1873–1903." *Buffalo Law Review* 29 (Fall 1980): 667-725.

Kelly, Alfred H. "The Fourteenth Amendment Reconsidered: The Segregation Question." *University of Michigan Law Review* 54 (June 1956): 986–1049.

———. "The Congressional Controversy over School Segregation, 1867–1875." *American Historical Review* 64 (April 1959): 537–63.

———. "Clio and the Court: An Illicit Love Affair." In *The Supreme Court Review 1965*, pp. 119–58. Edited by Philip B. Kurland. Chicago: University of Chicago Press, 1965.

———. "Constitutional Liberty and the Law of Libel: A Historian's View." *American Historical Review* 74 (December 1968): 429–52.

Kennedy, Randall. "Race Relations Law and the Tradition of Celebration: The Case of Professor Schmidt." *Columbia Law Review* 86 (December 1986): 1622–61.

Kousser, J. Morgan. "Separate but *not* Equal: The Supreme Court's First Decision on Racial Discrimination in Schools." *Journal of Southern History* 46 (February 1980): 17–44.

———. "Progressivism for Middle-Class Whites Only: North Carolina Education, 1880–1910." *Journal of Southern History* 46 (May 1980): 169–84.

Kutler, Stanley I. "Chief Justice Taft, Judicial Unanimity, and Labor: The Coronado Case." *Historian* 24 (November 1961): 68–83.

———. "Labor, the Clayton Act, and the Supreme Court." *Labor History* 3 (Winter 1962): 19–38.

———. "*Ex parte McCardle*: Judicial Impotency? The Supreme Court and Reconstruction Reconsidered." *American Historical Review* 72 (April 1967): 833–51.

Lawrence, Thomas A. "Eclipse of Liberty: Civil Liberties in the United States during the First World War." *Wayne Law Review* 21 (November 1974): 33-112.

Lee, Frederic P. "The Origins of Judicial Control of Federal Executive Action." *Georgetown Law Journal* 36 (March 1948): 287–309.

Levy, Leonard W. "Liberty and the First Amendment: 1790–1800," *American Historical Review* 68 (October 1962): 22–37.

———. "The Right Against Self-Incrimination: History and Judicial History." *Political Science Quarterly* 84 (March 1969): 1–29.

Levy, Leonard W., and Harlan B. Phillips. "The *Roberts* Case: Source of the 'Separate but Equal' Doctrine." *American Historical Review* 56 (April 1951): 510–18.

Lindgren, Janet S. "Beyond Cases: Reconsidering Judicial Review." *Wisconsin Law Review* 1983, no. 3 (1983): 583–638.

Lucie, Patricia. "On Being a Free Person and a Citizen by Constitutional Amendment." *Journal of American Studies* 12 (December 1978): 343–58.

Lurie, Jonathan. "The Fourteenth Amendment: Use and Application in Selected State Court Civil Liberties Cases, 1870–1890—A Preliminary Assessment." *American Journal of Legal History* 28 (October 1984): 295–313.

Magrath, C. Peter. "Chief Justice Waite and the 'Twin Relic': *Reynolds v. United States.*" *Vanderbilt Law Review* 18 (March 1965): 507–43.

Maidment, Richard. "Plessy v. Ferguson Re-examined." *Journal of American Studies* 7 (August 1973): 125–32.

Margo, Robert A. "Race Differences in Public School Expenditures: Disenfranchisement and School Finance in Louisiana, 1890–1910." *Social Science History* 6 (Winter 1982): 9–33.

Mayers, Lewis. "The Federal Witness' Privilege Against Self-Incrimination: Constitutional or Common-Law?" *American Journal of Legal History* 4 (April 1960): 107–41.

———. "The Habeas Corpus Act of 1867: The Supreme Court as Legal Historian." *University of Chicago Law Review* 33 (Autumn 1965): 31–59.

Mayton, William T. "Seditious Libel and the Lost Guarantee of a Freedom of Expression." *Columbia Law Review* 84 (January 1984): 91–142.

McAllister, Breck P. "Ex Post Facto Laws in the Supreme Court of the United States." *California Law Review* 15 (May 1927): 269–88.

McCurdy, Charles W. "The Roots of 'Liberty of Contract' Reconsidered: Major Premises in the Law of Employment, 1867–1937." In *Supreme Court Historical Society Yearbook 1984*, pp. 20–33. Washington, D.C.: Supreme Court Historical Society 1984.

McPherson, James M. "Abolitionists and the Civil Rights Act of 1875." *Journal of American History* 52 (December 1965): 493–510.

Meyer, Alfred W. "The Blaine Amendment and the Bill of Rights." *Harvard Law Review* 64 (April 1951): 939–45.

Morrison, Stanley. "Does the Fourteenth Amendment Incorporate the Bill of Rights?

The Judicial Interpretation." *Stanford Law Review* 2 (December 1949): 140–73.

Murchison, Kenneth M. "The Entrapment Defense in Federal Courts: Emergence of a Legal Doctrine." *Mississippi Law Journal* 47 (April 1976): 211–36.

———. "Prohibition and the Fourth Amendment: A New Look at Some Old Cases." *Journal of Criminal Law and Criminology* 73 (Summer 1982): 471-532.

———. "Property Forfeiture in the Era of National Prohibition: A Study of Judicial Response to Legislative Reform." *Buffalo Law Review* 32 (Spring 1983): 417–63.

———. "The Dual Sovereignty Exception to Double Jeopardy." *New York University Review of Law & Social Change* 14, no. 2 (1986): 383–407.

Murphy, Paul L. "*Near v. Minnesota* in the Context of Historical Developments." *Minnesota Law Review* 66 (November 1981): 95–160.

Murphy, Walter F. "The Contempt Power of the Federal Courts." *Federal Bar Journal* 18 (January-March 1958): 34–55.

Nelson, William E. "Changing Conceptions of Judicial Review: The Evolution of Constitutional Theory in the States, 1790–1860." *University of Pennsylvania Law Review* 120 (June 1972): 1166–85.

———. "The Impact of the Antislavery Movement upon Styles of Judicial Reasoning in Nineteenth Century America." *Harvard Law Review* 87 (January 1974): 513–66.

Nerken, Ira. "A New Deal for the Protection of Fourteenth Amendment Rights: Challenging the Doctrinal Bases of the *Civil Rights Cases* and State Action Theory." *Harvard Civil Rights-Civil Liberties Law Review* 12 (Spring 1977): 297–366.

Note. "Civil and Criminal Contempt in the Federal Courts." *Yale Law Journal* 57 (November 1947): 83–107.

———. "The Strange Career of 'State Action' under the Fifteenth Amendment." *Yale Law Journal* 78 (July 1965): 1448–61.

———. "Developments in the Law—Federal Habeas Corpus." *Harvard Law Review* 83 (March 1970): 787–885.

Oaks, Dallin H. "The 'Original' Writ of Habeas Corpus in the Supreme Court." In *The Supreme Court Review 1962*, pp. 153–211. Edited by Philip B. Kurland. Chicago: University of Chicago Press, 1962.

———. "Legal History in the High Court—Habeas Corpus." *Michigan Law Review* 64 (January 1966): 451-72.

Oberst, Paul. "The Strange Career of Plessy v. Ferguson." *Arizona Law Review* 15, no. 2 (1973): 389–418.

Olsen, Frances. "From False Paternalism to False Equality: Judicial Assaults on Feminist Community, Illinois 1869–1895." *Michigan Law Review* 84 (June 1986): 1518–41.

Orth, John W. "The Fair Fame and Name of Louisiana." *Tulane Lawyer* 2 (Fall 1980): 2-15.

———. "The Interpretation of the Eleventh Amendment, 1798–1908: A Case Study of Judicial Power." *University of Illinois Law Review* 1983, no. 2: 423–55.

Packer, Herbert L. "Mens Rea and the Supreme Court." In *The Supreme Court Review 1962*, pp. 107–52. Edited by Philip B. Kurland. Chicago: University of Chicago Press, 1962.

Pollak, Louis H. "Advocating Civil Liberties: A Young Lawyer before an Old Court." *Harvard Civil Rights-Civil Liberties Law Review* 17 (Spring 1982): 1–30.

Poulson, B.W. "Criminal Conspiracy, Injunctions and Damage Suits in Labor Law." *Journal of Legal History* 7 (September 1986): 212–27.

Power, Garrett. "Apartheid Baltimore Style: The Residential Segregation Ordinances of 1910–1913." *Maryland Law Review* 42, no. 2 (1983): 289–328.

Rabban, David M. "The First Amendment in Its Forgotten Years." *Yale Law Journal* 90 (January 1981): 514–95.

———. "The Emergence of Modern First Amendment Doctrine." *University of Chicago Law Review* 50 (Fall 1983): 1205–1355.

———. "The Ahistorical Historian: Leonard Levy on Freedom of Expression in Early American History." *Stanford Law Review* 37 (February 1985): 795-856.

Rabinowitz, Howard N. "From Exclusion to Segregation: Southern Race Relations, 1865–1890." *Journal of American History* 63 (September 1976): 325–50.

Ragan, Fred D. "Justice Oliver Wendell Holmes, Jr., Zechariah Chafee, Jr., and the Clear and Present Danger Test for Free Speech: The First Year, 1919." *Journal of American History* 58 (June 1971): 24–45.

Reitz, Curtis R. "Federal Habeas Corpus: Impact of an Abortive State Proceeding." *Harvard Law Review* 74 (May 1961): 1315-73.

Reznick, Scott M. "Empiricism and the Principle of Conditions in the Evolution of the Police Power: A Model for Definitional Scrutiny." *Washington University Law Quarterly* 1978 (Winter): 1–92.

Rice, Roger L. "Residential Segregation by Law, 1900–1917." *Journal of Southern History* 34 (May 1968): 179–99.

Riegel, Stephen J. "The Persistent Career of Jim Crow: Lower Federal Courts and the 'Separate but Equal' Doctrine." *American Journal of Legal History* 28 (January 1984): 17–40.

Robb, Gary C. "The *Carroll* Case: The Expansion of the Automobile Exception in Warrantless Search and Seizure Cases." *Willamette Law Review* 15 (Winter 1978): 39–59.

Roche, John P. "Civil Liberty in the Age of Enterprise." *University of Chicago Law Review* 31 (Autumn 1963): 103–35.

———. "Entrepreneurial Liberty and the Fourteenth Amendment." *Labor History* 4 (Winter 1963): 3–31.

Rosenberg, Norman L. "The Law of Political Libel and Freedom of Press in Nineteenth Century America: An Interpretation." *American Journal of Legal History* 17 (October 1973): 336–52.

———. "The New Law of Political Libel: A Historical Perspective." *Rutgers Law Review* 28 (Summer 1975): 1141–83.

Saltzburg, Stephen A. "Habeas Corpus: The Supreme Court and the Congress." *Ohio State Law Journal* 44, no. 2 (1983): 367–91.

Scheiber, Harry N. "Public Rights and the Rule of Law in American Legal History." *California Law Review* 72 (March 1984): 217–51.

Schmidt, Benno C., Jr. "Principle and Prejudice: The Supreme Court and Race in the Progressive Era. Part 1: The Heyday of Jim Crow." *Columbia Law Review* 82 (April 1982): 444–524.

———. "Principle and Prejudice: The Supreme Court and Race in the Progressive

Era. Part 2: The *Peonage Cases.*" *Columbia Law Review* 82 (May 1982): 646–718.

―――. "Principle and Prejudice: The Supreme Court and Race in the Progressive Era. Part 3: Black Disenfranchisement from the KKK to the Grandfather Clause." *Columbia Law Review* 82 (June 1982): 835–905.

―――. "Juries, Jurisdiction, and Race Discrimination: The Lost Promise of *Strauder v. West Virgina.*" *Texas Law Review* 61 (May 1983): 1401–99.

Scott, John A. "Justice Bradley's Evolving Concept of the Fourteenth Amendment from the Slaughterhouse Cases to the Civil Rights Cases." *Rutgers Law Review* 25 (Summer 1971): 552–69.

―――. "Segregation: A Fundamental Aspect of Southern Race Relations, 1800–1860." *Journal of the Early Republic* 4 (Winter 1984): 421–41.

Siegan, Bernard H. "Rehabilitating *Lochner.*" *San Diego Law Review* 22 (May-June 1985): 453–97.

Smead, Elmer E. "*Sic Utere Tuo Ut Alienum Non Laedas*: A Basis of the State Police Power." *Cornell Law Quarterly* 21 (February 1936): 276–92.

Smith, Rogers M. "The Constitution and Autonomy." *Texas Law Review* 60 (February 1982): 175–202.

―――. "The Meaning of American Citizenship." *This Constitution: A Bicentennial Chronicle*, No. 8 (Fall 1985): 12–18.

Smith, W. Roy. "Negro Suffrage in the South." In *Studies in Southern History and Politics Inscribed to William Archibald Dunning*, 229–56. New York: Columbia University Press, 1914.

Spackman, S.P.F. "American Federalism and the Civil Rights Act of 1875." *Journal of American Studies* 10 (December 1976): 313–28.

Spector, Robert M. "Woman Against the Law: Myra Bradwell's Struggle for Admission to the Illinois Bar." *Journal of the Illinois State Historical Society* 68 (June 1975): 228–42.

Starr, Joseph R. "The Legal Status of American Political Parties," Parts I and II. *American Political Science Review* 34 (June 1940): 439–55, and (August 1940): 685–99.

Sterling David L. "In Defense of Debs: The Lawyers and the Espionage Act Case." *Indiana Magazine of History* 83 (March 1987): 17–42.

Stevens, John D., et al. "Criminal Libel as Seditious Libel, 1916–65." *Journalism Quarterly* 43 (Spring 1966): 110–13.

Surrency, Erwin C. "The Judiciary Act of 1801." *American Journal of Legal History* 2 (January 1958): 53–65.

―――. "A History of the Federal Courts." *Missouri Law Review* 28 (Spring 1963): 214–44.

Swinney, Everette. "Enforcing the Fifteenth Amendment, 1870–1877." *Journal of Southern History* 28 (May 1962): 208–18.

Tanenhaus, Joseph. "Picketing as a Tort: The Development of the Law of Picketing from 1880 to 1940." *University of Pittsburgh Law Review* 14 (Winter 1953): 170–98.

―――. "Picketing as Free Speech: Early Stages in the Growth of the New Law of Picketing." *University of Pittsburgh Law Review* 14 (Spring 1953): 397–418.

Tyack, David B. "The Perils of Pluralism: The Background of the Pierce Case." *American Historical Review* 76 (October 1968): 74–98.

Tyack, David B. and Aaron Benavot. "Courts and Public Schools: Educational Litigation in Historical Perspective." *Law & Society Review* 19, no. 3 (1985): 339-80.

Tyack, David B. and Thomas James. "Moral Majorities and the School Curriculum: Historical Perspectives on the Legalization of Virtue." *Teachers College Record* 86 (Summer 1985): 513–37.

Ulman, Francis J., and Frank H. Spears. " 'Dismissed for Want of a Substantial Federal Question': A Study in the Practice of the Supreme Court in Deciding Appeals from State Courts." *Boston Law Review* 20 (June 1940): 501–32.

Urofsky, Melvin I. "Myth and Reality: The Supreme Court and Protective Legislation in the Progressive Era." In *Supreme Court Historical Society Yearbook 1983*, 53-72. Washington, D.C.: Supreme Court Historical Society, 1983.

———. "State Courts and Protective Legislation during the Progressive Era: A Reevaluation." *Journal of American History* 72 (June 1985): 63–91.

Van Alstyne, William W. "A Critical Guide to Marbury v. Madison." *Duke Law Journal* 1969 (January): 1–47.

Vaughn, William P. "Separate and Unequal: The Civil Rights Act of 1875 and Defeat of the School Segregation Clause." *Southwestern Social Science Quarterly* 48 (September 1967): 146–54.

Waite, Edward F. "The Negro in the Supreme Court," *Minnesota Law Review* 30 (March 1946): 219–304.

Warren, Charles. "Legislative and Judicial Attacks on the Supreme Court of the United States—A History of the Twenty-Fifth Section of the Judiciary Act," *American Law Review* 47 (January-February 1913): 1–34, and (March-April 1913): 161–89.

———. "New Light on the History of the Federal Judiciary Act of 1789," *Harvard Law Review* 37 (November 1923): 49–132.

———. "The New 'Liberty' under the Fourteenth Amendment." *Harvard Law Review* 39 (February 1926): 431–65.

Watson, Edward M. "Use of Statutory Presumptions in Criminal Cases." *Michigan Law Review* 38 (January 1940): 366–81.

Watson, Richard L., Jr. "The Defeat of Judge Parker: A Study in Pressure Groups and Politics." *Mississippi Valley Historical Review* 50 (September 1963): 213–34.

Westin, Alan F. "Introduction: Charles Beard and the American Debate Over Judicial Review, 1790–1861." pp. 1–34. In Charles A. Beard, *The Supreme Court and the Constitution*. Spectrum Book ed., Englewood Cliffs, N.J.: Prentice-Hall, 1962.

———. "The Case of the Prejudiced Doorkeeper." In *Quarrels That Shaped the Constitution*, pp. 128–44. Edited by John A. Garraty. New York: Harper & Row, 1964.

Wiecek, William M. "The Reconstruction of Federal Judicial Power, 1863-1875." *American Journal of Legal History* 13 (October 1969): 333–59.

———. "The Great Writ and Reconstruction: The Habeas Corpus Act of 1867." *Journal of Southern History* 36 (November 1970): 530–48.

———. "The 'Imperial Judiciary' in Historical Perspective." In *Supreme Court Historical Society Yearbook 1984*, pp. 61–89. Washington, D.C.: Supreme Court Historical Society, 1984.

Woodward, C. Vann. "The Case of the Louisiana Traveler." In *Quarrels That Shaped the Constitution*, pp. 145–58. Edited by John A. Garraty. New York: Harper & Row, 1964.

Wyatt-Brown, Bertram. "The Civil Rights Act of 1875." *Western Political Quarterly* 18 (December 1965): 763-75.

Zuckert, Michael B. "Congressional Power Under the Fourteenth Amendment— The Original Understanding of Section Five." *Constitutional Commentary* 3 (Winter 1986): 123–56.

Index to Cases

Subject Index

About the Author

JOHN BRAEMAN is Professor of History at the University of Nebraska-Lincoln. He is the author of *Albert J. Beveridge: American Nationalist* and editor of numerous books including *Woodrow Wilson, American Politics in the Twentieth Century*, and *The Road to Independence*. His many articles have appeared in such publications as *Business History Review, Journal of American Studies, American Quarterly*, and *Review of Politics*.